THE UNIVERSAL DECLARATION OF HUMAN RIGHTS AT SEVENTY: A REVIEW OF SUCCESSES AND CHALLENGES

THE UNIVERSAL DECLARATION OF HUMAN RIGHTS AT SEVENTY:
A REVIEW OF SUCCESSES AND CHALLENGES

Edited by

Noelle Higgins

Amina Adanan

David M Doyle

Michael Doherty

CLARUS
PRESS

Published by
Clarus Press Ltd,
Griffith Campus,
South Circular Road,
Dublin 8.
www.claruspress.ie

Typeset by
Gough Typesetting Services, Dublin

Printed by
Sprint Print Ltd,
Dublin.

ISBN
978-1-911611-30-1

ABOUT THE CONTRIBUTORS

Amina Adanan

Dr Amina Adanan is Lecturer in Law in Maynooth University Law Department. In 2018, Amina was awarded a PhD in human rights from NUI Galway for her thesis, 'Allies and Enemies, past and present: An analysis of the rationale for the development of universal jurisdiction over serious crimes under international law'. Amina is a former holder of the EJ Phelan Fellowship in International Law, awarded by the National University of Ireland. Amina's research areas are international criminal law and the history of international law. She teaches modules in International Human Rights Law, Land Law and Fundamental Rights in Ireland.

Siobhan Barron

Siobhan Barron is the Director of the National Disability Authority (NDA) which is an independent statutory body established to provide information and advice to the Government on policy and practice impacting on the lives of people with disabilities. Through its research, advice and role, the NDA aims to support and monitor the effective development and delivery of co-ordinated cross-government action on disability and the implementation of the United Nations Convention on the Rights of Persons with Disabilities to ensure people with disabilities can participate as valued citizens in the mainstream of Irish society and can live the lives they want to lead.

Deirdre Clancy

Deirdre Clancy served four mandates as an expert on the United Nations Security Council's Somalia Eritrea Monitoring Group. Prior to that she spent twenty years working on human rights in conflict, particularly in Africa, at the International Refugee Rights Initiative (which she co-founded), the Lawyers Committee for Human Rights/Human Rights First, and the Council of Europe. Deirdre began her career at Irish Refugee Council, where she set up the first national legal assistance project for refugees in 1994. Deirdre has lectured on international law at universities in Ireland, Uganda and the United States of America.

Michael Doherty

Michael Doherty is Professor of Law, and Head of the Department of Law, at Maynooth University, with particular expertise in the areas of Irish and EU employment and labour law, industrial relations, and social dialogue. He has published widely in national and international outlets on these topics and presented his work at numerous domestic and international conferences. He has worked on a number of projects for the European Commission and European Parliament on cross-border working terms and conditions, and is a member of several European research networks. He is a frequent media contributor on labour relations issues.

David M Doyle

Dr David M Doyle is a Lecturer in Law at Maynooth University. He has been awarded Department of Justice Research Funding (2019), an Irish Human Rights and Equality Grant (2018), Irish Research Council (IRC) Elevate Fellowship (2013), IRC New Foundations Awards (2012, 2016, 2017), an IRC Research and Networking Grant (2012), an IRC Postdoctoral Fellowship (2011), an IRC New Ideas Award (2011) and an IRCHSS Doctoral Scholarship (2008) to conduct research in the areas of legal history, criminal law and education law. His research has been published in the *Irish Criminal Law Journal*, *The Irish Jurist*, *The Journal of British Studies*, *The Journal of Legal History*, *New Hibernia Review*, *The Howard Journal of Crime and Justice*, *The British Journal of Criminology* and *The Industrial Law Review*. His first book (with Liam O'Callaghan), *Capital Punishment in Independent Ireland: A Social, Legal and Political History*, was published by Liverpool University Press in December 2019

Keith Ewing

Professor Keith Ewing is Professor of Public Law at King's College London and co-author of two of Britain's leading textbooks in constitutional and administrative law, and labour law. He was educated at Edinburgh University and worked at Cambridge University in England, Monash University in Australia, Osgoode Hall in Canada, before joining the King's College London law school in 1989. Professor Ewing is recognised as a leading scholar in public law and labour law. He has written extensively on the funding of political parties. His most recent work relates to reforming labour law to strengthen trade union freedom, constitutional reform, relating to public participation in the political process and the status of social and economic rights.

Liam Herrick

Liam Herrick is currently the Executive Director for the Irish Council for Civil Liberties. Prior to this, he was the Executive Director of the Irish Penal Reform Trust from 2007 until the beginning of 2014, during which time he helped to establish the IPRT as the leading independent voice on penal matters in Ireland and oversaw an ambitious programme of research, awareness raising and campaigning work. In 2012, he was appointed by Minister Shatter as a member of the Strategic Review Group on Penal Policy. He holds a BCL and an LL.M. from University College Cork and a Diploma in European Human Rights Law from University College Dublin. In April 2013, he was appointed as a Commissioner Designate of the Human Rights and Equality Commission. In January 2014, Liam was appointed as Advisor to President Michael D Higgins.

Noelle Higgins

Noelle Higgins is an Associate Professor in Law at Maynooth University, where she specialises in public international law, and currently teaches and researches in international human rights law, international humanitarian law and international criminal law. Her recent publications focus mainly on the field of cultural rights. She is currently an 'Academic friend' of the United Nations Expert Mechanism on the Rights of Indigenous Peoples, and was previously the Vice-Chair of the Ethical, Political, Legal and Philosophical Studies Committee of the Royal Irish Academy and a member of the Irish Department of Foreign Affairs and Trade–NGO Forum on Human Rights.

Fiona McGaughey

Fiona McGaughey teaches International Human Rights Law and Theory, Method and Contemporary Issues in International Law on the Master of International Law at University of Western Australia (UWA). She also teaches in the undergraduate Law and Society Major. Her primary research areas are: non-governmental organisations in international human rights law, United Nations human rights mechanisms, business and human rights (including modern slavery), transitional justice and legal / human rights pedagogy. She has particular expertise in socio-legal methods. Fiona is originally from Northern Ireland and studied Common and Civil Law with French (LLB Hons) at Queen's University Belfast; she later completed her Masters in Human Rights and PhD in Western Australia. Fiona is a member of the Law Council of Australia's Business and Human Rights Committee and co-convenor of UWA's Modern Slavery Research Cluster.

Gerard Maguire

Gerard Maguire is a PhD Candidate with the Department of Law at Maynooth University. He has previously worked with Survival International on a research project focusing on the right to education of tribal children in their mother tongue. Gerard was appointed the 2019 recipient of the International Communities Organisation Research Scholarship and is one of the founding members of The International Justice Network which is a collective of international researchers who support the advancement of International Justice. As of November 2019, he is a member of the management committee for an EU COST Action project relating to Global Atrocity Crimes and Justice Constellations. Gerard's research interests are in the areas of Public International Law, International Human Rights Law, and Genocide Studies.

Jean Molloy

Jean Molloy is a PhD Candidate with the Department of Law at Maynooth University. She obtained a Bachelors of Arts from The University of Melbourne and an MSc (Criminology and Criminal Justice) from University College Dublin in 2012. Jean became a student of the Law Department at Maynooth University in 2015, undertaking an LLM in International Justice. Jean's research interests include international criminal law, terrorism and counter-terrorism, Islamic State, torture and genocide. She has lectured in international criminal law and international human rights law at Maynooth University Department of Law.

Clíodhna Murphy

Clíodhna Murphy is a lecturer at Maynooth University Department of Law. Clíodhna's research focuses on migration law and human rights. She has published widely in these fields, including in journals such as *International & Comparative Law Quarterly*; *Human Rights Quarterly*; *Industrial Law Journal*; and *British Journal of Criminology*.

Muiread Murphy

Muiread graduated from Maynooth University with a Bachelor in Laws degree (LLB) in 2017 and completed a Masters in Comparative Criminology and Criminal Justice in 2018. She began an Irish Research Council funded doctorate programme in September 2019, focusing on severe labour exploitation.

Maria Murphy

Dr Maria Murphy joined the Department of Law at Maynooth University in 2014. Dr Murphy researches in the areas of privacy law, surveillance, data protection, information technology law, and human rights. In addition to publishing in a variety of national and international journals, Dr Murphy has authored the book, *Surveillance and the Law: Language, Power and Privacy* (2019) and co-authored the book, *Information and Communications Technology Law in Ireland* (2017). Dr Murphy completed her PhD at University College Cork in 2013 and holds a *magna cum laude* LLM degree from Temple University (Philadelphia), and a First Class Honours BCL (International) degree from UCC.

TABLE OF CONTENTS

INTRODUCTION

The Universal Declaration of Human Rights (UDHR) was viewed by its drafters as 'a first step in a great evolutionary process.'[1] While the framers agreed that it would have no binding authority over states, it was nonetheless hoped that the instrument 'would define the human rights which states undertook to recognize and would serve as a criterion to guide and stimulate them.'[2] As he was introducing the UDHR to the General Assembly, that body's president, Dr Herbert Evatt, underlined that, although the instrument neither operationalises human rights nor contains an enforcement mechanism, its impact would still be profound because:

> [i]t is the first occasion on which the organized community of nations has made a declaration on human rights and fundamental freedoms, and it has the authority of the body of the United Nations as a whole, and millions of people, men, women, and children all over the world, many miles from Paris and New York, will turn for help, guidance and inspiration to this document.[3]

Over 70 years after its adoption, the aspiration of its drafters of inspiring a great evolutionary process can be said to have been fulfilled, although this is a still continuing and challenging process. Since its adoption in 1948, as a response to the atrocities committed during World War II, the UDHR has contributed to the creation of a multifaceted human rights framework within the United Nations (UN), and has inspired the development of regional systems of human rights protection.

Since the adoption of the UDHR, the UN has developed a bifurcated human rights protective framework, i.e. the Charter-based system and the Treaty-based system. The Treaty-based system consists of nine core human rights treaties, and their associated monitoring bodies, which were drafted with the aim of concretising the aspirational provisions of the UDHR, and requiring states

1 See Hersch Lauterpacht, The Universal Declaration of Human Rights, 25 BRIT YB INT'L L 354 (1948), (quoting the Verbatim Record of the General Assembly, U.N. GAOR, 3d sess., 183d plen. mtg. at 166, UN Doc A/PV (10 December 1948)).

2 Tai-Heng Cheng, The Universal Declaration of Human Rights at Sixty: Is It Still Right for the United States? 41 CORNELL INT'L L.J. 251, 262 (2008), p. 266 (quoting the Mexican Representative).

3 See Hersch Lauterpacht, The Universal Declaration of Human Rights, 25 BRIT. YB INT'L L 354 (1948), p. 354 (quoting the Verbatim Record of the General Assembly, UN GAOR, 3d sess., 183d plen. mtg. at 166, UN Doc A/PV (10 December 1948)).

parties to respect, protect and fulfil the rights enshrined within them. On the other hand, the Charter-based system emanates, as its name suggests, from the human rights provisions of the UN Charter. However, even in the Charter-based system the UDHR plays a central role, as a benchmark by which states' human rights laws and policies are measured, e.g. in the reporting obligations of all UN member states under the Universal Periodic Review (UPR) process, and thus the Declaration maintains a pivotal position in all aspects of the UN human rights mandate.

There has been significant progress in the field of human rights protection and promotion since the adoption of the UDHR, although violations and abuses occur with disappointing regularity. The 70th anniversary of the adoption of the UDHR was an occasion to review some of the successes which have occurred in the field, as well as highlight some of the challenges that still remain to ensure human right protection for all. Maynooth University Department of Law organised a conference to celebrate the 70th Anniversary of the Declaration in 2018. Contributors to the conference included academics, practitioners, and representatives of a number of human rights organisations, thus providing a holistic critique of the human rights framework. The conference provided an opportunity to assess various aspects of human rights protection and promotion, from the status of the Declaration under international law, to actors involved in human rights practice, including non-governmental organisations (NGOs), to the beneficiaries of the human rights framework. The conference sessions also encompassed analyses and critiques of the numerous gaps in the current human rights legal framework, including in relation to group rights and the protection of minorities, and current human rights challenges, with a particular emphasis on the fields of migration and the rights of workers. This volume is an output of that event, which includes 11 substantive chapters based on papers presented at, and ideas discussed in, Maynooth.

The first section of the volume is dedicated to a discussion of the history and context of the UDHR. Amina Adanan's chapter provides a comprehensive examination of the legal status of the UDHR under international law, and explores how the majority of its provisions have become legally binding. Noelle Higgins' chapter then provides a discussion of how the UDHR is currently used as a benchmark for human rights protection and promotion within the UN human rights framework as part of the UPR process, illustrating the enduring and continuing importance of the Declaration since 1948.

Section 2 then provides insights into the UDHR in action, focusing on specific areas of human rights law and practice. Group rights are dealt with in chapter 3 by Jean Molloy and chapter 4 by Ger Maguire. These contributions trace the history of the protection of minorities and indigenous peoples under international law, and challenges of group protection, in addition to referencing how the UDHR impacts on the protection of both minorities and indigenous peoples. Chapter 5 by Keith D Ewing focuses on the influence of the UDHR on the rights of workers, and argues that the battle to secure the rights laid down in the Charter cannot be won by law or lawyers alone, but by creating the economic and political conditions in which they can flourish. In chapter 6, Muiread Murphy, David Doyle and Clíodhna Murphy examine the difficulties associated with the identification of human trafficking victims in Ireland. Chapter 7, by Maria Murphy, takes the right to privacy as its focus and analyses the relevance and application of Articles 12 (right to privacy) and 19 (freedom of expression) of the UDHR in the digital age. In chapter 8 Siobhan Barron critically analyses the implementation of the UN Convention on the Rights of Persons with Disabilities in Ireland, noting the continued room for progress, notwithstanding the advances made in the area. The final contribution in this section, by Déirdre Clancy, provides an important analysis of the UN targeted sanctions regime and assesses how this framework can contribute to securing the human rights and fundamental freedoms, as set out in the UDHR.

Section 3 concludes the volume with a discussion of NGOs and the promotion and protection of human rights by these organisations. Chapter 10, by Liam Herrick, provides a discussion of the increasing difficulties that human rights NGOs organisations operating in Ireland and Europe face. The final chapter of the volume, by Fiona McGaughey, reviews the practice of NGOs in the UN framework over the lifetime of the UDHR.

CHAPTER 1

THE UNIVERSAL DECLARATION OF HUMAN RIGHTS AS CUSTOMARY INTERNATIONAL LAW

By Amina Adanan

1. INTRODUCTION

The drafting history of the UDHR demonstrates that when it was adopted on 10 December 1948, it was not created as a legally binding instrument.[1] At the time, the chair of the UDHR drafting committee, Eleanor Roosevelt, described the instrument as 'not a treaty... not an international agreement. It is not and does not purport to be a statement of law or of legal obligation'.[2] However, it was intended to be 'a common standard of achievement for all peoples and all nations',[3] which *all* states were to aim to realise.[4] Seventy years after its creation, most of its content has become binding under customary international law. There is ample evidence in support of this transformation, which can be found in the number of international instruments that cite it as a source of fundamental human rights law,[5] the case law of the International Court of

---

1 Louis B Sohn, 'The Human Rights Law of the Charter' (1977) 12 *Texas International Law Journal* 129; Krzysztof Drzewicki, 'Human Rights in the United Nations Charter and the Universal Declaration of Human Rights' (1998) 7 *Polish Quarterly of International Affairs* 9. The UDHR was codified as a resolution of the UNGA.

2 Cited in Adam McBeth, Justin Noland and Simon Rice, *The International Law of Human Rights* (2nd edn, OUP 2017) 22. See also the comments of the French representative, René Cassin, as cited in McBeth, Noland and Rice at 22.

3 Universal Declaration of Human Rights (adopted 10 December 1948) UNGA Res 217 A(III) (UDHR), preamble; see comments of Eleanor Roosevelt in McBeth, Noland and Rice, ibid 22.

4 Javaid Rehman, *International Human Rights Law* (2nd edn, Pearsons 2010) 79; LJ Macfarlane, *Human Rights: Realities and Possibilities: Northern Ireland, the Republic of Ireland and Hungary* (Macmillan 1990) 1.

5 Convention for the Protection of Human Rights and Fundamental Freedoms (adopted 4 November 1950, entered into force 3 September 1953) 213 UNTS 222 (as amended) (ECHR), preamble; Proclamation of Teheran, Final Act of the International Conference on Human Rights, Teheran, (22 April to 13 May 1968) UN Doc A/CONF. 32/41 (Tehran Proclamation); African Charter on Human and Peoples' Rights (adopted 27 June 1981, entered into force 21 October 1986) (1982) 21 ILM 58 (African Charter), preamble; Vienna Declaration and Programme of Action (12 July 1993) UN Doc A/CONF.157/23. The Helsinki Final Act refers to the UDHR consisting of obligations, see Conference on Security and Co-operation in Europe Final Act, Helsinki, 1 August 1975, section VII.

Justice (ICJ),[6] as well as in constitutions, legislation and case law at a national level.[7] In addition, States continuously rely on the UDHR in UN proceedings.[8] Indeed, the Declaration is now supported by States that originally opposed it.[9]

The question of whether the UDHR has become binding has received much attention from scholars.[10] As early as the 1960s, scholars asserted the customary law status of the UDHR.[11] On the occasion of the 20th anniversary of the UDHR, some States, NGOs, and the International Law Institute declared the Declaration to be reflective of customary international law.[12] More recently, Robert McCorquodale noted that '…states have accepted that the UDHR is a legitimate and lawful basis for binding customary international obligations of all states'.[13] On the other hand, some scholars argue that the UDHR is part of the general principles of international law.[14]

This chapter argues that the transition from a non-legally binding to a legally binding instrument has occurred through the Declaration's evolution under customary international law, its nexus to the human rights and fundamental freedoms referred to in the UN Charter, and the overlap of some of its content with *jus cogens* peremptory norms. This chapter reflects on how the UDHR has transformed into a legally binding document through these methods, in the absence of an up-to-date large-scale evidence based study to quantify the customary status of the UDHR.[15]

---

6 For example, see *Tehran Hostages Case (United States v Iran)* [1980] ICJ Rep 3, para 91.

7 Hurst Hannum, 'The Status of the Universal Declaration of Human Rights in National and International Law' (1995) 25 *Georgia Journal of International & Comparative Law* 287.

8 Tehran Proclamation; Vienna Declaration and Programme of Action.

9 Louis B Sohn, 'The Universal Declaration of Human Rights: A common standard of achievement? The Status of the Universal Declaration in International Law' (1967) 8 *Journal of the International Commission of Jurists* 17, 23.

10 For example see Sohn, ibid; Theodor Meron, *Human Rights and Humanitarian Norms* (Clarendon Press 1989); Hannum (n 7); RB Lillich, 'The Growing Importance of Customary International Human Rights Law' (1995/96) 25 *Georgia Journal of International & Comparative Law* 1; Bruno Simma and Philip Alston 'The Sources of Human Rights Law: Custom, Jus Cogens, and General Principles' (1992) 12 *Australian Yearbook of International Law* 82; Michael Woods in 'Customary International Law and Human Rights' EUI working Papers, (AEL 2016/03 Academy of European Law, Distinguished Lectures of the Academy).

11 As noted by Lillich, ibid 1 and McBeth, Noland and Rice (n 2) 22. See also Egon Schwelb, *Human Rights and the International Community: the Roots and Growth of the Universal Declaration of Human Rights 1948-1963* (Quadrangle Books 1964) 36-37.

12 Hannum (n 7) 322-23. See also n 35.

13 Robert McCorqoudale, 'A Future for Human Rights law' in Manisuli Ssenyonjo and Mashood A Baderin (eds), *International Human Rights Law: Six Decades After the UDHR and Beyond* (Routledge 2016) 541-42.

14 As noted in Rhona KM Smith, *Textbook on International Human Rights* (7th edn, OUP 2016) 39; Simma and Alston (n 10) 104.

15 Perhaps the most extensive evidence based examination was carried out by Hurst Hannum (n 7), which provides a detailed list of the citing of the Declaration at an international level and a national level.

2. The UDHR and the Traditional Elements of Customary Rule Formation

Customary international rule formation plays an important part in the creation of humanitarian based norms in international law.[16] This trajectory should not be underestimated, given that systematic human rights abuses are often committed with the instigation of a governing State. In order to ensure that fundamental human rights of individuals are protected, it is appropriate that binding rules be created and developed outside of the formal State codified rule based system. The required components of customary rule formation have been addressed a number of times by the ICJ and other legal bodies.[17] For a rule to have evolved into a binding norm, there must be the requisite State practice (or *usus* or *diuturnitas*) and *opinio juris* (or *opinio necessitatis*).[18] The former consists of the conduct of States,[19] while the latter refers to conduct that is carried out in the belief that a rule should be followed.[20]

The extent of State practice that is required for a customary rule to become binding has been referred to by the ICJ on a number of occasions. Originally, the Court declared that State practice should be '...both extensive and virtually uniform in the sense of the provision invoked...'.[21] This stringent test was relaxed somewhat in the famous ICJ *Nicaragua* litigation, where it was held that '[t]he Court does not consider that, for a rule to be established as customary, the corresponding practice must be in absolutely rigorous conformity with the rule'.[22] This statement is cited as evidence that State practice need not be absolutely uniform.[23] One of the arguments cited by scholars who contest the

---

16 Its significance can be seen in the extensive corpus of rules that have developed under customary international humanitarian law, see International Committee of the Red Cross, Customary IHL database at <https://ihl-databases.icrc.org/customary-ihl/eng/docs/home> accessed 28 October 2018.

17 See *North Sea Continental Shelf Case (Federal Republic of Germany/ Denmark; Federal Republic of Germany/ Netherlands)* (Judgment) [1969] ICJ Rep 3; *Nicaragua Case* (*Nicaragua v United States of America*) (merits) [1986] ICJ Rep 14. Since 2012, the International Law Commission (ILC) has included the topic, 'the Identification of Customary International Law' in its programme of work, see <http://legal.un.org/ilc/guide/1_13.shtml> accessed 22 October 2018.

18 Antonio Cassese, *International Law* (2nd edn, OUP 2005) 157; American Law Institute, 'Restatement of the Law, Third, Foreign Relations Law of the United States' (1987) (Third Restatement of Foreign Relations Law), s 102(1)(a); ILC, 'Draft conclusions on identification of customary international law 2018' UN Doc A/73/10, conclusion 5.

19 Conduct that amounts to State practice is defined by the ILC as 'conduct of the State, whether in the exercise of its executive, legislative, judicial or other functions', see 'Draft conclusions on identification of customary international law 2018', ibid, conclusion 5.

20 In respect of *opinio juris*, conclusion 9 of the ILC draft conclusions reads: 'The requirement, as a constituent element of customary international law, that the general practice be accepted as law (*opinio juris*) means that the practice in question must be undertaken with a sense of legal right or obligation'. It is integral that States carry out the conduct in the conscious belief that a rule should be followed, see *North Sea Continental Shelf Case* (n 17) para 77.

21 *North Sea Continental Shelf Case*, ibid, para 74.

22 *Nicaragua Case* (n 17) para 186.

23 Cassese (n 18) 157.

customary status of the UDHR is the number of breaches of its provisions.[24] However, it should be noted that the *Nicaragua* test does not mean that because a State breaches a rule of international law, that the norm does not have legal status.[25] As renowned UDHR scholar, Oscar Schachter, noted, '[o]ccasional violations do not nullify a rule that is widely observed'.[26] Schachter also noted that '[w]hether human rights obligations have become customary law cannot readily be answered on the basis of the usual process of customary law formation'.[27] This is partly so because 'States do not usually make claims on other States or protest violations that do not affect their nationals. In that sense, one can find scant State practice accompanied by *opinio juris*'.[28]

Support for the proposition that *opinio juris* is more persuasive than State practice in the formation of customary international human rights can be found in scholarly writing.[29] Recently, ILC Chairperson, Sir Michael Wood, who argues that allowing *opinio juris* to be the sole requirement for the formation of a fundamental human rights norm would fragment the rules of customary international rule formation, critiqued this position.[30] The problem with applying the traditional two element test is that it does not include the fact that in some cases *opinio juris* is stronger than State practice in the formation of customary international human rights law. The history of the development of humanitarian norms in international law shows that *opinio juris* is often the impetus for the declaration of the existence of a fundamental human right. The outcry that followed the atrocities committed during the Second World War gave rise to prosecutions under customary international law in respect of international crimes that were not codified under international law at the time of their commission. Similarly, State practice in respect of the crime of apartheid is difficult to pinpoint. However, it would be difficult to argue that the crime is not prohibited under customary international law due to the significant amount of *opinio juris* to that effect.

The question also arises whether it is appropriate to permit State-created

---

24 Simma and Alston (n 10) 91-93.

25 *Nicaragua Case* (n 17) para 74.

26 Oscar Schachter, *International Law in Theory and Practice* (Martinus Nijhoff Publishers 1991) 338.

27 ibid 336.

28 ibid.

29 Meron (n 10); Louis Henkin, *The Age of Rights* (Columbia University Press 1990); Schachter (ibid); Nigel Rodley and Matt Pollard, *The Treatment of Prisoners under International Law* (3rd edn, OUP 2009). Indeed, Theodor Meron has suggested an alternative two prong test to identify whether a human right meets the status of international custom, which includes '... the degree to which a statement of a particular right in one human rights instrument, especially a human rights treaty, has been repeated in other human rights instruments' and 'the confirmation of the right in national practice, primarily through the right in national law', at p 94. Meron notes that the Human Rights Committee also adopted this approach.

30 Woods (n 10) 7. Woods criticises the approach taken by Meron, Henkin and others that customary rule formation in respect of human rights only has one requirement, namely *opinio juris*.

human rights norms as the sole method of forming humanitarian rules? As Louis B Sohn noted, '… it would be very dangerous to leave the making of international law to states, especially where human rights are concerned'.[31] The reality of systematic human rights abuses is that they are committed with the support or acquiescence of the governing authority in the State. A further rationale for not applying the traditional criteria to the UDHR is because international human rights law applies between a State and its subjects, rather than between States themselves. Thus, the two-pronged test for customary international law formation is not as relevant for human rights rules, as it is for the creation of international legal rules that apply between States.[32] The purpose of international human rights law is to protect the individual from State injustice.[33]

Finally, the frequency at which the UDHR is relied on in international and national courts, as well as international and regional fora adds to its customary status.[34] What is more, certain international instruments have referred to the binding nature of the UDHR. As was declared in the Tehran Proclamation:

> The Universal Declaration of Human Rights states a common understanding of the peoples of the world concerning the inalienable and inviolable rights of all members of the human family and constitutes an obligation for the members of the international community.[35]

The UDHR is a unique human rights document and is not comparable to other UN Declarations. The high regard in which it is held is evident from its reference in international instruments in the 70 years since it was created.[36]

---

31 Louis B Sohn, 'Sources of International Law' (1995) 25 *Georgia Journal of International and Comparative Law* 399, 399 citing Jordan Paust.

32 This point was noted by Woods (n 10) 3.

33 Sohn, 'Sources of International Law' (n 31).

34 For example, see instruments cited in note 5. See also UNGA Res, UN Millennium Declaration (8 September 2000) UN Doc A/55/ L2, part 5; UNGA Res, Declaration on the Granting of Independence to Colonial Countries (14 December 1960) UN Doc 1514 (XV), para 7. See also Smith (n 14) 39; Rehman (n 4) 80-82; Gudmundur Alfredsson and Asbørn Eide (eds), *The Universal Declaration of Human Rights: A Common Standard of Achievement* (Kluwer 1999) xxxi.

35 Tehran Proclamation para 2. In 1968, the International Conference on Human Rights convened in Tehran to assess the implementation of the UDHR on its 20th anniversary. This group consisted of representatives from 86 States, UN bodies and specialized agencies, NGOs and inter-governmental organisations. The Conference adopted the Tehran Proclamation, by consensus on 13 May 1968.

36 ECHR, preamble; International Covenant on Civil and Political Rights (adopted 16 December 1966, entered into force 23 March 1976) 999 UNTS 171 (ICCPR), preamble; International Convention on Economic, Social and Cultural Rights (adopted 16 December 1966, entered into force 3 January 1976) 993 UNTS 3, preamble; Tehran Proclamation; African Charter, preamble; Vienna Declaration and Programme of Action; Helsinki Act; Arab Charter on Human Rights (adopted 22 May 2004, entered into force 15 March 2008) *reprinted in* (2005) 12 *Int'l Hum Rts Rep* 893, preamble. Rehman notes that the reference to the UDHR in significant regional human rights treaties affirms the satisfaction of the *opinio juris* criteria being fulfilled. See Rehman (n 4) 80.

In addition, many of the rights listed in the UDHR have been reproduced in binding human rights treaties. Moreover, the UN bodies with important human rights responsibilities have reaffirmed the provisions of the UDHR on numerous occasions.[37] All of this amounts to persuasive evidence in support of the argument that *opinio juris* exists to the effect that the UDHR has reached customary status. As Louis B Sohn notes, 'consistent practice of the United Nations, which has imbued the Declaration with a status almost equal to that of the Charter itself'.[38]

3. The Provisions of the UDHR as Customary International Law

Within the debate as to the customary status of the UDHR, the question arises as to whether it achieves customary status as a whole, or in part. In the past, some writers have asserted that the UDHR has reached the status of customary international law in its entirety. However, more recent analysis suggests that this is not the case and, in fact, the provisions must be explored individually in terms of their customary status.[39] It is accepted that the UDHR provisions considered to be fundamental human rights have reached customary status.[40] However, there is a lack of agreement as to what rights are in the category of fundamental rights.[41] For example, Hurst Hannum notes that it would be difficult to argue that the right to rest and leisure provided in Art 24,[42] or the right to protection from unemployment in Art 23(1), have reached customary law status.[43] Conversely, it is clear that provisions such as the prohibitions on

---

37 See UNGA Res 60/251, 3 April 2006, which relates to the Human Rights Council.

38 Sohn (n 9) 25.

39 Smith (n 14) 39; Patrick Thornberry, *International Law and the Rights of Minorities* (Clarendon Press 1991) 322.

40 James Crawford, *Brownlie's Principles of Public International Law* (8th edn, OUP 2012) 642. Indeed, when the UDHR was being drafted, some delegates were cognisant that some of the principles inserted into the Declaration were already customary law, see Sohn (n 9) 21.

41 Crawford, ibid 642.

42 UDHR, Art 24 reads: 'Everyone has the right to rest and leisure, including reasonable limitation of working hours and periodic holidays with pay'.

43 UDHR, Art 23 (1) reads: 'Everyone has the right to work, to free choice of employment, to just and favourable conditions of work and to protection against unemployment'. Hannum (n 7) 340.

slavery,[44] torture,[45] discrimination,[46] and the right to a fair trial[47] have reached the status of customary international law. Applying this 'provision-by-provision' approach, the vast majority of the UDHR provisions have reached customary status.[48]

The rights that are agreed to have reached the status of customary international law are, for the most part, civil and political in nature.[49] It has proved difficult for economic, social and cultural rights (ESCR) to reach customary status.[50] One of the fundamental human rights principles held to exist is to wrongfully deprive '...human beings of their freedom and to subject them to physical constraint in conditions of hardship...' as was declared by the ICJ in the *Tehran Hostages case*.[51] What is more, in its memorandum as part of the case proceedings, the US affirmed that:

> The existence of such fundamental rights for all human beings, nationals and aliens alike, and the existence of a corresponding duty on the part of every State to respect and observe them, are now reflected, *inter alia,* in the Universal Declaration of Human Rights....'.[52]

Similarly, in the *Barcelona Traction* case, the ICJ cited freedom from slavery and racial discrimination as obligations *erga omnes*, declaring them to be included among the 'principles and rules concerning the basic rights of the human person'.[53] Importantly, this list is not conclusive.[54]

---

44 UDHR, Art 4 reads: 'No one shall be held in slavery or servitude; slavery and the slave trade shall be prohibited in all their forms'.

45 UDHR, Art 5: 'No one shall be subjected to torture or to cruel, inhuman or degrading treatment or punishment'.

46 UDHR, Art 2 reads, 'Everyone is entitled to all the rights and freedoms set forth in this Declaration, without distinction of any kind, such as race, colour, sex, language, religion, political or other opinion, national or social origin, property, birth or other status. Furthermore, no distinction shall be made on the basis of the political, jurisdictional or international status of the country or territory to which a person belongs, whether it be independent, trust, non-self-governing or under any other limitation of sovereignty'.

47 UDHR, Art 10 reads: 'Everyone is entitled in full equality to a fair and public hearing by an independent and impartial tribunal, in the determination of his rights and obligations and of any criminal charge against him'. See also Arts 7 and 11.

48 Rchman (n 4) 80.

49 Lillich (n 10) 8. Writing in 1983, Philip Alston noted that there was persuasive evidence to suggest that the first 21 articles of the UDHR had reached customary status, see, Philip Alston 'The Universal Declaration at 35: Western passé or alive and universal' (1983) 31 *International Commission of Jurists Review* 60, 69.

50 Rehman (n 4) 82. However, Schachter asserted that some ESCR have reached the status of customary rules, Schachter (n 26) 340.

51 As noted by Schachter, ibid 337. See Tehran Hostages case (n 6) para 92. Here, the Court specifically referred to the human rights principles within the UN Charter and the UDHR.

52 Memorial of the Government of the United States of America in Tehran Hostages Case, p 182. See also Lilich (n 10) 3.

53 *Barcelona Traction Case (Belgium v Spain)* [1970] ICJ Rep 4, para 34.

54 See the wording used by the Court, ibid.

The American Law Institute's Third Restatement of Foreign Relations Law of the United States is often cited in support of some UDHR provisions having reached customary status. Section 702 concerning 'Customary International Law of Human Rights' provides a list that the organisation considers to be customary international law. It reads:

> A state violates international law if, as a matter of state policy, it practices, encourages, or condones
> (a) genocide,
> (b) slavery or slave trade,
> (c) the murder or causing the disappearance of individuals,
> (d) torture or other cruel, inhuman, or degrading treatment or punishment,
> (e) prolonged arbitrary detention,
> (f) systematic racial discrimination, or
> (g) a consistent pattern of gross violations of internationally recognized human rights.

There is considerable overlap between the rights listed here and the rights declared to be customary international law by the ICJ.[55] Support for the rights in this list having become customary rules can be found in academic writing.[56] Meron adds due process rights to this list.[57] Significantly, the list is non-exhaustive.[58]

It is well established that the provisions of the UDHR that are *jus cogens* peremptory norms have reached customary status.[59] What is more, as Schachter notes, the concept of *jus cogens* is virtually accepted by all States.[60] It is certain that the prohibitions on torture,[61] genocide,[62] slavery, racial discrimination and

---

55 See for example, *Barcelona Traction Case* (n 53) para 34 and *Questions relating to the Obligation to Prosecute or Extradite (Belgium v Senegal)* (Judgment) [2012] ICJ Rep 2012, 422, para 99.

56 Meron (n 10) 96-97; Lillich (10) 6.

57 Meron, ibid.

58 Meron, ibid 99. The American Law Institute is in the process of drafting the Fourth Restatement of the Foreign Relations Law of the United States.

59 Rehman (n 4) 82.

60 Schachter (n 26) 342. Art 53 of the Vienna Convention on the Law of Treaties (adopted 23 May 1969, entered into force 27 January 1980) 1155 UNTS 331 (Vienna Convention) supports this point. It reads: 'A treaty is void if, at the time of its conclusion, it conflicts with a peremptory norm of general international law. For the purposes of the present Convention, a peremptory norm of general international law is a norm accepted and recognised by the international community of States as a whole as a norm from which no derogation is permitted and which can be modified only by a subsequent norm of general international law having the same character'. The Vienna Convention is considered to be customary international law.

61 *Questions relating to the Obligation to Prosecute or Extradite* (n 55) para 99; *Furundzija Case* (Trial Judgment) IT-95-17/1-T (10 December 1998) para 144.

62 Final Report of the Commission of Experts established pursuant to Security Council Resolution 780 (27 May 1994) UN Doc. S/1994/674, para 107.

the crime of aggression are among the list of *jus cogens* peremptory norms.[63] Indeed, Rehman asserts that more rights can be added to this list.[64] The concept of *jus cogens* has yet to be dealt with in a substantive way by an international tribunal. However, in his separate opinion as part of the ICJ judgment in *Questions relating to the Obligation to Prosecute or Extradite*, Judge Antônio Cançado Trindade asserted that *jus cogens* consists of the 'very foundations of a truly universal international law'.[65]

4. The Nexus Between the UDHR and the UN Charter

The drafting history of the UDHR suggests that its content was intended to codify the human rights element of the UN Charter.[66] One of the first tasks for the newly formed United Nations was to compose a Bill of Rights,[67] and the formation of the UDHR was part of this initiative. In 1948, René Cassin stated that the UDHR would be 'an authoritative interpretation for the Charter of the United Nations'.[68] The UN Charter is a binding international agreement that creates obligations on the UN Member States.[69] The opening sentences of the Charter declare that the peoples of the UN 'reaffirm faith in fundamental human rights, in the dignity and worth of the human person, in the equal rights of men and women and of nations large and small'.[70] Article 55 is considered to be 'the human rights provision' of the UN Charter, [71] which Member States have pledged to achieve through separate and joint UN action.[72] However, it is clear that the references to human rights within the Charter are made with the maintenance of international peace and security in mind.[73]

Despite its references to human rights and fundamental freedoms, other

63 *Barcelona Traction Case* (n 53) para 34.

64 Rehman asserts that rights such as the right to life, liberty and security, equality, the right to a fair trial, the presumption of innocence and the prohibition of retroactive criminal law have reached the status of *jus cogens*, see Rehman (n 4) 82.

65 *Questions relating to the Obligation to Prosecute or Extradite* (n 55) para 102.

66 Sohn (n 9) 23.

67 ibid.

68 Cited in McBeth, Noland and Rice (n 2) 22. This was one reason why South Africa abstained from the vote, see Rehman (n 4) 79-80.

69 Drzewicki (n 1) 14.

70 UN Charter, preamble.

71 UN Charter, Art 55 reads: 'With a view to the creation of conditions of stability and well-being which are necessary for peaceful and friendly relations among nations based on respect for the principle of equal rights and self-determination of peoples, the United Nations shall promote:

a. higher standards of living, full employment, and conditions of economic and social progress and development;
b. solutions of international economic, social, health, and related problems; and international cultural and educational cooperation; and
c. universal respect for, and observance of, human rights and fundamental freedoms for all without distinction as to race, sex, language, or religion'.

72 UN Charter, Art 56. See also Schachter (n 26) 335.

73 See UN Charter Art 55(c) in note 71.

than non-discrimination, the Charter is silent as to the identification of these rights, nor does it specify how human rights are to be enforced and achieved.[74] Moreover, vague terminology is used in terms of how human rights are to be respected.[75] The adoption of the UDHR has been described as 'the first, and possibly the singularly most important, step taken by the United Nations in furtherance of the incumbent obligation to promote respect for human rights and fundamental freedoms'.[76] It is this linkage to the UN Charter that adds to the legally binding nature of the Declaration. The superior position it holds is evidenced by its reference in subsequent human rights treaties.[77] There appears to be consensus now that the UDHR provisions proclaim the human rights and fundamental freedoms mentioned in Articles 55 and 56 of the UN Charter.[78] Moreover, the nexus between the UDHR and the UN Charter has been recognised by the ICJ.[79] As Nigel Rodley noted, 'The Universal Declaration of Human Rights was the document that ensured that the Charter's human rights clauses did not remain a dead letter'.[80]

5. The Role of the UDHR in the Implementation and Monitoring of International Human Rights

The customary status of the UDHR is also evident in its role in the implementation and monitoring of fundamental human rights worldwide. One of the ways in which some of the provisions of the UDHR have become legally binding is by their repetition and codification in international human rights treaties. The provisions of the international treaties, which have stemmed from the UDHR are legally binding on the States that have ratified them.[81] What is more, some of these provisions have reached the status of customary international law.[82] The publication of these rights in the UDHR before the binding international treaties (such as the ECHR and ICCPR), contributed to their customary status. The reliance on the UDHR as a means of assessing State implementation of fundamental human rights also demonstrates the customary status of the UDHR. In particular, the role of the UDHR in the Universal

---

74 Drzewicki (n 1) 13; Schachter (n 26) 335. Art 1(3) of the UN Charter reads: 'To achieve international cooperation in solving international problems of an economic, social, cultural, or humanitarian character, and in promoting and encouraging respect for human rights and for fundamental freedoms for all without distinction as to race, sex, language, or religion'.

75 Drzewicki, ibid 14.

76 Smith (n 14) 38.

77 See treaties cited in notes 5 and 36.

78 Nigel Rodley, 'Can Armed Opposition Groups Violate Human Rights?' in Kathleen E Mahoney and Paul Mahoney (eds), *Human Rights in the Twenty-first Century: A Global Challenge* (Martinus Nijhoff Publishers 1993) 305.

79 See note 51.

80 Nigel Rodley, 'The Universal Declaration of Human Rights: Learning from Experience' in Barend Van Der Heijden and Bahia Tahzib-Lie (eds), *Reflections on the Universal Declaration of Human Rights* (Martinus Nijhoff Publishers 1998) 261.

81 McBeth, Noland and Rice (n 2) 181.

82 See the rights listed as being customary international law in sections 2 and 3 above.

Periodic Review (UPR) is often cited in support of the Declaration having achieved customary status. Through their routine reliance on the Declaration, the Treaty Monitoring Bodies (and indeed the UPR) extend the customary reach of the UDHR, which in turn develops and reinforces its customary status.[83] As part of the UPR, States have to report on the realisation of the UDHR provisions.[84] Moreover, it can be argued that this procedure is evidence that States view the UDHR as legally binding.[85]

On a national level, the Declaration is automatically applicable in all States because of its status as a resolution of the UN General Assembly, as opposed to an international treaty.[86] This is particularly important when it comes to enforcing human rights in dualist States.[87] Notwithstanding that the UDHR cannot be relied on directly in the courts of dualist States,[88] such as Ireland, its provisions can be found in the national legislation of such States.[89] Moreover, UN Special Rapporteurs can rely on the Declaration in situations where international human rights treaties do not apply.[90]

Finally, it must also be noted that fundamental human rights have had an influence on international criminal law. As William A Schabas notes, 'Evolving concepts of international human rights law have also played a role in the creation of the *ad hoc* tribunals'.[91] The provisions of the UDHR have played a significant role in this regard, as they epitomise fundamental human rights. What is more, the UDHR has been referred to in case law of the international criminal tribunals,[92] and its influence can be found in Art 21(3) of the Rome Statute of the International Criminal Court.

---

83 UN Human Rights Council, Institution-building of the United Nations Human Rights Council (18 June 2007) UN Doc A/HRC/RES/5/1, annex.

84 McBeth, Noland and Rice (n 2) 181; Oliver De Schutter, *International Human Rights Law* (2nd edn, CUP 2014) 63.

85 McBeth, Noland and Rice, ibid. For more on the nexus between the UDHR and the UPR please see Noelle Higgins, 'Implementing Universal Declaration of Human Rights Standards through the Universal Periodic Review Mechanism' in this volume.

86 See also Alfredsson and Eide (n 34) xxxi.

87 Hannum (n 7) 292-93.

88 Hannum, ibid.

89 For example, freedom from torture is criminalised under Irish law under the Criminal Justice (United Nations Convention Against Torture Act) 2000. The prohibition also exists as an unenumerated right under the Constitution, see Elaine Dewhurst, Noelle Higgins and Los Watkins, *Principles of Irish Human Rights Law* (Clarus Press 2012). Similarly, modern day slavery is criminalised in Irish law under the Criminal Law (Human Trafficking) Act 2008. In the UK, modern day slavery is criminalised under the Modern Slavery Act 2015.

90 Alfredsson and Eide (n 34) xxxi.

91 William A Schabas, *The UN International Criminal Tribunals: The former Yugoslavia, Rwanda and Sierra Leone* (CUP 2006) 8. See also Paola Gaeta and Antonio Cassese, *Cassese's International Criminal Law* (3rd edn, OUP 2013) 6.

92 *Kunarac case* (Trial Judgment) IT-96-23-T (22 February 2001) paras 477, 533; *Blaškić Case* (Trial Judgment) IT-95-14 (3 March 2000) para 220.

6. Conclusion

One of the effects of the UDHR provisions having reached the status of customary international law is that they are binding on all States, except for persistent objectors.[93] Moreover, reservations to international conventions cannot affect the application of the same rule in customary law.[94] Importantly, reservations are not permitted in respect of *jus cogens* norm.[95] A further effect of a rule becoming part of customary international human rights law is that it '…allows not only the treaty non-parties, but also the parties to have recourse to international law remedies not provided for in the treaties'.[96]

It is arguable that those provisions that have yet to crystalise into customary international law are in the process of doing so. As Mary Robinson noted on the occasion of the 50th anniversary, the UDHR:

> … has become an elevating force on the events of our world because it can be seen to embody the legal, moral and philosophical beliefs held true by all peoples and because it applies to all.[97]

This chapter has argued that provisions of the UDHR have reached customary status on a number of grounds. It is contended that in order to quantify the scope of the UDHR under customary international law, a large-scale study is needed in order to examine the scope of the Declaration at a national and an international level.[98]

7. Bibliography

Alfredsson, Gudmundur and Eide, Asbørn (eds), *The Universal Declaration of Human Rights: A Common Standard of Achievement* (Kluwer 1999)

Alston, Philip, 'The Universal Declaration at 35: Western passé or alive and universal' (1983) 31 *International Commission of Jurists Review* 60

Baderin, Mashood A, (eds), *International Human Rights Law: Six Decades After the UDHR and Beyond* (Routledge 2016)

Cassese, Antonio, *International Law* (2nd edn, OUP 2005)

Crawford, James *Brownlie's Principles of Public International Law* (8th edn, OUP 2012)

93 As Hammun notes, 'Almost no state has specifically rejected the principles proclaimed in the Universal Declaration'. Hannum (n 7) 340-41.

94 Meron (n 10) 7.

95 Myres S McDougal, Harold D Lasswell and Lung-Chu Chen, *Human Rights and World Public Order* (Yale University Press 1980) 274.

96 Schachter (n 26) 335.

97 Mary Robinson, 'The Universal Declaration of Human Rights: The International Keystone of Human Dignity' in Barend Van Der Heijden and Bahia Tahzib-Lie (eds), *Reflections on the Universal Declaration of Human Rights* (Martinus Nijhoff Publishers 1998) 257.

98 The need for a large study has been recognised by Meron (n 10) 94.

De Schutter, Oliver, *International Human Rights Law* (2nd edn, CUP 2014)

Dewhurst, Elaine, Higgins, Noelle and Watkins, Los, *Principles of Irish Human Rights Law* (Clarus Press 2012)

Drzewicki, Krzysztof, 'Human Rights in the United Nations Charter and the Universal Declaration of Human Rights' (1998) 7 *Polish Quarterly of International Affairs* 9

Hannum, Hurst, 'The Status of the Universal Declaration of Human Rights in National and International Law' (1995) 25 *Georgia Journal of International & Comparative Law* 287

Henkin, Louis, *The Age of Rights* (Columbia University Press 1990)

International Committee of the Red Cross, Customary IHL database at https://ihl-databases.icrc.org/customary-ihl/eng/docs/home, accessed 28 October 2018

Lillich, RB, 'The Growing Importance of Customary International Human Rights Law', (1995/96) 25 *Georgia Journal of International & Comparative Law* 1

Macfarlane, LJ *Human Rights: realities and Possibilities: Northern Ireland, the Republic of Ireland and Hungary* (Macmillan 1990)

McBeth, Adam, Justin Noland and Simon Rice, *The International Law of Human Rights* (2nd edn, OUP 2017)

McDougal, Myres S, Lasswell, Harold D and Chen, Lunh-Chu, *Human Rights and World Public Order* (Yale University Press 1980)

Meron, Theodor, *Human Rights and Humanitarian Norms* (Clarendon Press 1989)

Rehman, Javaid, *International Human Rights Law* (2nd edn, Pearsons 2010)

Rodley, Nigel, 'The Universal Declaration of Human Rights: Learning from Experience' in Barend Van Der Heijden and Bahia Tahzib-Lie (eds), *Reflections on the Universal Declaration of Human Rights* (Martinus Nijhoff Publishers 1998) 261

Rodley, Nigel, 'Can Armed Opposition Groups Violate Human Rights?' in Kathleen E Mahoney and Paul Mahoney (eds), *Human Rights in the Twenty-first Century: A Global Challenge* (Martinus Nijhoff Publishers 1993)

Rodley, Nigel and Pollard, Matt, *The Treatment of Prisoners under International Law* (3rd edn, OUP 2009)

Schabas, William A, *The UN International Criminal Tribunals: The former Yugoslavia, Rwanda and Sierra Leone* (CUP 2006)

Schachter, Oscar, *International Law in Theory and Practice* (Martinus Nijhoff Publishers 1991)

Schwelb, Egon, *Human Rights and the International Community: the Roots and Growth of the Universal Declaration of Human Rights 1948-1963* (Quadrangle Books 1964)

Simma, Bruno and Alston, Philip, 'The Sources of Human Rights Law: Custom, Jus Cogens, and General Principles' (1992) 12 *Australian Yearbook of International Law* 82

Smith, Rhona KM, *Textbook on International Human Rights* (7th edn, OUP 2016)

Sohn, Louis B., 'Sources of International Law' (1995) 25 *Georgia Journal of International and Comparative Law* 399

Sohn, Louis B., 'The Human Rights Law of the Charter' (1977) 12 *Texas International Law Journal* 129

Sohn, Louis B., 'The Universal Declaration of Human Rights: A common standard of achievement? The Status of the Universal Declaration in International Law' (1967) 8 *Journal of the International Commission of Jurists* 17

Thornberry, Patrick, *International Law and the Rights of Minorities* (Clarendon Press 1991)

Van Der Heijden Barend and Tahzib-Lie, Bahia, (eds), *Reflections on the Universal Declaration of Human Rights* (Martinus Nijhoff Publishers 1998)

Woods, Michael, 'Customary International Law and Human Rights', EUI working Papers, (AEL 2016/03 Academy of European Law, Distinguished Lectures of the Academy)

CHAPTER 2

IMPLEMENTING UNIVERSAL DECLARATION OF HUMAN RIGHTS STANDARDS THROUGH THE UNIVERSAL PERIODIC REVIEW MECHANISM

By Noelle Higgins

1. INTRODUCTION

The Universal Declaration of Human Rights (UDHR)[1] is the foundation stone of modern human rights discourse and practice, and has served as the inspiration behind developments within the United Nations (UN) human rights treaty system. States have aspired to respect the norms enshrined in the UDHR since it was adopted in 1948, and it has been revisited consistently, as the basis of UN[2] and regional human rights frameworks since.[3] In 2006, almost sixty years after its adoption, attention was again focused on the UDHR as a standard setter for states' human rights practices and policies, with the adoption of the Universal Periodic Review (UPR) mechanism. The UPR has as its aim the monitoring and assessment of the fulfilment by each state of its human rights obligations and commitments.[4] Also within its remit is the measurement of positive developments within States in the field of human rights, and the facilitation

---

1 UN General Assembly, Universal Declaration of Human Rights, 10 December 1948, 217 A (III).

2 See for example, the Vienna Declaration and Programme of Action, Adopted by the World Conference on Human Rights in Vienna on 25 June 1993, reaffirms, in its Preamble, states: 'commitment to the purposes and principles contained in the Charter of the United Nations and the Universal Declaration of Human Rights'. It further states that 'Emphasizing that the Universal Declaration of Human Rights, which constitutes a common standard of achievement for all peoples and all nations, is the source of inspiration and has been the basis for the United Nations in making advances in standard setting as contained in the existing international human rights instruments, in particular the International Covenant on Civil and Political Rights and the International Covenant on Economic, Social and Cultural Rights'. In addition, it refers to the UDHR throughout – paras 23, 31, 33, 38, and 57.

3 See, for example, the Convention for the Protection of Human Rights and Fundamental Freedoms, better known as the European Convention on Human Rights, Rome, 4.XI.1950., which recognises the UDHR as a source of inspiration for the work of the Council of Europe and that European countries, through the ECHR are taking 'the first steps for the collective enforcement of certain of the rights stated in the Universal Declaration.'

4 UN Human Rights Council, 'Institution-building of the United Nations Human Rights Council', HRC Res 5/1 UN GAOR, 5th Sess, 9th mtg, (2007) 1 UN Doc A/HRC/5/1.

of sharing of best practices in human rights protection between States.[5] The UDHR serves as a basis for the review, in addition to any other human rights instruments which have been ratified by the State under review, as well as applicable international humanitarian law, and any other commitments or pledges concerning human rights issues made by it.[6] The aim of this chapter is to analyse the development of the UPR mechanism to date and its contribution to the promotion of human rights standards worldwide, and also to examine the importance of the UDHR in this process.

2. The Foundations of the Universal Human Rights System at the United Nations

The UDHR is a milestone document in the history of human rights, adopted by the UN General Assembly in 1948, three years after the establishment of the UN. The drafters of the UN Charter agreed that the organisation should focus on promoting human rights as one of its primary aims. While Art 55 of the Charter refers to human rights, providing that 'the United Nations shall promote . . . universal respect for, and observance of, human rights and fundamental freedoms for all without distinction as to race, sex, language, or religion',[7] the Charter itself did not expand on the concept of human rights and fundamental freedoms or seek to enumerate them.[8] That task was given to the newly established Commission on Human Rights, which was asked to prepare an international bill of rights. This bill of rights began with the UDHR, and was later followed, and complemented, by the International Covenant on Civil and Political Rights and the International Covenant on Economic, Social and Cultural Rights adopted in 1966.[9] The UDHR was drafted by State representatives with different legal and cultural backgrounds from different areas of the world. While the drafting process was not without its difficulties,[10] the Declaration was finally adopted by the General Assembly in Paris on 10 December 1948,[11] by a vote of forty-eight in favour, none opposing, and eight abstaining.[12] It was deemed to be a common standard of achievements for all peoples and all nations, as it set out, for the first time, fundamental human rights which were to be universally protected.[13] Since then, this instrument has

---

5 ibid.

6 ibid, annex at 1.A.1.

7 United Nations, Charter of the United Nations, 24 October 1945, 1 UNTS XVI, art 55(c).

8 Oscar Schachter, 'The Genesis of the Declaration: A Fresh Examination' (1999) 11 *Pace Int'l Law Rev* 27, 53, where he discusses differing opinions on the inclusion of specific rights and freedoms in the UN Charter.

9 The Covenants were adopted by the United Nations General Assembly Resolution 2200A (XXI) of 16 December 1966.

10 See Hersch Lauterpacht, 'The Universal Declaration of Human Rights' (1948) 25 *Brit Yb Int'l L* 354; Oscar Schachter, n 8; Mary Ann Glendon, 'Knowing the Universal Declaration of Human Rights' (1998) 73 *Notre Dame L Rev* 1153.

11 UNGA Res 217A, 10 December 1948.

12 Mary Ann Glendon, n 10, 1162.

13 Eleanor Roosevelt, US Representative to the General Assembly, Statement during the General Assembly's Adoption of the UDHR (9 December 1948), in Department of State

been translated into over 500 languages and has served as an inspiration for the development of the human rights universally, regionally and domestically. It has also served as the progenitor for the current UN human rights treaty system, which now consists of 9 treaties focusing on various aspects of human life.[14] While the UDHR was intended as the first step in the process of creating binding human rights instruments, which would place obligations on States in respect of their citizens, the ICCPR and ICESCR did not come into force until 1976. In between times, the UDHR served as the guide for the development of States' human rights laws, policies and practices, even though it was drafted as a non-binding instrument. Despite the adoption of a number of binding human rights instruments since the UDHR was adopted, it has remained of central importance as a yardstick by which to measure States' human rights practices and policies.[15] This is highlighted by its role in the UPR process.

3. The UPR Mechanism

The UN established the Human Rights Council (the Council) in 2006[16] in response to criticism of the Human Rights Commission,[17] and in an attempt

Bulletin, 19 December 1948, 751 (underlining that the UDHR is not intended to be a treaty or an international agreement but a set of broad principles of rights and freedoms).

14 These instruments are: the Convention on the Elimination of all forms of Racial Discrimination, adopted 21 December 1965, United Nations, Treaty Series, vol. 660, p 195; the International Covenant on Civil and Political Rights, adopted 16 December 1966 by the United Nations General Assembly Resolution 2200A (XXI); the International Covenant on Economic, Social and Cultural Rights, adopted 16 December 1966 by the United Nations General Assembly Resolution 2200A (XXI); the Convention on the Elimination of all forms of Discrimination Against Women, adopted 18 December 1979, United Nations, Treaty Series, vol. 1249, p 13, the Convention Against Torture, and Other Cruel, Inhuman or Degrading Treatment or Punishment, adopted 10 December 1084, United Nations, Treaty Series, vol.1465, p 85; the Convention on the Rights of the Child, adopted 20 November 1989, United Nations, Treaty Series, vol 1577, p 3; the International Convention on the Protection of the Rights of All Migrant Workers and Members of Their Families, adopted 18 December 1990, A/RES/45/158; Convention on the Rights of Persons with Disabilities, adopted 24 January 2007, A/RES/61/106 and the International Convention for the Protection of all Persons from Enforced Disappearance, adopted 12 January 2007, A/RES/61/177.

15 Malik comments: 'Whenever the question of human rights has arisen throughout the world, the appeal has been far more to the Declaration than to the covenants.' Charles Malik, '1948 – The Drafting of the Universal Declaration of Human Rights' (1986) 97 *UN Bull Hum Rts* 18, quoted in Mary Ann Glendon, 'The Rule of Law in the Universal Declaration of Human Rights' (2004) 2(1) *Nw J Int'l Hum Rts* 1, p 12.

16 UNGA Res 60/251, 15 March 2006. With regard to the history and functions of the Human Rights Council, see Patrick J Flood, 'The U.N. Human Rights Council: Is its Mandate well-designed?' (2008-2009) 15 *ILSA J Int'l & Com L* 472 and Jarvis Matiya, 'Repositioning the international human rights protection system: the UN Human Rights Council' (2010) 36(2) *Commonwealth L Bull* 313.

17 See Hening Boekle, 'Western States, the UN Commission on Human Rights and the "1235" procedure: the question of bias revisited' (1995) 13 NQHR 367 and Thomas Franck, 'Of Gnats and Camels: Is there a Double Standard in the United Nations?' (1984) 78 *AJIL* 811. For a discussion of the transition from the Human Rights Commission to the Human Rights Council, see Paul Gordon Lauren, 'To Preserve and Build on its

to improve the organisation's standing as a promoter of human rights.[18] The Council was charged with undertaking 'a universal periodic review (UPR), based on objective and reliable information, of the fulfilment by each State of its human rights obligations and commitments in a manner which ensures universality of coverage and equal treatment with respect to all States'.[19] Thus, the UPR mechanism was established,[20] through the adoption by the Council of its 'institution-building package' in 2007, with its main aim being the assessment of states' human rights policies and practices,[21] as well as measuring positive developments within States in the field of human rights, and facilitating the sharing of best practices between States.[22] Every member State of the UN undergoes a review at the Human Rights Council every four-and-a-half to five years. The UDHR plays an important role in the UPR as it serves as a basis for the review. States are also reviewed as to how they live up to their obligations under other human rights instruments which they have ratified, in addition to applicable international humanitarian law, and any other commitments or pledges concerning human rights issues made by them.[23] Despite its status as a non-binding document, the UDHR still plays a very significant role in measuring states' human rights practices and policies. It applies equally to all States, unlike other UN and international humanitarian law treaties, which States can choose to ratify or not. In addition, States can make reservations to provisions in human rights treaties, and can, at times, derogate from their obligations under such treaties, thus diluting their impact.[24] However, the UDHR is universally applicable to all States, and thus serves as a constant in the UPR assessment process.

Cycle 1 of the UPR process began in 2008 and ended in 2011, with every member State of the UN undergoing a review. The process was tweaked before

---

Achievements and to Redress its Shortcomings: The Journey from the Commission on Human Rights to the Human Rights Council' (2007) 28 *HRQ* 307.

18 The Human Rights Council replaced the Human Rights Commission by virtue of UN General Assembly Resolution 60/251 (2006). See generally, Bertrand G Ramcharan, *The UN Human Rights Council* (Routledge 2011); Marc Bossuyt, 'The Human Rights Council: A First Appraisal' (2006) 24(4) *NQHR* 551 and Nico Schrijver, 'The UN Human Rights Council: A New "Society of the Committed" or Just Old Wine in New Bottles?' (2007) 20(4) *Ldn J Int'l L* 809.

19 UNGA Res 60/251, 15 March 2006. For a discussion of the UPR see Patrick J Flood, n 16, and Edward McMahon and Marta Ascherio, 'A Step Ahead in Promoting Human Rights? The Universal Periodic Review of the UN Human Rights Council' (2012) 18 *Glob Gov* 231.

20 Different States had varying views on the format they hoped the UPR would take. See Human Rights Peer Review, Draft Concept and Opinions Paper, prepared by Canada, (29 April 2005), para 9: <www.humanrightsvoices.org/assets/attachments/documents/human_rights_peer_review_canada.pdf> accessed August, 2018.

21 UN Human Rights Council, 'Institution-building of the United Nations Human Rights Council', HRC Res 5/1 UN GAOR, 5th Sess., 9th mtg., (2007) 1 UN Doc A/HRC/5/1.

22 ibid.

23 ibid, annex at 1.A.1.

24 See Liesbeth Lijnzaad, *Reservations to UN-Human Rights Treaties* (Martinus Nijhoff 1995); Rosalyn Higgins; 'Derogations under Human Rights Treaties' (1977) 48(1) *Br Yb Int'l L* 281.

the beginning of Cycle 2 (2012-2016), with some minor amendments being made to the procedures, including an increase in the time dedicated to each State's review before the Human Rights Council and the subsequent extension of the timeframe of each cycle from four to four-and-a-half years.[25] Cycle 3, which began in 2017 is currently ongoing, and will be completed in 2021. A combined total of 57,686 recommendations were made during the first two cycles. All States participated in their reviews and there has been substantial engagement by States generally with the process to date.[26]

4. The UPR in Action

There are various different phases in the UPR process: Preparation, Interaction, Consideration, Adoption, and Implementation.[27] The UDHR is an important benchmark during each phase, by which States' commitments to human rights can be measured.

Preparation phase

The preparation phase focuses on information gathering, and 3 reports on States' human rights policies and practices are compiled. The first report is compiled by the State under review, the second is a summary of reports from other human rights actors, including non-governmental organisations (NGOs), which is collated by the Office of the High Commissioner for Human Rights, and the final report is compiled from information provided by independent human rights experts, human rights treaty bodies and other UN entities. The

---

25 See resolution 16/21, 15 March 2011 and decision 17/119.

26 Almost all States also engaged in the UPR process by making recommendations to other States on a variety of issues, with only 22 States failing to make any recommendations at all. See <www.upr-info.org/database/statistics> accessed July 2018. However, in January 2013 Israel did not deliver its second UPR report on time, but in March Israel clarified that it sought a mere postponement of its report and dismissed rumours of UPR repudiation. See Phoebe Greenwood, 'Israel Refuses to Appear before UN Human Rights Review' *The Telegraph* (29 January 2013) Israel's request for a postponement was not as a result of dissatisfaction with the UPR process itself, but was rather a product of its feelings towards the Human Rights Council in general. See Barak Ravid, 'Israel to negotiate renewal of cooperation with UN Human Rights Council' *Haaretz* (7 May 2013). Some other States have experienced difficulties in engaging with the UPR on schedule or as per the guidelines. For example, Cape Verde did not submit a national report for its first review in 2008 (it subsequently submitted a report for the second UPR cycle in April 2013) but the review still continued, while Haiti's first review was postponed from the eight to the twelfth session due to the earthquake which had devastated the region. South Africa failed to submit its written report on time for its first review and thus took the option of presenting its report orally. It did, however, then distribute a written report during its oral submission.

27 See Joshua Cooper, 'Universal Periodic Review: A Potent Process for the Realization of Human Rights in Indigenous Homelands' (2014) 28(2) *Cultural Survival Quarterly Magazine*: <www.culturalsurvival.org/publications/cultural-survival-quarterly/universal-periodic-review-potent-process-realization-human> accessed July 2018.

UDHR can be referred to in these reports, as the principles enshrined therein are the standard to which States should aspire in their practices and policies.

Interaction phase

The second phase of the UPR, also known as the 'interactive dialogue' phase, takes place at the Human Rights Council in Geneva, when every State under review provides an oral report on their human rights policies and practices on a rolling basis. Reviews are carried out by the UPR Working Group, which consists of the 47 members of the Human Rights Council. Representatives of any UN member state can ask questions from, and make recommendations to, the State under review. However, tight time restrictions apply to this session and States under review have just 70 minutes for presentation and discussion, and other states have a combined total of 140 minutes to ask questions and make recommendations. This results in 'many States not being able to speak at all, and diplomats lining up in the pre-dawn darkness to register to speak.'[28] Sweeney and Saito comment that this leads to 'a negative trend … of "friendly States" filling the speakers' list to compliment the State under review.'[29] However, States which do not have a chance to speak during the interactive dialogue stage can submit their comments later, via the UPR's extranet.[30] During this phase references may be made to the UDHR by the State under review as to how this instrument may have guided its policies and practices, and other States may also refer to it to underline where States are not living up to the standards espoused in the instrument.

Consideration and adoption phases

Once a State under review has delivered its oral report and received recommendations from other States, they then have time to consider these recommendations and whether they should adopt them. A report is then completed by three members of the Council, a 'Troika', tasked with the role of preparing an 'outcome report', with the assistance of the Office of the High Commissioner for Human Rights. This includes a summary of the dialogue between the State under review and other States, as well as recommendations and questions put to the State under review. No sooner than 48 hours after the interactive dialogue session there is another 30-minute discussion on the adoption of the outcome report, during which the State under review may make preliminary comments on recommendations. The State under review can 'support' or 'note' recommendations. When a state notes recommendations,

---

28 Edward McMahon, 'Herding Cats and Sheep: Assessing State and Regional Behavior in the Universal Periodic Review Mechanism of the United Nations Human Rights Council' (2010): <www.upr-info.org/IMG/pdf/McMahon_Herding_Cats_and_Sheeps_July_2010.pdf>, 12, accessed February 2018.

29 Gareth Sweeney and Yuri Saito, 'An NGO assessment of the new mechanisms of the UN Human Rights Council' (2009) 9(2) *HRLRev* 203, 210.

30 The UPR Extranet is available at: <www.ohchr.org/EN/HRBodies/UPR/Pages/UPRRegistration.aspx> accessed July 2018.

it can include an explanation setting out why it does not support them.[31] The recommendations made are included in the final plenary session report of the council and the outcome report is adopted by the UPR Working Group. The State under review presents its response in an addendum to the Working Group, which is officially adopted at the Council during a plenary session three to four months later. During this phase, the UDHR can be used as a guide to assess the recommendations made to a State under review and justify a State's decision to support recommendations made to it.

Implementation phase

The expected outcome of the UPR process is that human rights practices will improve, and align with the standards set out in the UDHR. Therefore, the implementation of the recommendations made during the process at the domestic level is at the core of this process. Unfortunately, there can be a disconnect between what States say at the Human Rights Council in Geneva and the recommendations they support there, and their human rights laws and practices in reality. Regrettably, the UPR does not include an official follow up framework, whereby States' progress in implementing recommendations is recorded. States can choose to undergo a mid-term review after two years, which consists of them writing a report on how they have implemented the recommendations they supported. As of 30 July 2018, 71 States had submitted UPR mid-term reports. 55 States submitted reports in relation to recommendations put forward during the first cycle of the UPR, 34 submitted reports in respect of Cycle 2 and 18 States submitted mid-term reports in relation to recommendations put forward during both cycles.[32] Civil society and NGOs can also submit mid-term reports, commenting on the progress of State implementation of UPR recommendations.[33] However, the main follow-up on recommendations happens during the next review, which happens four and a half years later. The lack of a strong implementation apparatus is problematic. While some States take recommendations seriously and adjust their national laws and practices in accordance with recommendations, other States are slow to implement recommendations.[34] It is important, therefore, that NGOs continue to assert pressure on States to implement recommendations between UPR cycles, and the UDHR can be utilised as the standard by which progress can be judged.

---

[31] UN Human Rights Council, 'Institution-building of the United Nations Human Rights Council', HRC Res 5/1 UN GAOR, 5th Sess., 9th mtg., (2007) 1 UN Doc A/HRC/5/1.

[32] See United Nations Human Rights Council, 'UPR Mid-term Reports': <www.ohchr.org/EN/HRBodies/UPR/Pages/UPRImplementation.aspx> accessed July 2018.

[33] ibid.

[34] The NGO called UPRInfo has attempted to address some of these problems by creating the Follow-up Programme in 2011 which encourages all UPR stakeholders to more actively participate in the follow-up to the UPR recommendations. UPRInfo, 'Follow-up Programme': <https://www.upr-info.org/followup/> accessed July 2018. It also developed the Implementation of the Recommendation Index in order to categorise the level of implementation for the UPR recommendations.

5. Assessing the Effectiveness of the UPR

Early on, the potential of the UPR was highlighted by UN officials. For example, the former UN Secretary General Ban Ki-moon stated that the UPR had 'great potential to promote and protect human rights in the darkest corners of the world',[35] and in a similar vein, Louise Arbour, the former UN High Commissioner for Human Rights, commented that the UPR could 'provide a vehicle for scrutiny for the implementation of rights and norms beyond anything ever attempted by the Commission on Human Rights'.[36] Academics have also noted the positive aspects of the UPR. Frazier, who analysed the implementation of UPR recommendations on the part of nine States, commented that:

> [T]he UPR has been effective in promoting human rights in the short term. It has helped to highlight serious human rights violations and has done so in a public forum that allows debate to occur on the best way to address those problems. The UPR has also helped to give countries specific guidance, and individualized, achievable goals to meet in progressing respect for human rights; goals which many countries have met or are in the process of meeting.[37]

One of the greatest benefits of the UPR process is its universality, as every State in the world is required to undergo a similar review and is judged by the same standards, as set out in the UDHR, and other human rights instruments. The process was designed to treat every State equally, despite the general inequality of States as regards size, power and resources. Smith comments that 'there is evidence of a real attempt to treat every State the same in terms of the process of universal periodic review'.[38] In order to facilitate universality, the UN has a fund to assist poorer States to attend and participate in the UPR meetings in Geneva.[39] Furthermore, the UPR requires a review of State practice in all spheres, not just those which are the subject of a UN treaty, and therefore, '[c] ommon themes emerge from the interactive dialogue, themes not prevalent

---

35 UN Secretary-General Ban Ki-moon, 'Address to the 4th session of the UN Human Rights Council by UN Secretary-General' (Geneva, 12 March 2007): <www.un.org/apps/news/story.asp?NewsID=21834#.UYD0q6JayPc> accessed August 2018.

36 UN Press Release, 'Address by Louise Arbour, UN High Commissioner for Human Rights on the occasion of the eighth session of the Human Rights Council' (Geneva, 2 June 2008): <www.unhchr.ch/huricane/huricane.nsf/0/06B91AC08630D980C125745C00304584?opendocument> accessed August 2018.

37 David Frazier, 'Evaluating the Implementation of UPR Recommendations: A Quantitative Analysis of the Implementation Efforts of Nine UN Member States' (2011): <www.upr-info.org/IMG/pdf/david_frazier_paper_upr_implementation_2011-2.pdf> accessed May 2018.

38 Rhona Smith, 'Equality of "Nations Large and Small": Testing the Theory of the Universal Periodic Review in the Asia-Pacific' (2011) 2 *Asia-Pacific J HR & Law* 36, 53.

39 Human Rights Council Resolution 6/17, 28 November 2007, UPR Voluntary Trust Fund, UN Doc. A/HRC/RES/6/17. However, it should be noted that the level at which a State can engage in the interactive dialogue with other States under review can be restricted if States do not have a permanent mission in Switzerland.

in the work of the treaty bodies.'[40] Another positive aspect of the UPR is its peer-review approach, which can facilitate an open discussion, rather than an adversarial approach.[41] States may be more receptive to recommendations made by other States as a result of the dialogic nature of the process where there is a spirit of co-operation, rather than confrontation as regards human rights standards.[42] States can also learn from past experience of other States on specific human rights issues. In this context, Smith observes that:

> ... [i]t is apparent that universal periodic review is intended to be something more than a "report card" identifying strengths and weaknesses. Rather there is clear intention on the part of the Council that the process will result in an improvement of the human rights situation generally through sharing good practices, cooperation with other UN mechanism [*sic.*] (notably the UN special procedures) and the identification of areas in which technical assistance could be provided. This is conducive to the inter-governmental nature of the process and should support the entire UN human rights system.[43]

Some commentators are less convinced of the merits of the UPR. A number of issues are underlined in critiques of the process, including the theme of bargaining and block voting within the UPR framework, with claims of States congratulating like-minded States and condemning others.[44] This problem of unwarranted mutual praise was highlighted by UN Watch in a 2009 report which analysed the behaviour of 55 States during the first part of the UPR cycle. The Report stated that '[t]ragically, a majority of 32 out of 55 countries acted as a mutual praise society, misusing the process in order to legitimize human rights abusers, instead of holding them to account.'[45]

Ultimately, the success of the UPR will be measured by changes in domestic human rights law, policies and practices. This is, as referred to above, a weakness of the UPR system, as there is a lack of an enforcement and oversight

---

40 Rhona Smith, 'More of the Same or Something Different? Preliminary Observations on the Contribution of Universal Periodic Review with reference to the Chinese Experience' (2011) 10 *Chinese J Int'l L* 565, 583.

41 See Frederick Cowell and Angelina Milon, 'Decriminalisation of Sexual Orientation through the Universal Periodic Review' (2012) 12(2) *HRL Rev* 341, 346, who state: 'While the process gives no guarantee that the recommendations agreed are followed through, the soft law approach can be advantageous when considering issues that are culturally sensitive or controversial, or have not been previously under active consideration in a state's domestic political or constitutional institutions'.

42 See ibid 352, where it states that '... the dialogic process can be instrumental in tackling contentious human rights issues ... in a way that was not previously possible. By providing a channel for views and strategies, the peer review process allows us to see reform from a different angle and to give it stronger force.'

43 Rhona Smith, n 38.

44 Edward McMahon, n 28.

45 UN Watch, 'Mutual Praise Society. Country scorecard and evaluation of the Universal Periodic Review system of the UN Human Rights Council', presented at the United Nations Human Rights Council (Geneva, February 6 2009).

mechanism. While States may seem to be engaged with the UPR by supporting various UPR recommendations, they may not match this enthusiasm in Geneva with action at home. The role of NGOs in maintaining pressure on States to implement recommendations is vital in this context. In addition, the Council could modify the UPR process in order to incorporate a more effective implementation aspect. This could include making the mid-term report process mandatory. Furthermore, some States have adopted implementation templates, where recommendations can be traced directly to practical actions, in the form of legislative changes or the establishment of human rights institutions. For example, Kenyan civil society stakeholders developed a document outlining how the recommendations received by the Kenyan government should be implemented.[46] The Working Group on Human Rights in India and the UN (WGHR) also developed a table incorporating information regarding the UPR recommendations, as well as possible actions on the recommendations, indicators that could help to monitor implementation, in addition to the government department or ministry responsible for the implementation. This document also includes a column that indicates the type of measures that have been taken by the State, thus helping to keep track of the progress made to date.[47] If the Council put in place a similar template as part of the UPR process, it is likely that States would have to take the implementation of UPR recommendations more seriously, and States' progress would be more easily managed and monitored. To date, there have been some positive improvements, however, and UPR recommendations are often finding their way, in various shapes and forms, into domestic practice through amendment of domestic laws, ratification of international instruments and changes in governmental policies,[48] and State practice is moving closer to the ideals set out in the UDHR.

6. Conclusion

Over time, the general consensus is that, while the UPR is not perfect,[49] it has added to the promotion and protection of human rights domestically. This seems to be supported by research into the implementation of recommendations.[50]

46 See Kenya National Commission on Human Rights, 'Accounting For Human Rights Protection Under The UPR: The Difference Kenya's Stakeholders Made' (September 2011): <www.upr-info.org/sites/default/files/general-document/pdf/knchr_accounting_for_human_rights_protection_under_the_upr_2011.pdf> accessed August 2018.

47 See WGHR Press Release, 'Comprehensive review of India's human rights record at the UN Human Rights Council: Glaring Omissions, Some Progress' (September 21, 2012): <www.wghr.org/pdf/WGHR%20UPR%20press%20release%20 21.09.2012.pdf > accessed July 2018.

48 Noelle Higgins, 'Advancing the Rights of Minorities and Indigenous Peoples: Getting UN Attention via the Universal Periodic Review' (2014) 32(4) *NQHR* 379.

49 See, for example, Rachel Brett, 'A Curate's Egg', Quaker United Nations Office (August 2009): <https://www.upr-info.org/sites/default/files/general-document/pdf/-acuratesegg200908.pdf> accessed August 2018.

50 See, for example, UPRInfo, 'Universal Periodic Review; On the Road to Implementation' (2012): <www.upr-info.org/sites/default/files/general-document/pdf/2012_on_the_road_to_implementation.pdf> accessed August 2018. See also Elaine Dewhurst and Noelle

While there is much work left to do by States in order for their human rights practices and policies to align with the standards set out in the UDHR, the UPR process has made important strides in this direction for some, if not all, States.

7. Bibliography

Boekle, Henning, 'Western States, the UN Commission on Human Rights and the "1235" procedure: the question of bias revisited' (1995) 13 *NQHR* 367

Bossuyt, Marc, 'The Human Rights Council: A First Appraisal' (2006) 24(4) *NQHR* 551

Brett, Rachel, 'A Curate's Egg', Quaker United Nations Office (August 2009): <https://www.upr-info.org/sites/default/files/general-document/pdf/-acuratesegg200908.pdf> accessed August 2018

Cooper, Joshua, 'Universal Periodic Review: A Potent Process for the Realization of Human Rights in Indigenous Homelands' (2014) 28(2) *Cultural Survival Quarterly Magazine*: <https://www.culturalsurvival.org/publications/cultural-survival-quarterly/universal-periodic-review-potent-process-realization-human> accessed July 2018

Cowell, Frederick and Angelina Milon, 'Decriminalisation of Sexual Orientation through the Universal Periodic Review' (2012) 12(2) *HRL Rev* 341

Dewhurst, Elaine and Higgins, Noelle, 'Ireland and the Universal Periodic Review: A Two Way Process' (2012) 1 *Socio-Legal Studies R* 140

Flood, Patrick J., 'The U.N. Human Rights Council: Is its Mandate well-designed?' (2008-2009) 15 *ILSA J Int'l & Com L* 472

Franck, Thomas 'Of Gnats and Camels: Is there a Double Standard in the United Nations?' (1984) 78 *American Journal of International Law* 811

Frazier, David, 'Evaluating the Implementation of UPR Recommendations: A Quantitative Analysis of the Implementation Efforts of Nine UN Member States' (2011): <www.upr-info.org/IMG/pdf/david_frazier_paper_upr_implementation_2011-2.pdf> accessed May 2018

Glendon, May Ann, 'Knowing the Universal Declaration of Human Rights' (1998) 73 *Notre Dame L Rev* 1153

Greenwood, Phoebe, 'Israel Refuses to Appear before UN Human Rights Review', *The Telegraph* (29 January 2013)

Higgins, Noelle, 'Advancing the Rights of Minorities and Indigenous Peoples: Getting UN Attention via the Universal Periodic Review' (2014) 32(4) *NQHR* 379 .

Higgins, Rosalyn; 'Derogations under Human Rights Treaties' (1977) 48(1) *Br Yb Int'l L* 281

Kenya National Commission on Human Rights, 'Accounting For Human Rights Protection Under The UPR: The Difference Kenya's Stakeholders Made' (September 2011): <https://www.upr-info.org/sites/default/files/general-document/pdf/knchr_accounting_for_human_rights_protection_under_the_upr_2011.pdf> accessed September 2018

Lauren, Paul Gordon, 'To Preserve and Build on its Achievements and to Redress its Shortcomings: The Journey from the Commission on Human Rights to the Human Rights Council' (2007) 28 *HRQ* 307

Higgins, 'Ireland and the Universal Periodic Review: A Two Way Process' (2012) 1 *Socio-Legal Studs Rev* 140.

Lauterpacht, Hersch, 'The Universal Declaration of Human Rights' (1948) 25 *Brit Yb Int'l L* 354

Lijnzaad, Liesbeth, *Reservations to UN-Human Rights Treaties* (Martinus Nijhoff 1995)

Malik, Charles, '1948- The Drafting of the Universal Declaration of Human Rights' (1986) 97 UN Bull Hum Rts. 18, quoted in Mary Ann Glendon, 'The Rule of Law in the Universal Declaration of Human Rights' (2004) 2(1) *Nw J Int'l Hum Rts* 1

Matiya, Jarvis, 'Repositioning the international human rights protection system: the UN Human Rights Council' (2010) 36(2) *Commonwealth L Bull* 313

McMahon, Edward, 'Herding Cats and Sheep: Assessing State and Regional Behavior in the Universal Periodic Review Mechanism of the United Nations Human Rights Council': <www.upr-info.org/IMG/pdf/McMahon_Herding_Cats_and_Sheeps_July_2010.pdf> accessed February 2018

McMahon Edward and Marta Ascherio, 'A Step Ahead in Promoting Human Rights? The Universal Periodic Review of the UN Human Rights Council' (2012) 18 *Glob Gov* 231

Ramcharan, Bertrand, *The UN Human Rights Council* (Routledge 2011)

Ravid, Barak, 'Israel to negotiate renewal of cooperation with UN Human Rights Council' *Haaretz* (7 May 2013)

Schachter, Oscar, 'The Genesis of the Declaration: A Fresh Examination' (1999) 11 *Pace Int'l Law Rev* 27

Schrijver, Nico, 'The UN Human Rights Council: A New "Society of the Committed" or Just Old Wine in New Bottles?' (2007) 20(4) *Ldn J Int'l L* 809

Smith, Rhona, 'Equality of "Nations Large and Small": Testing the Theory of the Universal Periodic Review in the Asia-Pacific' (2011) 2 *Asia-Pacific J HR & Law* 36

Smith, Rhona, 'More of the Same or Something Different? Preliminary Observations on the Contribution of Universal Periodic Review with reference to the Chinese Experience' (2011) 10 *Chinese J Int'l L* 565

Smith, Rhona, 'To see Themselves as Others see Them': The Five Permanent Members of the Security Council and the Human Rights Council's Universal Periodic Review', *Human Rights Quarterly*, Vol 35, 2013, pp 1-32

Sweeney Gareth and Yuri Saito, 'An NGO assessment of the new mechanisms of the UN Human Rights Council' (2009) 9(2) *HRL Rev* 203

UN Watch, 'Mutual Praise Society. Country scorecard and evaluation of the Universal Periodic Review system of the UN Human Rights Council', presented at the United Nations Human Rights Council (Geneva, 6 February 2009)

UPRInfo, 'Universal Periodic Review; On the Road to Implementation' (2012): <https://www.upr-info.org/sites/default/files/general-document/pdf/2012_on_the_road_to_implementation.pdf> accessed August 2018

UPRInfo, 'Follow-up Programme' <https://www.upr-info.org/followup/> accessed July 2018

WGHR Press Release, 'Comprehensive review of India's human rights record at the UN Human Rights Council: Glaring Omissions, Some Progress' (21 September 2012): <http://www.wghr.org/pdf/WGHR%20UPR%20press%20release%20 21.09.2012.pdf> accessed July 2018

Chapter 3

MINORITY RIGHTS AND THE UNIVERSAL DECLARATION OF HUMAN RIGHTS

By Jean Molloy

1. Introduction

The protection of the rights of ethnic, religious, and linguistic groups is one of the oldest concerns of international law.[1] Originally, the law was concerned with the protection of religious minorities only, which was provided through a series of *ad hoc* treaties, in order to protect lands that had been ceded through war and the redrawing of territorial boundaries.[2] Over time though, the approach to the protection of minority groups has broadened to now include ethnic, cultural and linguistic groups. While the adoption of the Universal Declaration of Human Rights 1948 (UDHR) was a landmark event, this instrument does not make specific reference to the protection of minorities, because the United Nations (UN) focused on the rights of individuals and emphasised the inherent dignity of each individual person.

While there is not one universally accepted definition of minority under international law, a generally recognised definition was provided by Francesco Capotorti, the Special Rapporteur of the United Nations Sub-Commission on Prevention of Discrimination and Protection of Minorities, which states:

> A group numerically inferior to the rest of the population of a State, in a non-dominant position, whose members—being nationals of the State—possess ethnic, religious or linguistic characteristics differing from those of the rest of the population and show, if only implicitly, a sense of solidarity, directed towards preserving their culture, traditions, religion or language.[3]

Despite the lack of protection for minorities in the UDHR, this instrument later provided the inspiration for the legal protections that were granted to

1 Patrick Thornberry, *International Law and the Rights of Minorities* (Clarendon Press 1991); McCartney, *National States and National Minorities* (OUP 1934); Modeen, *The International Protection of National Minorities in Europe* (Abo Akademi 1969).

2 Thornberry, ibid.

3 Francesco Capotorti, Study on the Rights of Persons Belonging to Ethnic, Religious and Linguistic Minorities, 242, UN Doc E/CN.4/Sub.2/384/Rev.1.UNHR Office of the High Commissioner, *Minority Rights: International Standards and Guidance for Implementation*, (HR/PUB/10/3, UN: New York and Geneva, 2010) 2.

minority groups through the International Covenant on Civil and Political Rights (ICCPR, adopted in 1966),[4] which forms part of the International Bill of Human Rights[5] and United Nations Declaration on the Rights of Persons Belonging to National or Ethnic, Religious and Linguistic Minorities (adopted in 1992).[6] Yet, the issue of minority protection in international law is constantly challenged. Providing protection for cultural, linguistic and ethnic minorities, in addition to the rights of individuals, is of particular importance, as minority groups have specific needs and requirements, the most basic being the actual recognition of the existence of minorities. Additional issues of concern are the promotion of multicultural and intercultural education, nationally and locally; the lack of participation by minority groups in all aspects of public life; disparities in social indicators such as employment, health and housing and the concerns of women and children belonging to minorities, particularly when they are refugees and internally displaced persons.[7]

Persons belonging to national or ethnic, religious and linguistic minorities are also often victims of multiple discrimination and they may lack access to, among other things, adequate housing, land and property, and even a nationality.[8] One such group are the Rohingya minority of Myanmar. In September 2018, the United Nations Human Rights Council published a report entitled *Report on the Detailed Findings of the Independent International Fact-Finding Mission on Myanmar*.[9] The Report established consistent patterns of serious human rights violations and abuses in Kachin, Rakhine and Shan States. These included unlawful killings, torture and other ill-treatment, sexual and gender-based violence and forced labour and forced recruitment of adults and children, in violation of international humanitarian law and international human rights law. One of the critical issues that the targeting of Rohingya people is the lack of a forceful regime in international law that guarantees the rights of minority peoples.[10] The aim of this chapter is to examine the international legal framework that is in place to protect minority groups, from

---

4 Adopted by General Assembly Resolution 2200A (XXI) of 16 December 1966; entry into force 23 March 1976, in accordance with Art 49; Gaetano Pentassuglia, *Minorities in International Law: An Introductory Study*, (Strasbourg: Council of Europe Publishing, 2002).

5 The International Bill of Human Rights consists of the Universal Declaration of Human Rights (1948), the International Covenant on Civil and Political Rights (ICCPR, 1966) with its two Optional Protocols and the International Covenant on Economic, Social and Cultural Rights (ICESCR, 1966).

6 Adopted by General Assembly Resolution 47/135 of 18 December 1992.

7 UNHCR Office of the High Commissioner, *Minority Rights: International Standards and Guidance for Implementation* (HR/PUB/10/3, UN, New York and Geneva, 2010).

8 UNHCR Office of the High Commissioner, *Minority Rights: International Standards and Guidance for Implementation* (HR/PUB/10/3, UN: New York and Geneva, 2010).

9 UNHRC, *Report on the Detailed Findings of the independent International Fact-Finding Mission on Myanmar*, September 2018. Available at: https://www.ohchr.org/Documents/HRBodies/HRCouncil/FFM-Myanmar/A_HRC_39_CRP.2.pdf .

10 Joshua Castellino and Kathleen A Cavanaugh, *Minority Rights in the Middle East,* (OUP 2013).

its development as a system that protected religious minorities only, to the one that now encompasses national and ethnic, religious and linguistic minorities.

2. Early Historical Background

The belief that everyone, by virtue of her or his humanity, is entitled to certain human rights is a recent development in the international arena.[11] The inception of the protection of minorities was based only on religion; cultural, linguistic and ethnic minorities were not considered during the period of the development of minority protection that occurred prior to the sixteenth century. The history of, and concern for, the protection of minorities developed through 'protective' treaties, which although similar in their purpose, did not produce anything resembling a comprehensive scheme.[12] Minority rights developed through agreements such as the Promise of St Louis of France (1250), which was an early example of the protective regime concerning minorities. The Instrument highlighted the condition of the Maronites as an issue of concern. St. Louis pledged to protect the Maronite Christians[13] in the Holy Land in the year 1250, a promise which was periodically renewed by French monarchs.[14]

The growth of minority rights was further refined through a series of regional bilateral treaties in the seventeenth and eighteenth centuries. The rival European powers of Austria and Russia, Austria and Turkey and Greece and Turkey sought to contain the divided loyalties that arose from populations swearing allegiance to one ruler whilst living in the territory of another jurisdiction. The Treaty of Oliva in 1660,[15] was signed between the Polish-Lithuanian Commonwealth, the Habsburgs and Brandenburg-Prussia. Poland ceded the regions of Pomerania and Livonia to Sweden, guaranteeing religious freedom to the inhabitants of those ceded territories, as outlined in Art 2(3) of the Treaty.[16] The Convention of 1881 for the Settlement of the Frontier between Greece and Turkey provided that 'the lives, property, honour, religion, and customs of those of the inhabitants of the localities ceded to Greece who shall remain under the Hellenic administration will be scrupulously respected.[17] They will

---

[11] With the adoption of the UDHR in 1948, the rights of the individual were affirmed as a fundamental part of the international legal regime.

[12] Thornberry (n 1).

[13] The Maronites are a Christian group who adhere to the Syriac Maronite Church.

[14] Kheinkor Lamarr, 'Jurisprudence of Minority Rights: The Changing Contours of Minority Rights', *Proceedings of the Research Association for Interdisciplinary Studies,* 26-27 March 2018.

[15] Thornberry (n 1); *Malcolm Evans, Religious Liberty and International Law in Europe*, Cambridge Studies in International and Comparative Law (CUP 2008); Robert I Frost, *The Northern Wars. War, State and Society in Northeastern Europe 1558-1721* (Longman 2000).

[16] Treaty of Oliva 1660, Art 2(3).

[17] Convention for the Settlement of the Frontier between Greece and Turkey, and Convention to Regulate the Evacuation of the Territories ceded by Greece between Austria-Hungary, France, Germany, Great Britain, Italy, Russia and Turkey, signed at Constantinople, 24 May 1881.

enjoy exactly the same civil and political rights as Hellenic subjects of origin'. Other Treaties relating to minorities include the Treaty of Paris 1763, which was signed between Great Britain and France. Article 4 provided that the King of Great Britain:

> [A]grees to grant to the inhabitants of Canada the freedom of the Catholic religion: consequently [he] will give the most precise and most effectual order, that his new Roman Catholic subjects may profess the worship of religion according to the rites of the Roman church, as far as the laws of Great Britain permit.[18]

The Treaty of Dresden, 1745, between the King of Prussia and the Elector of Saxony specified that Protestantism would be preserved in the territories of Prussia and Saxony, in accordance with the Treaty of Westphalia.[19]

The Protestant Reformation and the Thirty Years War were instrumental in granting the freedom of religious practise to minority groups, such as Lutherans and Calvinists, as they paved the way for the use of religious tolerance as a means of ending religious conflicts.[20] The Peace of Westphalia 1648 was adopted during this period of turmoil when Europe was plagued with religious wars, primarily between Catholicism and the Reformation religions. Importantly, Westphalia recognised the three major Christian religions (Catholic, Lutheran and Calvinist) and bestowed particular entitlements relating to religious and political participation.[21] Essentially, the Peace of Westphalia bestowed the freedom to worship privately, granted the liberty of conscience, and the right of emigration to all religious minorities and dissidents.[22]

3. Minorities and Non-Treaty Systems

Although European influence on the development of minority rights is evident in the treaties discussed above, sophisticated and advanced systems of tolerance towards minorities flourished outside of Europe. The Millet system of the Ottoman Empire was one such arrangement. The Ottoman Empire, founded by Othman, ruled the Middle East for 400 hundred years.[23] It was vast in its landmass and was multi-ethnic in its composition. The political organisation of the Empire allowed members of differing ethnic communities to prosper, so long as they pledged allegiance to the Ottoman Empire.[24] *Ottomanism* was encouraged among the diverse ethnic groups of the Empire with the aim of promoting equality among the Millets by treating all subjects of the empire

---

18 Treaty of Paris 1763, Art 4.
19 Treaty of Dresden, 1745.
20 Gaetano Pentassuglia, *Minorities in International Law: An Introductory Study* (Council of Europe Publishing 2002).
21 ibid.
22 ibid.
23 Philip Robins, *The Middle East* (Oneworld Publications 2016).
24 ibid.

equally before the law, in a move designed to emancipate the empire's non-Muslim subjects. The Millet system was one of the most advanced early sources of these rights that existed in the Ottoman Empire. It granted religious freedom and legal protection to non-Muslim minority groups within the Ottoman Empire, reflecting religious pluralism based on customs rather than treaties,[25] and is 'possibly the first manifestation of what could be deemed "minority rights law"'.[26] While the Millet system asserted the rights of minority religious groups, the American Revolution of 1765 was concerned with tenet of individual rights and the consent governed people,[27] whereas the French Revolution combined the notion of fundamental rights with the concept of a culturally homogenous State. [28]

4. The League of Nations

At the time of the establishment of the League of Nations in 1920, the rights of minorities had garnered a central prominence in European politics.[29] The break-up of the empires of Austria-Hungary, Prussia and the Ottoman Empire and the reconfiguration of nation-States in Europe created minority groups in newly formed or enlarged States who now required protection.[30] The League developed a minority rights regime, under Art 23 of the Covenant of the League of Nations, which included the just treatment of native inhabitants and protection of minorities in Europe.[31] It was the most extensive minority rights regime to have been developed by the international community at that time. It included fourteen instruments dealing with minority groups in Europe and established special treaties on minorities between the allied and associated powers, and a number of countries, including Poland (1919), Czechoslovakia (1919), Austria (1919), Bulgaria (1919), Hungary (1920), Finland (1921), Albania (1921), Lithuania (1922), Estonia (1923), Turkey (1923) and Iraq (1932).[32]

The protections afforded to minorities included recognising the basic right to life, liberty and free exercise of any creed, religion or belief not incompatible with public order or morals of all inhabitants of the abovementioned territories; and guarantees for the benefit of 'nationals who belong to racial, religious or linguistic minorities'.[33] This was a crucial and far-reaching development in the understanding and approach to the legal regulation of minorities from

---

25 Bruce Masters, *Christians and Jews in the Ottoman Arab World: The Roots of Sectarianism* (CUP 2001).
26 Castellino and Cavanaugh (n 10) 268.
27 n 20.
28 n 20; Gregory *Fremont-Barnes, Encyclopedia of the Age of Political Revolutions and New Ideologies, 1760-1815* (Greenwood 2007).
29 Pentassuglia (n 20).
30 Pentassuglia (n 20).
31 Art 23 of the Covenant of the League of Nations 1919.
32 Thornberry (n 1).
33 Pentassuglia (n 20).

the previous treaties to the League of Nations treaties. It was no longer only religious groups who would be protected as minorities; the law now extended the protection of minorities to cultural, linguistic and ethnic groups under the League of Nations mandate. The League's guarantee for the protection of minority rights was both internal and external. Internally, States were obliged to regard treaty provisions as fundamental laws invalidating all other laws and regulations that conflicted with them. Externally, the treaty provisions were applied in a more limited fashion, being relevant only 'so far as they affect persons belonging to racial, religious or linguistic minorities'.[34]

The League established the Permanent Court of International Justice (PCIJ), under Art 14 of the Covenant of the League of Nations, to hear and determine disputes referred to it by the Assembly or Council of the League, which arose from the application of relevant minority treaties. In 1935, the PCIJ issued its Advisory Opinion on the *Minority School in Albania* case,[35] relating to the application of non-discrimination and the protection of minors. Here, the Court recognised Albania's positive obligation to 'ensure for the minority element suitable means for the preservation of their racial peculiarities, their traditions and their national characteristics', which entailed facilitation of the right to establish and control 'charitable, religious and social institutions, schools and other educational establishments, with the right to use their own language and to exercise their religion freely therein'.[36] These obligations were intended to ensure 'the possibility of living peacefully alongside the population and co-operating amicably with it, while at the same time preserving the characteristics which distinguish them from the majority, satisfying the ensuing special needs'.[37] The Advisory Opinion of the PCIJ reinforced the League of Nation's recognition of cultural, religious and linguistic minorities and further established the right of minorities to practise their religion, language and traditions.

Ultimately however, the League of Nations failed in its primary purpose, which was the prevention of another world war. Minority groups criticised the League of Nations for its lack of effective representation of their claims, as they could not appear before it to make oral presentations and had no *locus standi* vis-á-vis the League Council.[38] Treaty provisions could not be amended with the consent of the majority of Council members. Hitler's *Machtergreifung* or appointment as chancellor on 30 January 1933, combined with negative sentiments towards minority groups in Germany, Hungary, Austria, and Bulgaria all contributed to a fundamental revision of the Treaty of Versailles,[39] and to the demise of the League of Nations. However, the idea of an international organisation to

---

[34] Art 12 of the Polish Treaty. Thornberry (n 1) 44.

[35] PCIJ, *Minority Schools in Albania Greece vs. Albania*, Advisory Opinion 26, Series A./B., No. 64, 1935.

[36] ibid.

[37] Pentassuglia (n 20) 28.2.

[38] ibid; The Council and the PCIJ represented the political and legal pillars of the League. The PCIJ delivered a number of advisory opinions during its tenure.

[39] Patrick Thornberry, *International Law and the Rights of Minorities* (Clarendon Press

maintain international peace and security was accepted as vital during WWII, leading to the establishment of the United Nations in 1945.

5. The UDHR 1948

The UDHR is a milestone documents in the field of human rights. The Declaration was adopted by the UN General Assembly on 10 December 1948, by forty-eight votes to none, with eight abstentions.[40] With the adoption of the UDHR, the rights of the individual, rather than a focus on the rights of minorities, emerged as a fundamental part of the international legal regime, shifting the focus from the League of Nations group centred approach, which enshrined the right of minorities. Whilst the initial preliminary draft of the Declaration proposed enshrining rights to minority educational, religious, and cultural institutions as well as minority-language protection, political opposition from many States, who themselves had minority groups within their borders and did not welcome interference in their affairs, resulted in these provisions being omitted from the final version of the UDHR adopted by the UN General Assembly.[41]

Instead, the General Assembly referred the issue of minority protection to the *Sub-Commission on Prevention of Discrimination and Protection of Minorities*, tasking the Commission to undertake a thorough study of the problem of minorities'.[42] Commenting on this, Peter Hilpold stated that the General Assembly's 'reluctance to act coupled with a request for more knowledge was a characterizing trait of the entire development of minority rights within the UN system'.[43] The conclusions of a study conducted by the United Nations Secretariat in 1950[44] demonstrates this new approach:

> If the problem is regarded as a whole, there can be no doubt that the whole minorities protection regime was in 1919 an integral part of the system established to regulate the outcome of the First World War and create an international organization, the League of Nations. One principle of that system was that certain States and certain States only (chiefly States that had been newly reconstituted or considerably enlarged) should be

1991); Bischoff, *Nazi Conquest Through German Culture* (Harvard University Press 1942).

40 *Universal Declaration of Human Rights*, UNGA Res. 217A(III)., *GAOR, 3rd Session, Part 1, Resolutions, 71,* UN GAOR, 3d Sess., 1st plen. Mtg., UN Doc A/810, 12 December 1948.

41 *Universal Declaration of Human Rights*, UNGA Res. 217A (III), at 71, UN GAOR, 3d Sess., 1st plen. Mtg., UN Doc A/810, 12 December 1948.

42 *The Fate of Minorities*, G.A. Res. 217C (III), at 77, U.N. GAOR, 3d Sess., 1st plen. Mtg., UN Doc. A/810, 12 December 1948.

43 Peter Hilpold, 'UN Standard-Setting in the Field of Minority Rights', (2007) 14 *International Journal of Minority & Group Rights*, 181, 183.

44 *Study of the Legal Validity of the Undertakings Concerning Minorities,* UN Doc E/CN.4/367.

> subject to obligations and international control in the matter of minorities. But this whole system was overthrown by the Second World War. All the international decisions reached since 1944 have been inspired by a different philosophy. The idea of a general and universal protection of human rights and fundamental freedoms is emerging. It is therefore no longer only the minorities in certain countries which receive protection, but all human beings in all countries who receive a certain measure of international protection.[45]

Analysis conducted by Bruegel and Feinberg suggest that the authors of the United Nations Secretariat Study believed a new era of individual protection and the affirmation of individual rights had been ushered in by the United Nations Charter, the Potsdam decision on the administration of Germany and population transfer, and ultimately by the UDHR.[46]

The Declaration sets out the rights that are ascribed to each individual person but makes no explicit mention of minority or group rights. The right to life, for example, is expressed as an individual right but not as a group right.[47] The instrument does, however, contain civil, political, economic, social and cultural rights, and refers to the principles of non-discrimination in Art 2 and equality in Art 7, all of which are relevant to minorities. These Articles are of particular relevance and importance to minority groups as they enshrine the rights that are of central importance to the promotion and protection of their distinctive identity. Despite the absence of specific minority protection, the UDHR does guarantee freedom of expression, freedom of religion, rights of cultural and political participation, and equality rights to 'everyone', thereby securing equal citizenship to members of minorities and protection from discrimination by State powers. Art 2 states that '[e]veryone is entitled to the rights and freedoms set forth in this Declaration without distinction of any kind, such as race, colour, sex, language, religion, political or other opinion, national or social origin, property, birth or other status'. Article 7 declares that '[a]ll are equal before the law and are entitled without any discrimination to equal protection of the law. All are entitled to equal protection against discrimination in violation of this Declaration and against any incitement to such discrimination'.

Additionally, several articles deal with issues that are of particular concern to minority groups, namely the right to marry (Art 16), the right to freedom of thought, conscience and religion (Art 18), the right to freedom of opinion and expression (Art 19), the right of peaceful assembly and association (Art 20), and the right to equal pay for equal work 'without any discrimination' (Art 23(2)). The right to marry should be 'without any limitation due to race, nationality or religion'. The Declaration further outlines the rights and freedoms

---

45 Thornberry (n 1) 53-54.

46 Bruegel, 'A Neglected Field: The Protection of Minorities' (1971) 4 *RDH* 413; Feinberg, 'The Legal Validity of the Undertakings Concerning Minorities and the Clausula Rebus Sic Stantibus' 5 *Scripta Hierosolymitana: Studies in Law* 95 (1958).

47 UDHR, Art 3.

that each individual person is entitled to and which are of particular relevance to minorities, including the right to education (Art 26) and the right to freely participate in the cultural life of the community (Art 27). The UN General Assembly affirmed in Resolution 217 (III) 1948[48] that the United Nations '[could not] remain indifferent to the fate of minorities'.[49] The UDHR has, thus, served as a springboard for the development of a number of legislative initiatives concerning minorities, including the International Convention on the Elimination of All Forms of Racial Discrimination 1965,[50] the International Covenant on Civil and Political Rights[51] and the International Covenant on Economic, Social and Cultural Rights,[52] both of which were adopted in 1966, and the UN Declaration on the Rights of Persons Belonging to National or Ethnic, Religious and Linguistic Minorities 1992.[53] The UDHR has also been influential in the implementation of additional instruments that provide protections for minority groups (listed below).

6. ICCPR

While the UDHR framed rights in individualistic terms, the rights in Art 27 of the ICCPR refer to 'persons belonging to' minorities, but not to minority groups. They are therefore, as such, not group rights. However, the insertion of the sentence 'in community with the other members of their group' maintains the idea of a group.[54] According to Patrick Thornberry, the rights affirmed in Art 27 may be described as the rights of individuals premised on the existence of a community.[55] The Article declares that its stated purpose is to affirm civil and political rights in 'recognition of the inherent dignity and of the equal and inalienable rights of all members of the human family'. Article 27 of the ICCPR echoes the League of Nations approach by protecting the national, ethnic, religious or linguistic identity of minority groups. The Article states that:

> [i]n those States in which ethnic, religious or linguistic minorities exist,

---

48 United Nations General Assembly Resolution 217A was adopted on 10 December 1948, to ratify the Universal Declaration of Human Rights.

49 n 20, 97.

50 International Convention on the Elimination of All Forms of Racial Discrimination. Adopted and opened for signature and ratification by General Assembly resolution 2106 (XX) of 21 December 1965 entry into force 4 January 1969, in accordance with Art 19.

51 International Covenant on Civil and Political Rights, G.A. Res., 2200A (XXI), prmbl, 21 UN GAOR, Supp. No 16, UN Doc A/6316 (1966) 999 U.N.T.S. 171 (entered into force 23 March 1976).

52 International Covenant on Economic, Social and Cultural Rights, Adopted and opened for signature, ratification and accession by General Assembly resolution 2200A (XXI) of 16 December 1966 (entry into force 3 January 1976) (ICESCR).

53 *Declaration on the Rights of Persons Belonging to National or Ethnic, Religious and Linguistic Minorities* by consensus. Adopted by General Assembly Resolution 47/135 on 18 December 1992.

54 Thornberry (n 1) 100.

55 Patrick Thornberry, "Minority Rights" in *Collected Courses of the Academy of European Law*, VI-2, 1995a, 307; ibid.

> persons belonging to such minorities shall not be denied the right, in community with the other members of their group, to enjoy their own culture, to profess and practise their own religion, or to use their own language.

States that have ratified the Covenant are obliged to ensure that all individuals under their jurisdiction enjoy their rights.

The UN Human Rights Committee's General Comment No 23 (1994) on the rights of minorities has provided an interpretation of Art 27, which reads:

> This article establishes and recognizes a right which is conferred on individuals belonging to minority groups and which is distinct from, and additional to, all the other rights which, as individuals in common with everyone else, they are already entitled to enjoy under the Covenant.[56]

Furthermore, Art 27 places positive obligations on States in furtherance of the protection of minorities, as explained in General Comment No 23:

> Although Article 27 is expressed in negative terms, that Article, nevertheless, does recognize the existence of a "right" and requires that it shall not be denied. Consequently, a State party is under an obligation to ensure that the existence and the exercise of this right are protected against their denial or violation.[57]

In summary, a State's obligations to its minorities, as outlined in Article 27 of the ICCPR are threefold: (i) enjoyment of culture, (ii) profession and practice of religion and (iii) use of language, reflecting a return to the League of Nations' approach, which extended the protection of minorities to include cultural, linguistic groups.

7. ICESCR

Although the ICESCR is not a legal instrument specifically pertaining to the rights of minorities *per se*, Art 2(2) explicitly deals with issues that are of particular relevance to minority groups. The Article states:

> The States Parties to the present Covenant undertake to guarantee that the rights enunciated in the present Covenant will be exercised without discrimination of any kind as to race, colour, sex, language, religion, political or other opinion, national or social origin, property, birth or other status.

---

[56] UNHROHC General Comment Adopted by the Human Rights Committee under Article 40, Paragraph 4, of the *International Covenant on Civil and Political Rights 1966*. CCPR/C/21/REV.1/Add.5.

[57] United Nations Human Rights Committee, General Comment No 23 1994, para. 6.1.

The Committee on Economic, Social and Cultural Rights adopted General Comment No 20 (2009), which provides guidance on the obligation of States parties to guarantee non-discrimination in the exercise of each of the economic, social and cultural rights enshrined in the Covenant. The implementation of the rights of persons belonging to minorities has highlighted the need not only to understand and redress inequality but also to accommodate difference and diversity. The Committee also adopted General Comment No 21 (2009) on the right of everyone to take part in cultural life, which obliges States parties to recognize, respect and protect minority cultures as an essential component of the identity of the States themselves.

8. United Nations Declaration on the Rights of Persons Belonging to National or Ethnic, Religious and Linguistic Minorities 1992

The international legal framework on minority protection is based on the concept of non-discrimination and equality with the majority population, whilst also safeguarding and promoting the right to culture of the minority. One of the landmark Declarations on minorities that forms an integral part of the framework for the protection of human rights is the Declaration on the Rights of Persons Belonging to National or Ethnic, Religious and Linguistic Minorities.[58] The Declaration is the main reference document for minority rights and sets essential standards to ensure the rights of persons belonging to minorities and as such is a key reference for United Nations work.

Similar to Art 27 of the ICCPR, the Declaration does not recognise minority groups as distinct right-holders, but rather rights are conferred on 'persons belonging to' minorities.[59] It offers guidance to States as they seek to manage diversity and ensure non-discrimination, and for minorities themselves, as they strive to achieve equality and participation. Article 1 refers to minorities as based on national or ethnic, cultural, religious and linguistic identity, and provides that States should protect their existence.[60] The Declaration therefore imposes a duty upon States to promote conditions for the protection of that identity. Article 2 of the Declaration describes minorities as Persons belonging to national or ethnic, religious and linguistic minorities (hereinafter referred to as persons belonging to minorities) and affirms that they have the right to enjoy their own culture, to profess and practise their own religion, and to use their own language, in private and in public, freely and without interference or any form of discrimination.[61]

---

[58] *Declaration on the Rights of Persons Belonging to National or Ethnic, Religious and Linguistic Minorities* by consensus. Adopted by General Assembly Resolution 47/135 on 18 December 1992 (G/A Resolution 47/135).

[59] Pentassuglia (n 20) 112.

[60] *Declaration on the Rights of Persons Belonging to National or Ethnic, Religious and Linguistic Minorities*, Art 1.

[61] ibid, Art 1.

Each subsequent Article in the Declaration enshrines the rights of minority groups to live without discrimination (Art 3(1)); to live in a State that protects and promotes the rights of minority groups (Art 4(1)); to develop their culture, language, religion, traditions and customs (Art 4(2)) and to be extended adequate opportunities to learn their mother tongue or to have instruction in their mother tongue (Art 4(3)). In 2005, the Working Group on Minorities adopted a commentary intended to guide the understanding and application of the United Nations Minorities Declaration. In addition, the Working Group considered the Minority Profile and Matrix, which provides a checklist of issues and measures based on the provisions and principles contained in the United Nations Minorities Declaration and the Commentary.[62]

Additional instruments of relevance to the rights of minorities include the Convention on the Prevention and Punishment of Genocide 1948,[63] Convention on the Rights of the Child 1990,[64] International Labour Organisation (ILO) Discrimination (Employment and Occupation) Convention 1958 (No. 111),[65] European Charter for Regional or Minority Languages 1992,[66] Council of Europe's Framework Convention for Protection of National Minorities 1998,[67] ILO Declaration on Fundamental Principles and Rights at Work 1998,[68] UNESCO Convention for the Safeguarding of the Intangible Cultural Heritage 2003,[69] UNESCO Convention on the Protection and Promotion of the

62 United Nations Minorities Declaration and the Commentary, E/CN.4/Sub.2/AC.5/2006/3; *Minority Rights: International Standards and Guidance for Implementation* (HR/PUB/10/3, UN: New York and Geneva, 2010).

63 Convention on the Prevention and Punishment of the Crime of Genocide. Approved and proposed for signature and ratification or accession by General Assembly resolution 260 A (III) of 9 December 1948. Entry into force 12 January 1951, in accordance with article XIII.

64 Convention on the Rights of the Child 1990. Adopted and opened for signature, ratification and accession by General Assembly resolution 44/25 of 20 November 1989 entry into force 2 September 1990, in accordance with article 49 (CRC).

65 ILO Discrimination (Employment and Occupation) Convention 1958, Arts. 1 and 2. Adopted on 25 June 1958 by the General Conference of the International Labour Organisation at its forty-second session entry into force 15 June 1960, in accordance with Art 8 status of ratifications.

66 European Charter for Regional or Minority Languages (ECRML) 1992. Adopted as a convention on 25 June 1992 by the Committee of Ministers of the Council of Europe and was opened for signature in Strasbourg on 5 November 1992. It entered into force on 1 March 1998.

67 Framework Convention for the Protection of National Minorities 1998. Adopted by the Committee of Ministers of the Council of Europe on 10 November 1994 and entered into force on 1 February 1998.

68 ILO Declaration on Fundamental Principles and Rights at Work 1998.

69 UNESCO Convention for the Safeguarding of the Intangible Cultural Heritage 2003. Adopted at the General Conference of the United Nations Educational, Scientific and Cultural Organization (UNESCO) 17 October 2003 at the 32nd session.

Diversity of Cultural Expressions 2005,[70] Yogyakasta Principles 2007/2017,[71] and the UN Human Rights Council Resolution on Discrimination and Sexual Orientation 2016.[72]

9. Regional Developments

In addition to the framework of protection for minorities that exists in international law, there are a number of developments at a regional level where the focus remains on religious, linguistic and cultural protection. These include Art 16(1) of the American Convention on Human Rights, which provides for freedom of association for cultural purposes,[73] Art 17(2) of the African Charter on Human and Peoples' Rights, which provides that every individual may freely take part in the cultural life of his community and Art 29(7), which imposes a duty on all individuals to preserve and strengthen African cultural values.[74] In addition, Art 38 of the Arab Charter provides for a right to participate in cultural life, to enjoy artistic works and literature, and to develop artistic, intellectual and creative talents.[75] Furthermore, the Council of Europe has adopted a Framework Convention for the Protection of National Minorities and European Charter for Regional and Minority Languages.[76]

10. Rohingya People

Despite the protections that exist in international law, for persons belonging to national, ethnic, religious and/or linguistic minorities, these rights are far from being a reality for millions of people who are victims of regular and systematic abuse and discrimination. One such minority is the Rohingya people of Myanmar, whose rights have been grossly violated in recent years.

Myanmar, formally known as Burma,[77] is a former British colony that received its independence on 4 January 1948. The country has a population

---

70 UNESCO Convention on the Protection and Promotion of the Diversity of Cultural Expressions 2005, adopted at the General Conference of the United Nations Educational, Scientific and Cultural Organization (UNESCO) 20 October 2005 at the 33rd session.

71 Yogyakarta Principles 2007/2017. The Yogyakarta Principles is a document about human rights in the areas of sexual orientation and gender identity, published as the outcome of an international meeting of human rights groups in Yogyakarta, Indonesia, in November 2006. The Principles were supplemented in 2017, expanding to include new grounds of gender expression and sex characteristics and a number of new principles.

72 UNHRC Resolution on Discrimination and Sexual Orientation 2016 (A/HRC/17/19).

73 American Convention on Human Rights 'Pact of San Jose, Costa Rica' 1969.

74 African Charter on Human and Peoples' Rights 1986.

75 Arab Charter on Human Rights 1994.

76 Council of Europe Framework Convention for the Protection of National Minorities and European Charter for Regional and Minority Languages 1998.

77 The name was changed from Burma to Myanmar in 1986.

of approximately 51.5 million.[78] Although it is predominately Buddhist, about 4.3 % of its people are Muslims.[79] The Rohingya people are a Muslim group and number about one million people of which 800,000 live in the north of the Rahkine State. Myanmar was ruled by the military until 2011. During its reign, the regime was accused of severe human rights abuses, including murder and arbitrary executions, torture and rape, recruitment of child soldiers, forced relocations, forced labour and political imprisonment. The military-backed Union Solidarity and Development Party (USDP) won the 2010 general election, which was boycotted by the NLD and other pro-democracy parties, who objected to what were perceived as unfair electoral laws. Retired General Thein Sein, the leader of the USDP, was installed as President.[80] The Thein Sein Government implemented a number of important reforms, including the freeing of political prisoners, relaxing censorship and restrictions on the media. NLD leader Aung San Suu Kyi was also released from house arrest shortly after the 2010 elections.[81] While there has certainly been an improvement in human rights, for a minority group like the Rohingya, the situation has actually deteriorated, particularly since 2016.

The Rakhine State, where the majority of the Rohingya population live, is one of the poorest States in Myanmar. The Rohingya self-identify as a distinct ethnic group with their own language and culture, and claim a long-standing connection to Rakhine State. Successive Governments have rejected these claims, and the Rohingya were not included in the list of recognized ethnic groups. Most Rohingya are Stateless.[82] The Rohingya population face discrimination owing to protracted displacement, restrictions on freedom of movement and access to education.[83] According to the *Report of the OHCHR Mission to Bangladesh*[84] the persecution of the Rohingya has resulted in the denial of freedom of movement, education and healthcare, eviction campaigns, controls over family size, forced labour, expulsion from their lands and property, violence, enforced disappearances, rape and other forms of sexual violence, torture, cruel, inhumane and degrading treatment and arbitrary detention. In 2014, the UN Special Rapporteur on the human rights situation in Myanmar,

---

[78] According to the 2014 Population and Housing Census, the first census undertaken in Myanmar in three decades. The census was controversial as it only allowed participants to identify as belonging to one of 135 officially recognised ethnic groups (under eight major ethnic races: Kachin, Kayah, Karen, Chin, Bamar, Mon, Rakhine and Shan) or as 'other'. It did not include 'Rohingya' and participants were not allowed to self-identify as such. This led to a significant part of the population in Rakhine State not participating in the count.

[79] UN Human Rights Council, *Report of the Independent International Fact-finding Mission on Myanmar*–A/HRC/39/CPR.2, 17 September 2018.

[80] ibid.

[81] ibid.

[82] Report of the High Commissioner for Human Rights, *Situation of Human Rights of Rohingya Muslims and Other Minorities in Myanmar,* 2016, A/HRC/32/18.

[83] ibid.

[84] UN HR Office of the High Commissioner, *Report of OHCHR Mission to Bangladesh: Interviews with Rohingyas Fleeing from Myanmar since 9 October 2016*, 3 February 2017.

Tomás Ojea Quintana, stated that 'recent developments in Rakhine State are the latest in a long history of discrimination and persecution against the Rohingya community which could amount to crimes against humanity'.[85] Azeem Ibrahim argues that 'the situation in Rakhine can be described as almost a text-book case of pre-genocide'.[86] In a UN Report of *The Independent International Fact-finding Mission on Myanmar*,[87] the Myanmar's military has been accused of genocide, crimes against humanity and war crimes against the Rohingya in Rakhine State. The Report alleged that the army, known as the Tatmadaw, was responsible for war crimes and crimes against humanity and that their actions 'undoubtedly amounted to the gravest crimes under international law'.[88]

A particular problem relating to minorities and citizenship is that all too often members of certain groups are denied or deprived of their citizenship because of their national or ethnic, religious and linguistic characteristics.[89] This practice is in contravention of Art 15 of the UDHR[90] and Art 9 of the *1961 Convention on the Reduction of Statelessness*, which states that 'a Contracting State may not deprive any person or group of persons of their nationality on racial, ethnic, religious or political grounds'.[91] The Citizenship Law of 1982 does not acknowledge the Rohingya population as one of the 135 legally recognised ethnic groups.[92] It violates the right of every child to acquire nationality,[93] as it fails to protect the acquisition of citizenship for children born in Myanmar with no 'genuine link' to another State.[94] The lack of citizenship of the Rohingya community heightens their vulnerability to a range of human rights violations.

85 UN News, *UN expert alarmed at worsening human rights situation in Myanmar's Rakhine State*, 7 April 2014. Available at: https://news.un.org/en/story/2014/04/465552-un-expert-alarmed-worsening-human-rights-situation-myanmars-rakhine-State#.Wb-Z8pUo5kA.

86 Azeem Ibrahim, *The Rohingyas: Inside Myanmar's Genocide* (Hurst 2018), 110.

87 *Report of the Independent International Fact-finding Mission on Myanmar*–A/HRC/39/64.

88 ibid.

89 Most of the world's estimated 15 million Stateless persons belong to ethnic, religious or linguistic minorities, as a result of discrimination perpetuated against these minorities. For further information, refer to UHCHR *Minority Rights: International Standards and Guidance for Implementation* (New York and Geneva, 2010).

90 Art 15 of the UDHR States that '[e]veryone has the right to a nationality' and '[n]o one shall be arbitrarily deprived of his nationality nor denied the right to change his nationality'.

91 Convention on the Reduction of Statelessness 1961, Art 9. The *Convention on the Reduction of Statelessness* is a United Nations multilateral treaty whereby sovereign States agree to reduce the incidence of Statelessness. The Convention was originally intended as a Protocol to the Convention Relating to the Status of Refugees, while the 1954 Convention Relating to the Status of Stateless Persons was adopted to cover Stateless persons who are not refugees and therefore not within the scope of the Convention Relating to the Status of Refugees. See also General Assembly Resolution 50/152, UDHR, Art. 15(2); CRC, Arts 7, 8; Convention on the Elimination of All Forms of Discrimination against Women, Art 9; Convention on the Rights of Persons with Disabilities, Art 18.

92 'Myanmar's Rohingya', *The Economist*, 20 October 2012.

93 Convention on the Rights of the Child, Art 7.

94 Report of the High Commissioner for Human Rights, *Situation of Human Rights of Rohingya Muslims and Other Minorities in Myanmar,* 2016, A/HRC/32/18.

In an unprecedented move in September 2018, the International Criminal Court (ICC) ruled that it can prosecute Myanmar leaders for alleged crimes against humanity on the Rohingya people. Myanmar is not party to the Rome Statute of the ICC (Rome Statute), so the Court does not have any jurisdiction over crimes committed in Myanmar.[95] However, its leaders could still be prosecuted for the crime of humanity of deportation, the forcible transfer of a population, based on territorial jurisdiction. The crime of deportation begins in the country *from* which a population is being deported and is only complete once that population is forced over an international border *into* another country. Thus, an essential element of the crime occurs in the State of arrival, which, in the case of the Rohingya people, is Bangladesh, which is a State party to the Rome Statute.[96] It is for this reason that ICC Prosecutor Fatou Bensouda has stated that her office does have the authority to investigate. The decision opens the doors for ICC prosecutors to apply for a full-blown investigation into Myanmar for deportation and other crimes against humanity, including persecution.

11. Conclusion

As the United Nations continues to strive for the protection of human rights, it is now generally accepted that the protection of the rights and freedoms of people belonging to national minorities form an integral part of the international protection of human rights. Estimates suggesting that 10 to 20 per cent of the world's population belong to minorities. This statistic equates to approximately 600 million and 1.2 billion people,[97] who are in need of protection of their rights, given the discrimination and disadvantages experienced by them. The root causes of these human rights violations are found in the inequalities that exist between majority and minority groups in their enjoyment of economic, social and cultural rights. Clearly however, there remains significant challenges to protecting minorities due to what Thornberry describes as the 'homogenising tendencies of states'.[98] While it is correct to say that the policies of assimilation and integration vary from State to State, a United Nations study on Racial Discrimination in the Political Economic, Social and Cultural Spheres[99] describes assimilation as being based on the idea of the superiority of the dominant culture, (aiming) to produce a homogenous society by getting groups to discard their culture in favour of the dominant one.[100] Thornberry elaborates that while there is a willingness on behalf of the dominant culture to accept minority cultures, it is contingent upon these minority groups accepting the culture of the majority.[101] However, this position

[95] Human Rights Watch, UN Security Council: Refer Burma to the ICC – Countries Should Develop Comprehensive Strategy for Justice, 3 November 2017.

[96] ibid.

[97] Gentian Zyberi, 'The International Court of Justice and the Rights of Peoples and Minorities', 2013. Available at: https://www.researchgate.net/publication/301093498.

[98] Thornberry (n 1).

[99] UN Sales No. 71.XIV.2.

[100] UN Sales No. 71.XIV.2; Thornberry (n 1).

[101] ibid.

disenfranchises minority groups, exacerbating the issues identified above. As the plight of the Rohingya people has demonstrated, the principle of equality is far from being realised by minority populations worldwide due to the systematic and entrenched discrimination. The promotion and protection of the rights of persons belonging to minorities is therefore of paramount importance for the international community in order to prevent the ongoing persecution of minority population. The extension of the protection of minorities from religious groups only to include cultural, linguistic and ethnic groups under the League of Nations mandate was a major move in the international landscape. The adoption of the UDHR was a further landmark event. Several decades later, the emergence of the ICC was transformative in the history of global governance. The ICC has the jurisdiction to prosecute individuals for the crimes of genocide, crimes against humanity and war crimes. Although these crimes are not always committed against minorities, minority peoples are particularly vulnerable to these atrocities. The ruling by the ICC to open an investigation into crimes against humanity by the Myanmar State against the Rohingya people is crucial if the protections afforded to minority groups in international law are to be upheld and honoured. The UDHR sets out the rights that are ascribed to each individual person, emphasising the inherent dignity and worth of each individual person. Although it makes no explicit mention of minority or group rights, it was the catalyst for subsequent Conventions and Declarations that do specifically provide for group rights. Given the precarious plight of millions of minority peoples, the protections ensconced in the ICCPR, the United Nations Declaration on the Rights of Persons Belonging to National or Ethnic, Religious and Linguistic Minorities 1992 and other legal instruments that protect minorities have their foundations firmly in the UDHR.

12. Bibliography

Bischoff, Ralph F, *Nazi Conquest Through German Culture* (Harvard University Press 1942)

Bruegel, J, 'A Neglected Field: The Protection of Minorities' (1971) 4 *RDH* 413

Capotorti, Francesco, *Study on the Rights of Persons Belonging to Ethnic, Religious and Linguistic Minorities* (United Nations 1991)

Capotorti, Francesco, *Study on the Rights of Persons Belonging to Ethnic, Religious and Linguistic Minorities*

Castellino, Joshua and Cavanaugh, Kathleen, *Minority Rights in the Middle East* (OUP 2013)

Croxton, Derek and Tischer, Anuschka, *The Peace of Westphalia: A Historical Dictionary* (Greenwood Publishing Group 2002)

Croxton, Derek, *Westphalia: The Last Christian Peace* (Palgrave 2013)

Evans, Malcolm, *Religious Liberty and International Law in Europe* (Cambridge Studies in International and Comparative Law 2008)

Feinberg, Nathan, 'The Legal Validity of the Undertakings Concerning Minorities and the Clausula Rebus Sic Stantibus' *Studies in Law* (1958) 5 *Scripta Hierosolymitana* 95

Fremont-Barnes, Gregory, *Encyclopedia of the Age of Political Revolutions and New Ideologies, 1760-181* (Greenwood 2007)

Frost, Robert I, *The Northern Wars. War, State and Society in Northeastern Europe 1558-1721* (Longman 2000)

Ganshof, François Louis, *Qu'est-ce que la féodalité* (1944). Trans. Philip Grierson, *Feudalism* (3rd edn, Longmans, Green & Co 1976)

Guiora, Amos N, 'Due Process and Counterterrorism' (2012) 26 *Emory International Law Review* 163

Hilpold, Peter, 'UN Standard-Setting in the Field of Minority Rights' (2007) 14 *International Journal of Minority & Group Rights*

Human Rights Watch, *UN Security Council: Refer Burma to the ICC – Countries Should Develop Comprehensive Strategy for Justice*, 3 November, 2017. Available at: https://www.hrw.org/news/2017/11/03/un-security-council-refer-burma-icc

Hurst, Michael, *Key Treaties of the Great Powers*, vol. 2 (David & Charles 1972)

Ibrahim, Azeem, *The Rohingyas*: *Inside Myanmar's Genocide* (Hurst 2018)

Lamarr, Kheinkor, 'Jurisprudence of Minority Rights: The Changing Contours of Minority Rights', *Proceedings of the Research Association for Interdisciplinary Studies,* March 26-27, 2018

Masters, Bruce, *Christians and Jews in the Ottoman Arab World: The Roots of Sectarianism* (CUP 2001)

Macartney, CA, *National States and National Minorities* (OUP 1934)

Modeen, Tore, *The International Protection of National Minorities in* Europe (Abo Akademi, 1969)

"Myanmar's Rohingya", The Economist, 20 Oct 2012

Pentassuglia, Gaetano, *Minorities in International Law* (Council of Europe Publishing 2002)

Robins, Philip, *The Middle East* (Oneworld Publications 2016)

Stevenson, Douglas K, *American Life and Institutions* (Klett 1987)

Tomuschat, Christian (ed), *The United Nations at Age Fifty: A Legal Perspective* (Martinus Nijhoff Publishers 1996)

Thornberry, Patrick, *International Law and the Rights of Minorities* (Clarendon Press 1991)

United Nations Human Rights Council, *Report of the Independent International Fact-finding Mission on Myanmar*, 17 September 2018

UN News, *UN expert alarmed at worsening human rights situation in Myanmar's Rakhine state*, 7 April 2014. Available at: https://news.un.org/en/story/2014/04/465552-un-expert-alarmed-worsening-human-rights-situation-myanmars-rakhine-state#.Wb-Z8pUo5kA

United Nations Secretariat, *Study of the Legal Validity of the Undertakings Concerning Minorities,* 1950

United Nations Human Rights Office of the High Commissioner, *Minority Rights: International Standards and Guidance for Implementation*, HR/PUB/10/3, UN: New York and Geneva, 2010

United Nations Human Rights Office of the High Commissioner, *Situation of Human Rights of Rohingya Muslims and Other Minorities in Myanmar,* 2016

Wilson, Peter H, *Europe's Tragedy: A New History of the Thirty Years War* (Penguin 2010)

Zyberi, Gentian. 'The International Court of Justice and the Rights of Peoples and Minorities', 2013. Available at: https://www.researchgate.net/publication/301093498

Chapter 4

HOW UNIVERSAL IS THE UNIVERSAL DECLARATION?: INDIGENOUS PEOPLES AS A CHALLENGE TO THE UDHR

By Gerard Maguire

1. Introduction

This chapter will lay out the role that the Universal Declaration of Human Rights (UDHR) has played in the context of the rights of indigenous peoples and examine how collective rights have been, and remain, a challenge to the UDHR. To evaluate the reasons behind the lack of group rights, and particularly, the rights of indigenous peoples under the UDHR it is important to understand what the claims of these peoples are, which factors, have shaped these peoples and what exactly international human rights law can offer in relation to their protection. Although exact figures of the world's population of indigenous communities may never be known, many indigenous communities are located in rural and remote areas and are often neglected by their States in terms of census data collection. There are also many tribal peoples who are 'uncontacted',[1] and the estimation of their numbers varies greatly. However, according to the United Nations (UN), '[i]t is estimated that there are more than 370 million indigenous peoples spread across 70 countries worldwide'.[2] With the collapse in power of the world's colonising countries and the welcomed and, hard fought for, process of decolonisation of many countries, the rights and protections of indigenous peoples have slowly began to surface within the sphere of international law and human rights.[3] The struggle in the face of indigenous peoples around the globe is manifold and their plight is furthered with the fact that '[i]ndigenous peoples often have much in common with other neglected segments of societies, i.e. lack of political representation and participation, economic marginalization and poverty, lack of access to social

1 Defined by Survival International as 'Peoples who have no peaceful contact with anyone in the mainstream or dominant society'. <www.survivalinternational.org/info/terminology> accessed 06 November 2018.

2 'Who are Indigenous Peoples?' UN Factsheet available at <www.un.org/esa/socdev/unpfii/documents/5session_factsheet1.pdf> accessed 07 September 2018, 'The Issues' available at <https://www.culturalsurvival.org/issues> accessed 03 October 2018.

3 CW Chen, 'Indigenous Rights in International Law' (2014) *Oxford Research Encyclopedia of International Studies* accessed at <http://internationalstudies.oxfordre.com/view/10.1093/acrefore/9780190846626.001.0001/acrefore-9780190846626-e-77> accessed 06 November 2018.

services and discrimination'.[4] This chapter will offer an insight into this new and ever-changing field within the greater context of international law and examine why subsequent legal instruments have failed to offer the same level of protections for indigenous peoples in group form as the UDHR offers the individual. In order to assess this, the chapter will focus on the claims of indigenous peoples and how those claims have played a part in their exclusion from the UDHR. It will address the historic elements relating to the evolution of the rights of indigenous peoples and how this sphere has developed over the last century and how indigenous peoples began to rely and utilize instruments of international law to realize their rights, the rights that were denied to them within the drafting of the UDHR and posing the question 'how universal is the universal declaration of human rights?'.

2. A History of Abuse and Inequality

Over five hundred years ago, Europeans arrived in 'America' and began to lay claim to lands already occupied by indigenous peoples.[5] With these land grabs came frequent violence and terror with colonizers often slaughtering the indigenous children, women, and men who opposed their arrival. Those indigenous peoples who survived the brute violence were then faced with the danger of diseases carried by European settlers, from which they had no immunity, and those who escaped disease were faced with slavery.[6] This point in history is, arguably, when the world began to see the beginning of genocidal patterns. There is a continuing debate on whether or not the actions of Christopher Columbus in his 'discovery' of the Americas can amount to an act of genocide. Under his rule policies of slavery and systematic extermination in respect of the native population were implemented. As Ward Churchill noted:

> Columbus's programs reduced Taino numbers from as many as eight million at the outset of his regime to about three million in 1496. Perhaps 100,000 were left by the time of his departure. His policies, however, remained, with the result that by 1514 the Spanish census of the island showed barely 22,000 Indians remaining alive.[7]

Questions and concerns regarding the protections of indigenous peoples has been debated for centuries. As far back as the fifteenth and sixteenth century scholars, such as Francisco de Vitoria,[8] applied natural law precepts and

---

4 ibid.

5 The Americas were not unique in the ill treatment of their native peoples with the arrival of European settlers, similar instances are recorded in Africa and Australasia.

6 T De Orbe Novo, *The Eight Decades of Peter Martyr D'Anghera* (BiblioBazaar 2009) p 143.

7 W Churchill, *Indians are Us* (Common Courage Press 1994) p 1.

8 It is important to note that de Vitoria was concerned with the legal process and custom that was being used by and against native peoples in the Americas rather than the abuses they were suffering at the hands of Spanish colonizers.

challenged the Spanish claims to native lands.[9] De Vitoria argued that the Indians of the Americas were the true owners of their lands,[10] with 'dominion in both public and private matters'.[11] De Vitoria wrote extensively on the issue, and in keeping with the Eurocentric bias of the time 'designed' a way in which native peoples' lands could be taken from them at the behest of the new European invaders. This was the beginning of colonizing nations displaying disregard for the rights of native peoples that would remain a worrying consistency throughout the following centuries. Theorists described the law of nations,[12] or international law, as concerning itself only with the rights and duties of European and similarly *civilized* States, and as having its source entirely in the positive, consensual acts of those states. Thus, reinforcing the idea that the maltreatment of indigenous peoples was, not only ok, but justified. It highlights that collective or group rights for vulnerable peoples was not a concern of the then considered great powers. As the next section will address, this was a contributing factor to the omission of group rights from the UDHR.

3. Drafting of the UDHR and Omission of Group Rights

Considering the historic maltreatment of indigenous peoples and the resulting nature of vulnerability these peoples continue to face, it is curious that specific group protections were not included in the UDHR. The UDHR is aimed in its entirety at individual aspects of human rights rather than focusing on any particular elements of collective or group protections. The move away from the idea of minority protection that had been included in the workings of the law of nations, had been replaced. This move is what is correctly described by Mattias Åhrén as 'when the foundation for a new world order was created in the wake of World War II, protection of minority rights that the League of Nations had promoted was substituted for a set of universal individual human rights'.[13] Why were group rights, or any form of minority protections, omitted

9 S J Anaya, *Indigenous Peoples in International Law* (OUP 2000) p 15.

10 In this context, the term applies to the indigenous peoples of the Americas. Although some consider it pejorative. According to *Survival International*, 'it is widely used by indigenous people themselves in parts of the Americas, especially the United States and Brazil'. Accessed at < www.survivalinternational.org/info/terminology> accessed 06 November 2018.

11 Anaya, 2000 (n 9) pp 18-19.

12 When referring to the 'The Law of Nations' de Vattel's explanation is most accurate: '[t] he Law of nations modifies the intercourse of independent commonwealths in peace, and prescribes limits to their hostilities in war. It prescribes, that in peace nations should do each other as much good, and in time of war as little harm as may be possible without injuring their own proper real interests. The laws of nations, in short, establish that principle and rule of conduct which should prevent the strongest nation from abusing its power, and induce it to act justly and generously towards other States, upon the broad principle, that true happiness, whether of a single individual or of several, can only result from each adopting conduct influenced by a sincere desire to increase the general welfare of all mankind', see E Vattel et al, *The law of nations* (Liberty Fund 2008) pp ix.

13 M Åhrén, *Indigenous peoples' status in the international legal system* (1st edn, OUP 2016) p 27.

from the drafting of the UDHR remains the question. The vulnerable status of these groups were well documented and widely known.[14] To address this question it is necessary to consider the time of drafting of the UDHR when the images of the atrocities of World War II were still ingrained within the conscience of many States and people. Áhrén alludes to this in his writing on the issue. He states that '[t]hese factors together had rendered the world community adverse to minority rights when it embarked on drafting a new world order in the wake of World War II'.[15] By 'these factors, Áhrén is referring to the fact that the Nazi regime had used alleged needs to protect German minority groups in neighbouring countries as justification for the aggression that finally resulted in the outbreak of the war… the general perception was that the German minorities had collaborated in these efforts'.[16] There was a wish to protect against any potential that a minority group might have to challenge State power if they were granted group rights as was the case with the German experience at the outset of World War II.

4. Claims of Indigenous Peoples

While the process of decolonisation could be argued to be the starting point for the development of the modern era's understanding and concept of human rights, the process did not recognise the precarious position of indigenous peoples that existed in colonised countries. As Hurst Hannum states, '[t]erritory not nationhood, was the determining factor in the decolonization process'.[17] Indeed, there appeared to be a more sinister concern on behalf of the States of 'power' when drafting the UDHR. There an element of fear regarding territorial integrity of states versus the right to seek self-determination again, influenced by the German occurrences at the beginning of World War II.

Self-determination can mean a multitude of possibilities depending on the eyes of the beholder and proves to be a constantly contentious and discussed issue within the sphere of international law and politics. There are various connotations associated with the right, liberation from a colonial power or emancipation for a disenfranchised national minority, liberty of person and survival. However in the context of indigenous peoples, the right of self-determination surpasses the want and need for simply autonomy or independence, Jérémie Gilbert has recognized this in his writings and has stated that '[s]elf-determination contains all the aspirations of freedom and represents the ideal of a people entitled to pursue its own destiny'.[18] The right to self-determination is instrumental in the quest for protection, rights and justice for world's indigenous populations.

---

14 The United Nations 'Lets Fight Racism' available at <http://www.un.org/en/letsfightracism/indigenous.shtml> accessed 08 November 2018.

15 Åhrén (n 13) p 27.

16 ibid.

17 H Hannum, *Autonomy, Sovereignty and Self-Determination: The Accommodation of Conflicting Rights* (University of Pennsylvania Press 1966) p 81.

18 J Gilbert, *Indigenous Peoples' Land Rights under International Law: From Victims to Actors* (Transnational Publishers 2006) p 200.

It is enshrined in numerous international legal and human rights instruments. Common Art 1 of the International Covenant on Civil and Political Rights (ICCPR) and the International Covenant on Economic, Social and Cultural Rights (ICESCR) both address the right to self-determination. The right is further stated in numerous other international and national human rights instruments, for example, the African Charter of Human and Peoples' Rights,[19] the Declaration on the Granting Independence to Colonial Territories and Peoples,[20] and the Helsinki Final Act 1975.[21]

The issue at the heart of the decolonization process was that the territories who had been bestowed the right of self-determination were the entire population of the colonized territory and little to no consideration was given to the indigenous peoples of the land. This was 'irrespective of pre-colonial ethnic and cultural patterns'[22] and this poses a further hindrance for indigenous peoples who are seeking the same right. As often the case with vulnerable populations, the predicaments and circumstances of these groups are not usually heard or understood on an international level. Firstly, indigenous populations 'argue that they are unlike other "nations" or "minorities" as understood in international law, and constitute a *sui generis* category which is entitled to self-determination'.[23] Secondly, this is most likely due to the perpetual cycle of past injustices and ill-treatment at the hands of colonial masters and 'despite the contemporary absence of colonial structures in the classical form, indigenous peoples have continued to suffer impediments or threats to their ability to live and develop freely as distinct groups in their original homelands'.[24] The key phrase is 'original homelands'. Many struggles faced by indigenous peoples are surrounded by conflicts with States and governments relating to ancestral lands. What is important to take into consideration when debating the issue at hand is that, within regard to indigenous peoples, self-determination is not necessarily seeking secession. It can encompass a level of autonomy and a greater level of control over traditional lands and natural resources.[25] Most of the discourse regarding indigenous peoples and state actors is in relation to this claim of ownership of said lands and States' concerns regarding territorial

19 The African Charter on Human and Peoples' Rights (also known as the Banjul Charter) is an international human rights instrument that is intended to promote and protect human rights and basic freedoms in the African continent.

20 The Declaration on the Granting of Independence to Colonial Countries and Peoples was adopted by the United Nations General Assembly on 14 December 1960.

21 International Working Group on Indigenous Affairs 'Self-Determination' available at <http://www.iwgia.org/human-rights/self-determination> accessed 09 October 2018.

22 Åhrén (n 13) p 35.

23 TD Musgrave, *Self-Determination and National Minorities* (OUP 1997) p 173.

24 Anaya, 2000 (n 9) p 86.

25 This is an important factor recognized by the UN General Assembly in the preamble to UNDRIP, in which it states 'Convinced that control by indigenous peoples over developments affecting them and their lands, territories and resources will enable them to maintain and strengthen their institutions, cultures and traditions, and to promote their development in accordance with their aspirations and needs'.

integrity, from which, States have protection against as laid out in Art 46 of United Nations Declaration on the Rights of Indigenous Peoples (UNDRIP).[26]

Gilbert addresses the unique connection indigenous peoples have with land stating '[i]ndigenous peoples' claims to their ancestral lands are manifold and are based on a social, religious and cultural approach to their relationship with territories'.[27] This is not the only relationship between indigenous peoples and territory, as often the issue surpasses cultural connections as the land occupied by indigenous groups is often the sole means for the group's survival and sustainability. There is an innate connection between indigenous peoples and the land they occupy, not only for the ritualistic, symbolic and historic connections to particular land but also, as Gilbert has described the connection between land and survival for many indigenous groups. He points out that 'without access to their land, indigenous communities would not access their means of livelihood',[28] and if these claims made by Gilbert are in fact the case, then land rights of indigenous peoples are instrumental for not only the cultural survival of indigenous groups, but also their physical survival. Article 3 of the UDHR underlines this core right, which states:

> [e]veryone has the right to life, liberty and security of person', and for indigenous peoples to achieve this right, land ownership is integral, further supported by the international working group on indigenous affairs, which maintains that '[t]he issue of land and resource rights is the most important question for the majority of the worlds indigenous peoples.[29]

The vulnerable societal position of indigenous peoples often results in this right being abused, usually at the hands of States who are concerned more so with the economic benefits of these lands than the fundamental connections indigenous groups have with said territory. According to the International Working Group on Indigenous Affairs '[m]any governments often oppose international recognition of indigenous peoples' right to self-determination more through fear of losing control over indigenous lands than fear of losing some their overall political power.[30] As previously stated, within the context of indigenous peoples, self-determination is not, generally, about independence or a claim of secession. Rather, it is usually in relation to land claims and it is for this particular reason that:

---

26 UNDRIP, Art 46(1) states 'Nothing in this Declaration may be interpreted as implying for any State, people, group or person any right to engage in any activity or to perform any act contrary to the Charter of the United Nations or construed as authorizing or encouraging any action which would dismember or impair, totally or in part, the territorial integrity or political unity of sovereign and independent States'.

27 Gilbert (n 18) p 128.

28 ibid, p 117.

29 International Working Group on Indigenous Affairs 'Self-Determination' available at <http://www.iwgia.org/images/stories/sections/human-rights/self-determ/docs/selfdetermination.pdf> accessed 06 October 2018.

30 ibid.

> [b]oth nationally and internationally, indigenous peoples are increasingly focusing their struggles on the right to self-determination, principally over their lands and resources which continue to be threatened by national and international economic interest.[31]

There is still an air of perceived inferiority evident when assessing the meaning of self-determination within the context of indigenous peoples, on the part of those who refuse to grant the right.

The special applicability of the right of self-determination to indigenous peoples is apparent as '[a]lthough self-determination presumptively benefits all human beings, its linkage with the term *peoples* in international instruments indicates the collective or group character of the principle'.[32] The collective nature of the right is further cemented into the international legal framework with its inclusion in UNDRIP, adopted in 2007, which states in Art 3 that '[i]ndigenous peoples have the right to self-determination. By virtue of that right they freely determine their political status and freely pursue their economic, social and cultural development'[33] The pursuit and indeed achievement of these economic, social and cultural goals are of paramount importance to indigenous peoples as these developments are the foundation blocks for the survival of many of the world's indigenous communities.

Although it can be claimed 'indigenous peoples' land claims breathe new life to the issue of land ownership within the human rights discourse, through the emerging recognition of a collective right of land ownership',[34] there is a further threat to indigenous peoples in the form of destruction of their lands. There have been instances when the destruction of indigenous lands has not been merely for economic gain of a particular State, 'environmental devastation is not only a by-product of war, but has also been a military strategy since ancient times'.[35] If it is considered that 'it is certain that if the land destruction can be associated with the intent to destroy, the definition of genocide may apply'.[36] This is the case in Guatemala during the civil war period, government planned scorched earth policies caused irreparable damage to indigenous Mayan land and resulted in the destruction of the group's livelihood.[37] In the report by the Commission for Historical Clarification, it was found that the government backed scorched earth policies amounted to an act of genocide as it sought

---

31 E Cirkovic 'Self-Determination and Indigenous Peoples in International Law' 2007 31(2) *American Indian Law Review* p 376.
32 Anaya (n 9) p 77.
33 UNDRIP 2007.
34 Gilbert (n 18) p 88.
35 B Leebaw, 'Scorched Earth: Environmental War Crimes and International Justice', 2014 12(4) *Perspectives on Politics*, 770-788.
36 Gilbert (n 18) p 119.
37 Report of the Commission for Historical Clarification, Guatemala; Memory of Silence (1999) p 23 accessed at <http://www.aaas.org/search/gss/guatemala> accessed 08 October 2016.

to erase the sustainability of the indigenous Mayan population.[38] A similar occurrence in relation to the removal of indigenous peoples from ancestral lands was in Brazil, the indigenous Xingu Indian population were forcefully removed from their land for the purpose of land development permitted by the State. Within months of the move, twenty five percent of the Xingu tribe had died, mostly as a result of disease and sickness, from which their bodies had no immunity.[39] The protection of indigenous lands is important on many levels, traditional and cultural values, ancestral and religious values and ultimately for the sustenance of the group at hand. In many cases indigenous groups have survived due to the land they inhabit and depend on for their livelihood and survival. As Daes puts it, 'indigenous peoples have... declared that the rights to land, territories and natural resources is the basis for their collective survival and thus inextricably linked to their right to self-determination'.[40] Usually in cases of land seizure and forced eviction from ancestral lands, there is an economic reason behind the States actions and that reason is often when lands are rich in natural resources.

As previously stated, the drafters of the UDHR omit group protections for indigenous peoples. It is plausible to suggest that the reason for this was due to the protection it would have allowed these peoples to their own land claims. There have been individual protections of lands in some subsequent legal instruments. Paragraph 2 of Common Art 1 of both the ICCPR and ICESCR that:

> [a]ll peoples may, for their own ends, freely dispose of their natural wealth and resources without prejudice to any obligations arising out of international economic co-operation, based upon the principle of mutual benefit, and international law. In no case may a people be deprived of its own means of subsistence.

Yet there is an endless list of times that lands of indigenous peoples have been exploited for the economic gain of the State. The *Lubicon Lake Band* case, in Canada, is a prime example of the issues surrounding the grabbing of indigenous lands for the purpose of natural resource extraction.[41] The claim made by the indigenous population of Lubicon Lake was that 'oil and gas development in traditional lands threatened the environmental and economic base of the band, including the potential loss of natural resource revenues'.[42] The case, unresolved at a national level, was submitted to the Human Rights Committee on claims of violation of Arts 1 and 27 of the ICCPR.[43] The Committee found

---

38 ibid.

39 Tribes Alive Newsletter available at <http://ipcst.org/tribesalive/more-information/history-of-the-xingu> accessed 08 October 2018.

40 E I Daes, 'An Overview of the History of Indigenous Peoples: Self-Determination and the United Nations' 2008 21(1) *Cambridge Review of International Affairs*, 3.

41 *Lubicon Lake Band v Canada*, Communication No 167/1984 (26 March 1990), UN Doc Supp No 40 (A/45/40) at 1 (1990).

42 ibid.

43 ibid.

that the group could claim individual rights for violation of Art 27, but not a collective right under Art 1 of the Convention.[44]

The above-mentioned case highlights the precarious nature of self-determination within the context of indigenous peoples and indeed within the international legal framework and highly publicised cases.[45] Resource extraction from indigenous territories around the world is continuously justified by governments but often there are empty promises of investment into indigenous communities and sustainability projects but very few come to fruition:

> revenue from the extractive sector can be used to fund social programmes for education and poverty alleviation... [b]ut unfortunately, more often than not, they also fund corruption, conflict and in the case of indigenous peoples, a slow cultural genocide.[46]

The issue of free, prior and informed consent should enter the equation more frequently in relation to resource extraction on indigenous land.[47] Deborah Delgado-Pugley has written extensively on this issue, and has said of the legal intent behind this process:

> National prior consultation acts are meant to enshrine the right, recognized by international law, of indigenous peoples to be consulted by the State before the adoption of legal and administrative reforms that will affect them, and before the implementation of investment projects, where the project's area of influence includes their lands.[48]

---

44 ibid.

45 Possibly one of the most well-known cases in relation to ethnic land ownership claims is that of Ogoni People in Nigeria. As Royal Dutch Petroleum (RDP) focused its eyes on the fertile lands of the Ogoni region for oil extraction, the Ogoni people were forcibly exiled with no form of reparation made. There was no free, prior and informed consent of this land exploitation and the Ogoni, an ethnic minority in the region, battled tirelessly to retain the land that was theirs. RDP's claim was aided greatly by the corrupt Nigerian government of the time, who once again were more concerned with the economic viability of the lands rather than the indigenous claims. The family of Ken Saro-Wiwa took their claim to the United States under the Alien Tort Act, and their claim was later settled out of court for a figure in excess of fifteen and a half million US dollars <http://digitalcommons.law.yale.edu/cgi/viewcontent.cgi?article=1033&context=yhrdlj> accessed 10 August 2018.

46 CounterPunch 'The Economics of Exploitation' available at <www.counterpunch.org/2015/08/20/the-economics-of-exploitation-indigenous-peoples-and-the-impact-of-resource-extraction> accessed 09 October 2018.

47 According to the UN Expert Mechanism on the Rights of Indigenous Peoples, 'Free, Prior and Informed Consent (FPIC) is one of the most important principles that Indigenous Peoples believe can protect their right to participation. It is embedded in the right to self-determination. The duty of States to obtain Indigenous Peoples' FPIC entitles Indigenous people to effectively determine the outcome of decision-making that affects them, not merely a right to be involved'. accessed at <www.culturalsurvival.org/publications/cultural-survival-quarterly/free-prior-and-informed-consent-protecting-indigenous> accessed 09 November 2018.

48 D Delgado-Pugley, 'Contesting the Limits of Consultation in the Amazon Region: On

The benefits brought to this by indigenous populations alone can be incredibly fruitful as 'indigenous peoples have an intuitive relationship with nature, a wealth of traditional knowledge and have used natural resource management practices for centuries to preserve their lands'.[49] Usually this is not the case and the negative effects of indigenous land exploitation are extensive, as 'the extraction of resources does not just leave an ugly physical imprint, the scarred landscape of indigenous and nomadic lands are almost mirrored by an equally negative cultural and social imprint – endemic poverty, low level conflict and ecological collapse'.[50] Within the context of indigenous peoples it appears that 'peoples have been recognised; but it is also clear that legal recognition does not mean that the rights, territories, resources and cultures of indigenous peoples are respected'.[51] Professor Erica Irene Daes has said of self-determination, in relation to indigenous peoples, that it is a system:

> [T]hrough which indigenous peoples are able to join with all other peoples that make up the state on mutually agreed upon and just terms after many years of isolation and exclusion. This process does not require the assimilation of individuals, as citizens like all others, but the recognition and incorporation of distinct peoples within the fabric of the state, on agreed terms.[52]

It is once again through the overarching goal of their right to self-determination that this process of exploitation of vulnerable groups can be counteracted.

5. Further Incorporation of Group Rights Post-UDHR

The right to exist is a prerequisite for other rights. Man is entitled to his fundamental freedoms because he exists. 'Existence' is a notion which has a special sense for a collective; first because of Physical Existence, and secondly because of the notion of existence for a minority through the shared consciousness of its members, manifested through language, culture, religion, a shared sense of history.[53] If these traits are restricted or denied, this is a direct threat to the existence and survival of the group. The UDHR

Indigenous Peoples' Demands for Free, Prior and Informed Consent in Bolivia and Peru' (2013) 43 *Revue Générale de Droit*, p 151-81.

49 M Mowforth, 'The Violence of Development: Resource Depletion, Environmental Crises and Human Rights Abuses in Central America', *The Guardian* (September 2014): <www.theguardian.com/global-development/2014/sep/23/indigenous-people-crisis-land-resources> accessed 09 October 2018.

50 M Keman 'The Economics of Exploitation: Indigenous Peoples and the Impact of Resource Extraction' (2015) accessed at: <www.counterpunch.org/2015/08/20/the-economics-of-exploitation-indigenous-peoples-and-the-impact-of-resource-extraction> accessed 09 September 2018.

51 Mowforth (n 49).

52 Daes (n 40).

53 The UN defines Indigenous peoples as "…inheritors and practitioners of unique cultures and ways of relating to people and the environment. They have retained social, cultural, economic and political characteristics that are distinct from those of the dominant

laid the groundwork for future developments in the codification of the rights of minorities and indigenous peoples, which are developed in Art 27 of the ICCPR and UNDRIP. However the latter recognized the danger of claiming human rights as universal as it ignores and undermines the cultural differences that exist between societies in different parts of the world.

If this is considered, then it could be said that the UDHR could not possibly hold the same meaning, value and protections for everyone in the world. Keeping this in mind, it is necessary to question how universal is the UDHR, if vast numbers of peoples around the globe, many of whom need these protections, cannot rely on the declaration for support? By emphasising the rights of individuals, the Declaration was meant as an attempt to transcend cultural bias in such a way that it became relevant to all, no matter what their upbringing. Nevertheless, the UDHR is viewed by some as a neo-colonialist attempt by the West to control the lives of those in the developing world.[54] Protections alluded to in the preamble of the Declaration include a 'recognition of the inherent dignity and of the equal and inalienable rights of all members of the human family is the foundation of freedom, justice and peace in the world' and are described as a foundational necessity for peace, freedom and justice. The preamble further states 'disregard and contempt for these human rights have resulted in barbarous acts which have outraged the conscience of mankind'. However, in the context of indigenous peoples, group entities could not rely on these protections for their cultural and physical survival.

6. Subsequent Development of Law Relating to Indigenous Peoples

The International Labour Organization (ILO), published a study on indigenous peoples in 1953,[55] and in 1957 adopted Convention No 107 and Recommendation No 104 on the Protection and Integration of Indigenous and Tribal Populations.[56] These were the first international legal instruments specifically created to protect the rights of peoples whose ways of life and existence were — then, as now — threatened by dominating cultures. While it was in fact the first time the rights of indigenous peoples were mentioned in a context separate of minority rights, it was aimed towards an assimilation approach.[57] The expert meetings and proceeding were held with no 'apparent

societies in which they live', <www.un.org/indigenous-peoples> accessed 10 September 2019. Thus highlighting the significance of cultural markers for the existence of a group.

54 W Osiatynski , 'On the Universality of the Universal Declaration of Human Rights', in Sajó A (eds) *Human Rights with Modesty: The Problem of Universalism* (Springer 2004) p 33.

55 Indigenous Peoples: Living and Working Conditions of Aboriginal Populations in Independent Countries in 1953.

56 Recommendation No 104 on the Protection and Integration of Indigenous and Tribal Populations 1957.

57 Anaya (n 9) p 57. Anaya maintains that Convention 107 'reflects the premise of

participation on the indigenous peoples' own designated representatives'.[58] The UN Special Rapporteur José Martinez Cobo compiled a report investigating the treatment of indigenous peoples, entitled 'The Problem of Discrimination against Indigenous Populations' in 1981 and vehemently rejected the assimilation approach alluded to and encouraged by ILO Convention 107. He maintained that 'the UN's work directed at indigenous peoples should rather place emphasis on their ethno-development and self-determination, and not on integration'.[59] Since its creation in 1919, ILO has defended the social and economic rights of groups whose customs, traditions, institutions or language set them apart from other sections of national communities. With the creation of ILO 169, for the first time, there was a distinction made between minority and indigenous rights. The focus of ILO 169 displays a shift toward the importance of collective rights rather than solely the individual, which had been the case previously.

The approach taken by ILO 169 has been labelled 'ethno-political self-government, as the convention foresees self-governing rights of indigenous peoples and calls for respect of their collective traditions and customary laws'.[60] Other advancements in law such as ICCPR Art 27 and ICESCR Art 3 offered a form of cultural protection for these groups. However, they lacked the political force and moral obligation that lay behind the UDHR, if it is considered that the UDHR is generally agreed to be the foundation of international human rights law. The UN invested in attempting to square the circle so to speak, in relation to strengthening the rights of indigenous peoples and in 1982 created a working Group on Indigenous Populations. This was followed by the creation of the Sub-Commission on the prevention of Discrimination and Protection of Minorities prepared a Study on the Problem of Discrimination against Indigenous Populations in 1986.[61] In 1994, the Indigenous Peoples and Minorities Unit (IPMU) and the Office of the UN High Commission for Human Rights (OHCHR) was established. One of the central goals of the OHCHR was 'to ensure that all issues concerning indigenous peoples and national and/or ethnic, religious and linguistic minorities are fully addressed in all activities of promotion, protection and technical cooperation'.[62] Arguably the most important legal instrument that has been drafted in relation to the rights of indigenous peoples is the UNDRIP. The purpose of this Declaration is, according to Art 43 of the document, to 'constitute the minimum standards for the survival, dignity and well-being of the indigenous peoples of the world'. This was followed by the United Nations Indigenous Peoples' Partnership

assimilation operative among dominant political elements in national and international circles at the time of the convention's adoption'.

58 ibid, p 55.

59 Åhrén (n 13) p 8.

60 ibid, p 95.

61 Also known as the Cobo Report, accessible at <www.un.org/development/desa/indigenouspeoples/publications/2014/09/martinez-cobo-study/> accessed 10 September 2019.

62 The United Nations <www2.ohchr.org/english/issues/indigenous/docs/IntDay/OHCHRandIndigenouseng.pdf> accessed 10 October 2018.

which was established in 2011. The most recent development in the area of the rights of indigenous peoples is resolution 71/321.[63]

7. Contemporary Practice: The Evolving Nature of the Rights of Indigenous Peoples

In September 2017, the United Nations General Assembly adopted, without a vote, a resolution titled, 'enhancing the participation of indigenous peoples' representatives and institutions in meetings of relevant United Nations bodies on issues affecting them'.[64] By its terms, the Assembly welcomed recent discussions on indigenous participation, and encouraged the Permanent Forum on Indigenous Issues, the Expert Mechanism on the Rights of Indigenous Peoples and the UN Special Rapporteur on the Rights of Indigenous Peoples to continue to address the issue of indigenous participation. It further requested the Secretary-General to report, by the end of the Assembly's seventy fourth session, on achievements, analysis and recommendations on ways to enable such participation. At the beginning of discussions at the UN regarding the participation of Indigenous Peoples, the UNGA President Miroslav Lajcak stated:

> [R]ights are not aspirational, ideals or best-case scenarios, but rather minimum standards. They are non-negotiable, and they must be respected and promoted, yet, here we are, over a decade after the adoption of the Declaration on the Rights of Indigenous Peoples with rights not being realized.[65]

It is also important to recognize that the new resolution does not offer full participation within the United Nations, rather it enhances 'the participation of indigenous peoples' representatives and institutions in meetings of relevant United Nations bodies on issues affecting them'.[66] While the participation of indigenous peoples within the UN framework, without having to work through the States in which they reside, is a welcome symbol of progression in the recognition of the status of indigenous peoples, it leaves a rather large gap for critique. For example, the lexicon of the Resolution displays a lack of recognition of sovereignty of indigenous peoples, only allowing their participation within 'relevant bodies' and only on 'issues affecting them', thus comprehensively restricting its scope of application, The UNGA also

---

[63] A/RES/71/321 Full title: Enhancing the Participation of Indigenous Peoples' Representatives and Institutions in Meetings of Relevant United Nations Bodies on Issues Affecting Them.

[64] The United Nations <www.un.org/en/ga/search/view_doc.asp?symbol=A/RES/71/321> accessed 08 September 2018.

[65] AM Lebada, 'Indigenous Peoples, Member States Express Dissatisfaction with UNGA Decision' at <http://sdg.iisd.org/news/indigenous-peoples-member-states-express-dissatisfaction-with-unga-decision/> accessed 08 September 2018.

[66] The United Nations (n 64).

encouraged branches of the UN infrastructure[67] relating to indigenous peoples 'to continue to address the issue of indigenous participation'.[68]

Michael A Murphy has argued that having a greater inclusion of indigenous people in electoral procedure and political institutions will further understanding of their needs and claims. He has further suggested that active co-operation will have a much more beneficial result for all parties involved, for both indigenous and non-indigenous groups.[69] He has stated:

> indigenous representation in shared rule institutions such as national legislatures need not be seen as short circuiting indigenous self-determination; instead, this form of political voice can be viewed as part of a broader strategy for involving indigenous self-determination by targeting a variety of parallel and complimentary access points to political power.[70]

It is generally accepted that '[p]arliaments as institutions, can do more to learn about minority/indigenous groups and the issues they face, to reach out to these groups, and to extend some procedural accommodation of their participation in the legislative process',[71] although this is not unanimous across the globe. One of the most successful examples of the political participation of indigenous peoples is that of the Sami People. The Sami occupy areas in northern Europe, mainly Scandinavia and their territory crosses international borders in some instances. Through the Sami Parliament the quest for recognition of Sami self-determination has remained a core value, and although not a body set up to distinctly tackle this issue, the presence of the parliament and success of the Sami participation in the political structure has resulted in recognition of their claims. It is 'now indisputable that the Sami have a right to cultural autonomy and this requires a certain degree of self-determination, was established in the Sami Parliament Investigation in considering the roll of the Sami Parliament in Swedish democracy 2002'.[72] The Sami parliament has been actively encouraging members of the indigenous Sami communities to take a more active role within the system and it has proven successful in terms of promoting political participation for indigenous peoples and most recent figures show that in Sweden, '[m]ore than 8000 of the Sweden's presumed 20,000

67 For example, The Permanent Forum on Indigenous Issues, the Expert Mechanism on the Rights of Indigenous Peoples and the UN Special Rapporteur on the Rights of Indigenous Peoples.

68 The United Nations <www.un.org/development/desa/indigenouspeoples/news/2017/08/general-assembly-draft-resolution-on-participation-of-indigenous-peoples-at-the-un/> accessed 25 June 2018.

69 MA Murphy 'Representing Indigenous Self-Determination' *University of Toronto Law Journal* (2008) 58(2) pp 185-216.

70 ibid.

71 O Protsyk, 'The Representation of Minorities & Indigenous Peoples in Parliament' Report for the Inter-Parliamentary Union (2010) accessed at: <http://www.ipu.org/splz-e/chiapas10/overview.pdf> accessed 10 October 2018.

72 Sami Community Website 'Background: The State and the Sami Parliament' available at <www.sametinget.se/9688> accessed 10 October 2018.

Sami population are now registered in the Sami Parliament electoral register'.[73] This is a hugely positive action and allows the group be their own catalyst for change. It is this form of empowerment that the right to self-determination promises and delivers for indigenous peoples. Had this right been incorporated and protected by the UDHR the landscape for the right of indigenous peoples would look incredibly different today.

8. The Universal Periodic Review

In order to sustain the current momentum that is shining the global spotlight on the rights of indigenous peoples, the Universal Periodic Review[74] should be utilized to not only monitor progress but to allow a metaphorical microscope to be applied to States with indigenous populations, to ensure compliancy. The UPR began in 2006 and the aim of system was to create interactive dialogue between States and relevant stakeholders, and to assist and review in the fulfilment of States obligations to human rights. The rights of indigenous peoples were topical at the time of the first UPR as UNDRIP was in the process of being drafted and was therefore given a chance to have the spotlight shone on the concerns and abuses. An argument put forward by Noelle Higgins in relation to this is that 'a comprehensive and universal examination of the rights of minorities and indigenous peoples could be possible through the UPR'.[75] This would be a huge step forward, again, in terms of the compliance of States and also instils an almost moral obligation upon those states who have indigenous populations to comply and be transparent in their own implementation of human rights infrastructure at a national level. However, the UPR has failed to define what non-cooperation is in relation to observations and recommendations and how it will be dealt with. Close monitoring of the UPR system in relation to non-cooperation is essential.

9. Conclusion

The UDHR lacked universality in its inception in relation to group rights, by directing rights solely to the individual. It facilitated the exploitation of many indigenous groups, as described in the earlier section of this chapter. By omitting group rights within the UDHR, it could not be relied upon by groups who were in need of the strong legal, political and moral obligation the UDHR had, and continues to have. However, in reality, it increased the vulnerability of an already vulnerable population. It did however pave the way for future developments. The issue remains that said developments lack the political and moral force that lay behind the UDHR. Recognition of

---

73 ibid.

74 Referred to hereafter as UPR.

75 N Higgins, 'Advancing the Rights of Minorities and Indigenous Peoples: Getting UN Attention via the Universal Periodic Review' *Netherlands Quarterly of Human Rights* (2014) 32(4) pp 379-407.

indigenous rights has improved greatly in the past two decades. In the United States, nine cities in varying states across the country have opted to celebrate Indigenous Peoples Day as a counter celebration to the traditional celebration of Columbus Day, celebrating the uniqueness and cultural significance of the indigenous American Indian population.[76] This is an incredible move forward for the indigenous populations of the US and furthermore, a benefit to society at large and especially those surrounding the indigenous communities. Through the raising of the profile of indigenous issues through changes like those previously mentioned, the next generation are beginning to see the importance of these native populations, not only in history but for the future. The world is witnessing many indigenous groups transitioning from vulnerable groups in need of protection to self-actualizing group who are demanding their rights be recognized. As peoples', the indigenous communities of the world continue to bring into question the original understanding of human rights within a collective context.

10. Bibliography

Åhrén, M, *Indigenous peoples' status in the international legal system* (1st edn, OUP 2016)

Anaya, SJ, *Indigenous Peoples in International Law* (OUP 2000)

Chen, CW, 'Indigenous Rights in International Law' (2014) *Oxford Research Encyclopedia of International Studies*

Cirkovic, E, 'Self-Determination and Indigenous Peoples in International Law' (2007) 31(2) *American Indian Law Review*

Churchill, W, *Indians are Us*, (Common Courage Press 1994)

Daes, EI, 'An Overview of the History of Indigenous Peoples: Self-Determination and the United Nations' (2008) 21(1) *Cambridge Review of International Affairs*

Delgado-Pugley, D, 'Contesting the Limits of Consultation in the Amazon Region: On Indigenous Peoples' Demands for Free, Prior and Informed Consent in Bolivia and Peru'. (2013) 43 *Revue Générale de Droit*

De Orbe Novo, T, *The Eight Decades of Peter Martyr D'Anghera* (BiblioBazaar 2009)

E I Daes, EI, 'Explanatory note concerning the draft declaration on the rights of Indigenous peoples' (1993) UN Doc E/CN. 4/Sub.2/1993/26/Add

Gilbert, J, *Indigenous Peoples' Land Rights under International Law: From Victims to Actors* (Transnational Publishers 2006)

Hannum, H, *Autonomy, Sovereignty and Self-Determination: The Accommodation of Conflicting Rights* (University of Pennsylvania Press)

Higgins, N, 'Advancing the Rights of Minorities and Indigenous Peoples: Getting UN Attention via the Universal Periodic Review' (2014) 32(4) *Netherlands Quarterly of Human Rights*

Keman, M, 'The Economics of Exploitation: Indigenous Peoples and the Impact of Resource

[76] '9 Cities Abolish Columbus Day' <www.rt.com/usa/318178-cities-abolish-columbus-day> accessed 25 September 2018.

Extraction' (2015) accessed at: <http://www.counterpunch.org/2015/08/20/the-economics-of-exploitation-indigenous-peoples-and-the-impact-of-resource-extraction>

Leebaw, B, 'Scorched Earth: Environmental War Crimes and International Justice' (2014) 12(4) *Perspectives on Politics*

Lebada, AM, 'Indigenous Peoples, Member States Express Dissatisfaction with UNGA Decision' at <http://sdg.iisd.org/news/indigenous-peoples-member-states-express-dissatisfaction-with-unga-decision/>

Mowforth, M, 'The Violence of Development: Resource Depletion, Environmental Crises and Human Rights Abuses in Central America'. The Guardian (September 2014) accessed at <http://www.theguardian.com/global-development/2014/sep/23/indigenous-people-crisis-land-resources>

Musgrave, TD, *Self-Determination and National Minorities* (OUP 1997)

Murphy, MA, 'Representing Indigenous Self-Determination' (2008) 58(2) *University of Toronto Law Journal*

Osiatynski, W, 'On the Universality of the Universal Declaration of Human Rights' in Sajó A (eds) *Human Rights with Modesty: The Problem of Universalism* (Springer 2004)

Protsyk, O, 'The Representation of Minorities & Indigenous Peoples in Parliament' Report for the Inter-Parliamentary Union (2010) accessed at: <http://www.ipu.org/splz-e/chiapas10/overview.pdf>

Report of the Commission for Historical Clarification, Guatemala; Memory of Silence (1999) p 23 accessed at <http://www.aaas.org/search/gss/guatemala>

The Cobo Report, accessible at <https://www.un.org/development/desa/indigenouspeoples/publications/2014/09/martinez-cobo-study/>

Vattel, E et al, *The Law of Nations*, (Liberty Fund 2008)

Chapter 5

THE RIGHTS OF WORKERS

By Keith D Ewing

1. Introduction

Article 23 of the UDHR states:

> (1) Everyone has the right to work, to free choice of employment, to just and favourable conditions of work and to protection against unemployment.
>
> (2) Everyone, without any discrimination, has the right to equal pay for equal work.
>
> (3) Everyone who works has the right to just and favourable remuneration ensuring for himself and his family an existence worthy of human dignity, and supplemented, if necessary, by other means of social protection.
>
> (4) Everyone has the right to form and to join trade unions for the protection of his interests.

Article 24 states:

> Everyone has the right to rest and leisure, including reasonable limitation of working hours and periodic holidays with pay.

2. From the ILO to the UDHR

Unlike other provisions of the UDHR, the labour provisions have deep roots in international law, particularly as a result of the work of the International Labour Organisation (ILO), which was founded at the Treaty of Versailles in 1919. A product of the First World War, the ILO survived the ideological polarisation of the world in the 1920s, the economic collapse of the 1930s, and the Second World War in the 1940s.[1] For that alone, the ILO was an extraordinary achievement. As part of the revival of the organisation after the Second World War, its members agreed the Declaration of Philadelphia in 1944,

[1] Antony Alcock, *History of the International Labour Organisation* (Palgrave 1971).

embracing many of the values subsequently to be found in the UN Declaration and the workers' rights provisions in particular.[2]

Apart from reminding us that workers' rights are human rights and, as such, already part of the international human rights agenda,[3] the Declaration of Philadelphia prepared us for the principle that human rights are indivisible, and that social rights are equally as important as economic rights. This principle is acknowledged in the preamble to the UDHR, where it is written, albeit in patronising terms that:

> Whereas disregard and contempt for human rights have resulted in barbarous acts which have outraged the conscience of mankind, and the advent of a world in which human beings shall enjoy freedom of speech and belief and freedom from fear and want has been proclaimed as the highest aspiration of the common people.

This principle is carried forward into the text of the UDHR itself, where the social rights of workers sit side by side with civil and political rights of everyone, and alongside other social rights, including the right to health care and education.[4]

3. UDHR and Workers' Rights

These principles embedded in the UDHR have been an inspiration for a number of other international and regional instruments, including in the former case the two great United Nations instruments of 1966 – the International Covenant on Civil and Political Rights (ICCPR) on the one hand and the International Covenant on Economic, Social and Cultural Rights (ICESCR) on the other. In terms of workers' rights, the ICESCR is more expansive, consisting of four dedicated articles, expanding the two articles is the UDHR. But the core is nevertheless to be found in the latter: the right to just and favourable remuneration; the right to just and favourable working conditions; and the right to equal pay for equal work. This is a paean to a different political era from today, reflecting ideas not about social inclusion but social equity. It is a commitment not to a minimum wage, or a living wage, or a decent wage, but to a just wage.

The idea of a just wage is no doubt highly contestable, but it is clear from the era when this document was drafted that it was not a wage to be determined by

---

2 See Alain Supiot, *The Spirit of Philadelphia: Social Justice vs. the Total Market* (Verso 2012).

3 On workers' rights as human rights, see Virginia Mantouvalou, 'Are Labour Rights Human Rights?' (2012) 3 *European Labour Law Journal* 151.

4 On the indivisibility of human rights, see European Social Charter (revised) (entered into force 3 May 1996) ETS 163, preamble.

the 'higgling of the market',[5] nor to adopt the language of the preamble that was designed only to address 'fear from want'. This was an era of social democratic politics and progressive economics, the cue in the text for determining wage levels being those that would secure 'an existence worthy of human dignity' (Art 23), and the 'free development of the worker's personality' (Art 22). The same idea is reflected in the Declaration of Philadelphia where the International Labour Conference committed to:

> policies in regard to wages and earnings, hours and other conditions of work calculated to ensure a just share of the fruits of progress to all.[6]

Also important in the UDHR is the commitment to the right of workers to form and join trade unions for the protection of their interests. This is important because it is through free trade unions that workers can secure many of the rights set out in the Declaration (though some — such as the right to work and free choice of employment — require active State promotion of economic policies). But it is important also because it is through trade unions that workers can take part in a process of industrial self-government, whether by means of collective bargaining in the industry and enterprise in which they are employed, or by means of trade union engagement with government to produce the laws that workers need for their protection.

That said, the trade union rights in the Declaration are very limited, though these have been fleshed out significantly by ICESCR to include not just the right to join a trade union, but also the right to trade union autonomy, as well as the right to strike. This is an essential feature of any system designed to address the abuse of power by employers.[7] Although the UNDHR is disappointing for its limited embrace of trade union rights, it is notable that earlier in the same year the ILO had concluded the preparation of Convention 87 on Freedom of Association and the Right to Organise (1948), and in the following year would conclude its preparation of Convention 98 on the Right to Organise and Collective Bargaining (1949). Both are regarded as core human rights instruments.

4. UDHR and the Indivisibility of Human Rights

An indication of the inspirational effects of the UDHR is to be found in the preamble to the ICESCR, which provides that:

---

5 A term used by HB Higgins in *ex parte H V McKay* (1907) 2 CAR 1 (the famous *Harvester* judgment). See discussion in Paul O'Higgins, 'Labour is not a Commodity – An Irish Contribution to International Labour Law' (1997) 26 *Industrial Law Journal* 225.

6 International Labour Organization, *Declaration of Philadelphia: Declaration Concerning the Aims and Purposes of the International Labour Organization* (ILO 1944), III(d).

7 International Covenant on Economic, Social and Cultural Rights (entered into force 3 January 1976) 993 UNTS 3, Art 8.

> in accordance with the Universal Declaration of Human Rights, the ideal of free human beings enjoying freedom from fear and want can only be achieved if conditions are created whereby everyone may enjoy his economic, social and cultural rights, as well as his civil and political rights.

The provisions of Arts 23 and 24 of the UDHR are to be found in these other instruments, which include not only the two UN instruments, but also regional instruments such as the European Social Charter. The latter does not acknowledge the UDHR, although the European Convention on Human Rights (ECHR) refers to it prominently in the preamble.

That said, the UDHR is in some respects a high-water mark, which has become more visible in the fifty years since it was adopted. In the first place, what we have seen since then has been an ideological split in the recognition of rights, in the sense that having been housed under a single roof in the UDHR, are now split into two different documents, with civil and political rights in one instrument and social and economic rights in another. While we had the unitary UDHR, we now have the binary ICCPR and the ICESCR. Prior to 1966, at a regional level, we had the ECHR but also the European Social Charter, with an eleven-year gap between them.

It may be said, of course, that it makes no difference whether the rights are in one or two instruments. What matters is their acknowledgement at international level. But it does matter, because the division of instruments typically conceals a difference in the means of supervision and enforcement, with the civil and political rights under both regimes above (UN and Council of Europe) embracing different methods of enforcement, with those relating to social and economic rights being inferior to those relating to civil and political rights. The European Court of Human Rights is thus misnamed: it is the European Court for *some* Human Rights.[8]

In fact, it was not until the European Charter of Fundamental Rights that we find the two categories of rights were brought together again under the same roof. This is all the more striking for the fact that social and economic rights have become greatly expanded beyond the two articles in the UNDHR — although the EU Charter embraces them both. However, while this was a hugely symbolic return to first principles, it remains likely that the sometimes opaquely drafted provisions relating to 'solidarity' as referred to in the EU Charter will — as

---

8 The European Social Charter in contrast is supervised by the European Committee of Social Rights, which has the power to accept 'collective complaints' from approved bodies in relation to countries which accept the complaints procedure (countries which include Ireland but not the UK). Otherwise, supervision is by monitoring member states regular reports.

a result of the jurisprudence of the CJEU — be forever subordinate to the overriding fundamental freedoms in the TFEU.[9]

5. Human Rights and Corporations

Despite the foregoing, the UDHR has nevertheless played an important part in the development of the International Bill of Rights — a seminal text of modern times. But it has also played a part in taking its social and economic rights in the modern era to the other great source of power over workers' lives, namely the corporation. The International Bill of Rights was drafted by the UN by States and is addressed to States. It imposes no direct obligations on private legal entities such as companies and creations of the State, though it may do so indirectly by requiring the State to discipline corporate power in relation to wages, working conditions and trade union rights.

The great challenge for the human rights community is how to bring corporate power within the framework of human rights principles. To this end, we now see a number of initiatives which reference the UDHR, beginning with the OECD Guidelines on Multinational Enterprises, the commentaries to which recognize that:

> while promoting and upholding human rights is primarily the responsibility of governments, where corporate conduct and human rights intersect enterprises do play a role, and thus MNEs are encouraged to respect human rights, not only in their dealings with employees, but also with respect to others affected by their activities, in a manner that is consistent with host governments' international obligations and commitments. The Universal Declaration of Human Rights and other human rights obligations of the government concerned are of particular relevance in this regard.[10]

Also important in this respect are the UN Guiding Principles on Business and Human Rights approved in 2011, based on the principles of 'Protect, Respect and Remedy'.[11] This is addressed to States *and* corporations, the latter being urged to respect human rights and to avoid infringing the human rights of others. The responsibility of businesses to respect human rights is said to refer to 'internationally recognized human rights – understood, at a minimum, as those expressed in the International Bill of Human Rights and the principles concerning fundamental rights set out in the ILO's Declaration on Fundamental

9 See Case C-438/05 *International Transport Workers' Federation and Finnish Seamen's Union v Viking Line ABP* [2007] ECR I-10779, and Case C-341/05 *Laval v Svenska Byggnadsarbetareforbundet* [2007] I-11767.

10 OECD, *Guidelines for Multinational Enterprises* (OECD 2011), Commentary 36.

11 UN High Commissioner for Human Rights, *Guiding Principles on Business and Human Rights* (United Nations 2011).

Principles and Rights at Work.[12] One of the commentaries to the Guiding Principles states explicitly that:

> An authoritative list of the core internationally recognized human rights is contained in the International Bill of Human Rights (consisting of the Universal Declaration of Human Rights and the main instruments through which it has been codified: the International Covenant on Civil and Political Rights and the International Covenant on Economic, Social and Cultural Rights), coupled with the principles concerning fundamental rights in the eight ILO core conventions as set out in the Declaration on Fundamental Principles and Rights at Work. These are the benchmarks against which other social actors assess the human rights impacts of business enterprises.[13]

There is thus an explicit recognition not only that governments should comply with the UDHR, but so too should corporations. While this means compliance will all aspects of the three UN instruments (including civil and political rights where they are relevant), this is an exhortation/expectation/obligation that has a particular resonance in relation to workers' rights in view of the nature of corporate activity and the role of workers in production and/or delivery. This would include UDHR, Arts 23 and 24. Of course, if States as signatories to international instruments were performing their solemn obligations, there would be no need at this level for a separate obligation on companies to respect human rights. But the reality is that there are States unable to comply, particularly where corporate investors demand limited regulation.

6. The Impact of the UDHR

The impact of the UDHR has thus been extensive. The battle for the recognition of human rights has been won. The UDHR has informed not only treaties but also a range of soft law initiatives addressed to both States and corporations. Its principles are enduring. Yet while the battle to recognize and reproduce human rights standards has been institutionalized and normalised, the battle to implement human rights standards has so far been lost, and indeed continues to regress. This is particularly true of workers' rights despite the impressive contemporary academic scholarship asserting that workers' rights are human rights. That said, however, at least concerning workers' rights, the impact of the UDHR has been limited, as has been the impact of the other instruments which it has helped inspire activists, civil servants and governments to create.

This regression can be illustrated in a number of ways. But for present purposes it is enough to take the core provisions of the UDHR, Arts 23 and 24 to illustrate the regression.

---

[12] ibid, Principle 12.

[13] ibid, Commentary to Principle 12.

The right to work and to just and favourable conditions of work

This is an era in which many governments now boast of full employment and labour shortages leading to a relaxation of immigration rules in some of the previously most closed countries. Paradoxically, it is also an era when immigration is apparently resented by home communities, despite the heavy dependence in these communities on manufacturing and service industries. In the European Union (EU) these latter contradictions have been exposed by Brexit. But although there is said to be high levels of employment (the United Kingdom for example posting the largest number of people in work ever recorded), there are also chronic problems of under-employment, with the growing commodification of labour reflected in different forms of casualization, such as agency employment and zero-hours contracts. These and other modern practices (which have parallels in earlier epochs) confound the commitment in the UDHR to 'just and favourable conditions of work'.

The right to equal pay for equal work

This principle — designed principally to eliminate gender discrimination on pay — has been recognized in international law since 1919, when it was included in the preamble to the ILO Constitution. It was endorsed not only by the UDHR, but also subsequently by ILO Convention 100 (Equal Remuneration Convention 1951), which was to inform the standards in other important documents, such as the ILO Declaration of the Fundamental Rights of Workers in 1998. Of course, it has also become the standard of the EU, as reflected in the original EEC Treaty, Art 119 and the Equal Pay Directive of 1975, together with the jurisprudence of the CJEU implementing these instruments. So it is a principle with a pedigree of almost 100 years at the time of writing. Yet the gender pay gap in most countries remains stubbornly wide, and at a median 18.4% in the United Kingdom.[14] Men are typically paid more than women.

The right to just and favourable remuneration

This principle can be met in a number of ways. But with the decline of collective bargaining coverage, the setting of wage rates is left increasingly to State minimum wage legislation, which the United Kingdom has tried to rebrand as a national living wage (albeit not a just wage). Few people could live on the national living wage in a manner that ensures 'an existence worthy of human dignity' to use the language of the UDHR, Art 23(3). The national minimum wage in the United Kingdom at the time of writing would produce an annual wage of about £16,246 for an adult working 40 hours a week on a standard contract.[15] This is higher than the minimum wage in a number of other

[14] Josh Holder, Alexandra Topping, Caelainn Barr, Feilding Cage and Antonio Voce, 'Gender pay gap: when does your company stop paying women in 2018?' *The Guardian* (4 April 2018).

[15] There is a voluntary 'real living wage', which at the of writing has been adopted by employers of only 180,000 workers. This would produce an annual salary for the worker on a stable 40-hour week contact of £18,720 and £21,944 in London.

countries. But it could hardly be said to be just when compared to the grossly inflated salaries of others: a university vice chancellor on £400,000 annually earns in just over two months what it takes a cleaner in the same institution on the NMW to earn in a year.[16]

The right to form and to join trade unions

Most countries recognize the right of workers to form and join trade unions for the protection of their interests. However, in most countries, there has been a sharp fall in levels of collective bargaining, some of it as a result of deliberate State neglect, and some of it sponsored by active State policies. In the case of the EU that latter policy has been co-ordinated by the Commission, using different powers to decentralize collective bargaining arrangements and deregulate employment standards. These steps were taken first as conditions of financial support to a number of countries (notably Greece) during the Euro crisis, but more recently in relation to a number of countries using economic governance powers under TFEU, Title VIII.[17] In the case of Greece, the intervention was so dramatic as to lead the ILO to conclude that it was likely to cause the destruction of an entire industrial relations system, which not only compromised international obligations, but also national constitutional arrangements.[18]

7. UDHR and Economic Liberalism

So here we have a contradiction: the extraordinary expansion of rights' recognition, but the equally extraordinary failure of rights' protection. Why has there been a regression from the standards in the UDHR? The answer lies in choices by governments which have adopted social, economic and political policies which either repudiate international legal obligations and workers' rights, or are indifferent to them. These choices include:

- The embrace of neo-liberal economics, and the commitment to 'open markets' rather than 'social markets', a commitment given legal effect in the TFEU;
- Globalisation and the free movement of capital-empowering corporations as investors, and corporations as exporters;
- Privatisation and out-sourcing, not only empowering corporations but also encouraging low wage competition for commercial contracts;
- Global supply chains also empowering corporations to drive down

16 Some Vice Chancellors are paid even more.

17 See Keith D Ewing, 'The Death of Social Europe' (2015) 26(1) *King's Law Journal* 76-98. Also See Alan Bogg and Keith D Ewing, 'A Tale of Two Documents: The Eclipse of the Social Democratic Constitution', in Eva Nanopoulos and Fotis Vergis (eds), *The Crisis Behind the Euro-Crisis: The Euro-Crisis as a Multi-Dimensional Systematic Crisis of the EU* (CUP 2019).

18 International Labour Office, *Report on the High Level Mission to Greece* (ILO 2011).

costs by sourcing cheap labour, with an impact on wages more widely;
- The conscious creation of 'labour markets', confounding the principle that 'labour is not a commodity'[19];
- The free movement of labour in a global labour market, exploited by businesses to import workers to do construction and service jobs that cannot be exported;
- Free trade agreements which encourage a race to the bottom, embodied in texts which empower corporations but have little by way of reciprocity for labour;
- The abandonment of the rule of law: almost every country is now in breach of core labour standards, as provided in international legal texts.

For lawyers, the latter is the most alarming, and all the more revealing for the fact that it was partly on rule of law grounds that the Right mounted their relentless campaign against the post-war social democratic settlement.[20] Claims about the abandonment of the rule of law are nevertheless easier to make from the Left. The rule of law means, at its most basic, that government should govern in accordance with legal obligations. As proponents of the rule of law as a liberal value make clear, these legal obligations include duties arising under both international and domestic law.[21] Yet even a perfunctory examination of the jurisprudence of the supervisory bodies of organisations like the ILO makes clear the extent to which many countries fall short of legal commitments on social rights of the kind to be found in UNDHR, Arts 23 and 24.[22]

None of the foregoing is inevitable; all reflect choices that have been made by governments and by others. But they do point to the myth of the universality of human rights, which are revealed to be no more than political claims, embedded in a particular legal instrument. The UDHR is no more and no less than the entrenchment of social democratic values in the ascendency at the time it was drafted (and expressed more explicitly in the ILO Declaration of Philadelphia of 1944). It is a statement of the ascendency of these values and a mark of their achievement, part of a superstructure that is underpinned by a body of economic values and political beliefs. But its universality cannot be demanded, but can only be accepted, and acceptance requires commitment.

Such rights are only as good as the systems they sustain continue to prevail.

---

19 On which see *Africa Personnel Services (Pty) Ltd v Namibia* [2009] NASC 17.

20 Friedrich A Hayek, *The Road to Serfdom* (University of Chicago Press 1944) 54: 'Nothing distinguishes more clearly conditions in a free country from those in a country under arbitrary government than the observance in the former of the great principles known as the Rule of Law'. Note also Friedrich A Hayek, *The Constitution of Liberty* (University of Chicago Press 1960) on trade union legal freedoms as a violation of these 'great principles'.

21 Lord Bingham, 'The Rule of Law' (2007) 66(1) *Cambridge Law Journal* 67-85.

22 See Keith D Ewing and John Hendy QC, 'The Eclipse of the Rule of Law: Trade Union Rights and the EU' (2015) 4 *Revista Derecho Social y Empresa* 80-112.

They offer no protection against change, and in a different economic and political system such as the one we now inhabit, they are tombstones to an age that has passed. Changing metaphors, these are now instruments in a guerrilla war against power rather than a consolidation of the subordination of power. If we were to draft a UNDHR for economic liberalism, it would be a very different one from that drafted for social democracy in 1948. The emphasis would be on economic freedom rather than social protection, a glimpse of contents being provided by the EU Charter of Fundamental Rights, Arts 16 and 17, which provide that:

> **Article 16**
> ***Freedom to conduct a business***
> The freedom to conduct a business in accordance with Union law and national laws and practices is recognised.[23]
>
> **Article 17**
> ***Right to property***
> 1. Everyone has the right to own, use, dispose of and bequeath his or her lawfully acquired possessions. No one may be deprived of his or her possessions, except in the public interest and in the cases and under the conditions provided for by law, subject to fair compensation being paid in good time for their loss. The use of property may be regulated by law in so far as is necessary for the general interest.

8. Conclusion

To conclude, it is true that superficially we have won the battle to recognize the rights of workers as fundamental human rights. They are widely expressed and continue to be re-affirmed paradoxically in free trade agreements and elsewhere.[24] This is perhaps the cruelest irony, with contemporary bilateral free trade agreements purporting to embrace the very rights they are calculated to destroy. Free trade agreements are visible symptoms of a new orthodoxy that has replaced the orthodoxy that created instruments like the UDHR and the ILO Declaration of Philadelphia. Rights which stand in the way of that new orthodoxy are swept aside, as revealed most brutally in the case of Greece during and after the Euro crisis from 2008 onwards.[25]

For all the multiple expressions of fundamental human rights, we have lost the battle to secure them, as reflected by many indicators including the rising levels of inequality between citizens in developed and developing countries

---

23 See Case C-426/11 *Parkwood-Leisure Ltd v Alemo-Herron,* 18 July 2013.

24 See Joo-Cheong Tham and Keith D Ewing, 'Labour Clauses in the TTP and TTIP – A Comparison without a Difference?' (2016) 17(2) *Melbourne Journal of International Law* 369.

25 See Ioannis Katsaroumpas, 'De-Constitutionalising Collective Labour Rights: The Case of Greece' (2018) 47(4) *Industrial Law Journal* 465-503.

alike. These rising levels of inequality are a symptom of 'rights' failure'. But as already suggested, the battle to secure rights will not be won by law or lawyers. On the contrary, if we want these rights, we will need to recreate the economic and political conditions in which they can flourish. That is to say a social market economy based on respect for workers, with a commitment to the distribution of wealth and opportunity. This is perhaps the final irony: rights such as those in UDHR are most effective when least needed, and least effective when most needed.

9. Bibliography

Alcock, A, *History of the International Labour Organisation* (Palgrave 1971)

Bingham, Lord, 'The Rule of Law' (2007) 66(1) *Cambridge Law Journal* 67

Bogg, Alan and Ewing, KD, 'A Tale of Two Documents: The Eclipse of the Social Democratic Constitution', in Eva Nanopoulos and Vergis, Fotis (eds), *The Crisis Behind the Euro-Crisis: The Euro-Crisis as a Multi-Dimensional Systematic Crisis of the EU* (CUP 2019)

Ewing, KD, 'The Death of Social Europe' (2015) 26(1) *King's Law Journal* 76

Ewing, KD and Hendy, John, 'The Eclipse of the Rule of Law: Trade Union Rights and the EU' (2015) 4 *Revista Derecho Social y Empresa* 80

Hayek, FA, *The Road to Serfdom* (University of Chicago Press 1944)

Hayek. FA, *The Constitution of Liberty* (University of Chicago Press 1960)

Holder, J, *et al*, 'Gender Pay Gap: When does your Company stop paying women in 2018?', *The Guardian* (4 April 2018)

International Labour Organization, *Declaration of Philadelphia: Declaration concerning the Aims and Purposes of the International Labour Organization* (ILO 1994)

International Labour Organization, *Report on the High Level Mission to Greece* (ILO 2011)

Mantouvalou, V, 'Are Labour Rights Human Rights?' (2012) 3 *European Labour Law Journal* 151

OECD, *Guidelines for Multinational Enterprises* (OECD 2011)

O'Higgins, P, 'Labour is not a Commodity – An Irish Contribution to International Labour Law' (1997) 26 *Industrial Law Journal* 225

Supiot, A, *The Spirit of Philadelphia: Social Justice Vs. The Total Market* (Verso 2012)

Tham, JC and Ewing KD, 'Labour Clauses in the TTP and TTIP – A Comparison without a Difference?' (2016) 17(2) *Melbourne Journal of International Law* 389

UN High Commissioner for Human Rights, *Guiding Principles on Business and Human Rights* (United Nations 2011)

Chapter 6

LABOUR TRAFFICKING AND THE CHALLENGES OF VICTIM IDENTIFICATION IN IRELAND: EXPLORING THE LEGACY OF ARTICLE 4 UDHR

By Muiread Murphy, David M Doyle and Clíodhna Murphy

No one shall be held in slavery or servitude; slavery and the slave trade shall be prohibited in all their forms.
(Universal Declaration of Human Rights, Article 4)

1. Introduction

The right to be free from slavery, servitude and forced labour is a fundamental human right that is provided for, and protected, both domestically and internationally.[1] Slavery and related forms of bondage were prohibited in the League of Nations Slavery Convention (1926)[2] and the International Labour Organisation (ILO) Forced Labour Convention (1930)[3], but it was not until the United Nations adopted the Universal Declaration of Human Rights (UDHR)[4] in 1948 that the right to be protected against these severe forms of exploitation was explicitly declared to be an international human right. Although not legally binding at the time of its adoption, the UDHR has served as a framework for subsequent international human rights treaties as well as many national constitutions.[5] Specifically in the context of severe labour exploitation, Art 4 UDHR can be seen as the genesis of what Jean Allain, Gillian Wylie and others have described as the 'neo-abolitionist era' of the twenty-first century.[6] The Art 4 formulation has since been expanded upon by many other human rights

---

1 Arjuna Naidu, 'The Right to Be Free from Slavery, Servitude and Forced Labor' (1987) 20 *Comparative and International Law Journal of Southern Africa* 108-113.

2 Slavery Convention (adopted 25 September 1926, entered into force 9 March 1927) 60 LNTS 253.

3 Forced Labour Convention (adopted 28 June 1930, entered into force 1 May 1932) ILO C29.

4 Universal Declaration of Human Rights (adopted 10 December 1948) UNGA Res 217 A(III) (UDHR).

5 Manisuli Ssenyonjo and Mashood A Baderin (eds), *International human rights law: six decades after the UDHR and beyond* (Ashgate Publishing Ltd 2010).

6 Jean Allain, *Slavery in International Law: Of Human Exploitation and Trafficking* (Brill 2012) 5. Ward and Wylie, 'Introducing Neo-abolitionism: Definition, Drivers and

instruments which address slavery, servitude, forced and compulsory labour and (perhaps most prominently) the related concept of human trafficking.[7] At a regional level, Art 4 of the European Convention on Human Rights (ECHR)[8] has been interpreted as imposing wide-ranging positive obligations on States to provide individuals with practical and effective protection against severe labour exploitation and trafficking.[9] Specific anti-trafficking measures also include a United Nations Protocol (2000)[10]; a Council of Europe Convention (2004)[11]; and various European Union (EU) Directives (2004,[12] 2011[13]). In Ireland, anti-trafficking legislation was passed in 2008 and forced labour was explicitly criminalised for the first time through this framework in 2013.[14]

Despite the existence of this plethora of human rights provisions, the 'assumption that slavery-like practices have been eliminated is far from real in the 21st Century'.[15] In this context, effective mechanisms for identifying victims of severe labour exploitation are a vital element of the positive obligation of States to protect individuals. Ireland, along with many other countries, has a comprehensive legal anti-trafficking regime but has struggled with establishing and implementing an effective system of victim identification. In 2018, the US Department of State *Trafficking in Persons Report* identified 'chronic deficiencies'[16] in Irish victim identification procedures and referral, including but not limited to, the effective exclusion of Irish and EEA citizens from formal victim identification procedures.[17] It is against this background that this chapter examines the difficulties associated with the identification of human trafficking victims in Ireland.

Debates', in Ward and Wylie (eds), *Feminism, Prostitution and the State: The Politics of Neo-Abolitionism* (Routledge 2017).

7 See generally, Vladislava Stoyanova, 'Article 4 of the ECHR and the Obligation of Criminalising Slavery, Servitude, Forced Labour and Human Trafficking' (2014) 3(2) *Cambridge Journal of International and Comparative Law* 407.

8 Convention for the Protection of Human Rights and Fundamental Freedoms (European Convention on Human Rights, as amended) (ECHR) Art 4.

9 See generally, Valentino Milano, 'The European Court of Human Rights' Case Law on Human Trafficking in Light of L.E. v Greece: A Disturbing Setback?' (2017) 17(4) *Human Rights Law Review* 710.

10 Protocol to Prevent, Suppress and Punish Trafficking in Persons Especially Women and Children (adopted 15 November 2000, entered into force 25 December 2003) 2237 UNTS 319.

11 Convention on Action against Trafficking in Human Beings (adopted 3 May 2005, entered into force 1 February 2008) CoETS 197.

12 Council Directive 2004/81/EC of 29 April 2004 on the residence permit issued to third-country nationals who are victims of trafficking in human beings or who have been the subject of an action to facilitate illegal immigration, who cooperate with the competent authorities [2004] OJ L261/19.

13 Council Directive 2011/36/EU of 5 April 2011 on preventing and combating trafficking in human beings and protecting its victims [2011] OJ L101/1.

14 Criminal Law (Human Trafficking) Act 2008, as amended by the Criminal Law (Human Trafficking) (Amendment) Act 2013.

15 Virginia Mantouvalou, 'Servitude and Forced Labour in the 21st Century: The Human Rights of Domestic Workers' (2006) 35(4) *Industrial Law Journal* 395, 414.

16 US Department of State, *Trafficking in Persons Report* (June 2018) 235.

17 ibid 236.

1.1 Delineating State obligations of identification

Accurate and timely identification is necessary to ensure that trafficking victims, who may have been subjected to traumatic physical and psychological experiences, receive adequate assistance and support to which they are entitled under international, European and national law. The obligations of States parties, to ensure compliance with the duty to identify and provide assistance to victims, have been stipulated in international provisions.[18] The significance of this identification stage, in the wider process of victim protection, has been 'extolled as a cornerstone of anti-trafficking efforts'.[19] At an international level, it is noteworthy that the UN *Protocol to Prevent, Suppress and Punish Trafficking in Persons, especially Women and Children*[20] does not outline specific obligations in relation to identifying victims of human trafficking. Article 18 of the United Nations Model Law against Trafficking in Persons, designed to 'assist States in implementing the provisions contained in the Protocol',[21] as well as to 'facilitate review and amendment of existing legislation and adoption of new legislation by States themselves', attempts to fill this gap.[22] It states that:

> 2. The national coordinating body shall develop and disseminate to professionals who are likely to encounter victims of trafficking information and materials concerning trafficking in persons.
>
> 3. With a view to the proper identification of victims of trafficking in persons, the competent authorities shall collaborate with relevant state and non-state victim assistance organizations.

This represents a non-binding attempt to highlight the need for States to establish appropriate procedures and authorities to achieve a comprehensive victim identification system.

In contrast, at a European level, the Council of Europe Convention on Action against Trafficking in Human Beings 2005 (ETC), comprehensively outlines the obligations on Contracting States relating to the identification of victims of human trafficking. Article 10(1) states:

> ... each Party shall provide its competent authorities with persons who are trained and qualified in preventing and combating trafficking in human beings, in identifying and helping victims, including children, and shall

---

18 European Migration Network, *Trafficked Persons As Asylum-Seekers: The Process of Identification and Access to Residence Rights in Austria* (EMN, February 2014) 23.

19 Marika McAdam, 'Who's Who at the Border? A rights-based approach to identifying human trafficking at international borders' (2013) 2 *Anti-Trafficking Review* 33-49, 34.

20 Protocol to Prevent, Suppress and Punish Trafficking in Persons Especially Women and Children (n10).

21 United Nations Office on Drugs and Crime, *Model Law against Trafficking in Persons* [2009 V.09-81990 (E)] Introduction, 1.

22 ibid.

> ensure that the different authorities collaborate with each other as well as with relevant support organisations, so that victims can be identified in a procedure duly taking into account the special situation of women and child victims and, in appropriate cases, issued with residence permits under the conditions provided for in Article 14 of the present Convention.

This Convention thus advocates inter-agency collaboration in ensuring that all victims of human trafficking can be efficiently identified and provided with assistance, and emphasises the importance of training and qualifications for relevant State personnel. However, the Convention, with the exception of the recovery and reflection period, fails to 'impose an obligation upon states to have a clear statutory basis regulating how victims of human trafficking can be identified'.[23]

Significantly, Art 4 of the ECHR has been interpreted by the European Court of Human Rights (ECtHR) as requiring that Contracting States must take appropriate operational measures to protect victims of trafficking,[24] which encompasses a duty to effectively investigate potential or suspected cases of human trafficking.[25] In *Chowdury and others v Greece*,[26] for example, the ECtHR drew directly on Art 10(1) ETC in finding that the Greek authorities' unresponsiveness to the plight of 42 migrant strawberry pickers engaged in forced labour was inadequate to meet the positive measures required by Art 4 ECHR. In this way, the Strasbourg Court has integrated the positive obligations contained in the various Council of Europe instruments[27] and imbued Article 4 ECHR with greater specificity than its rather broad literal assertion that:

> 1. No one shall be held in slavery or servitude.
> 2. No one shall be required to perform forced or compulsory labour.

Finally, at EU level, Directive 2011/36/EU on Preventing and Combating Trafficking in Human Beings and Protecting its Victims echoes the ETC. It imposes an obligation on Member States under Art 11(4) to:

> . . . take the necessary measures to establish appropriate mechanisms aimed at the early identification of, assistance to and support for victims, in cooperation with relevant organisations.

---

23 Vladislava Stoyanova, *Human Trafficking and Slavery Reconsidered: Conceptual Limits and State's Positive Obligations in European Law* (CUP 2017) 92.

24 *Rantsev v Cyprus and Russia*, App no 25965/04 (ECtHR, 7 January 2010).

25 *CN v The United Kingdom* App no 4239/08 (ECtHR, 13 November 2012).

26 App no 21884/15 (ECtHR, 30 March 2017).

27 See commentary by Vladislava Stoyanova, '*Chowdury and Others v. Greece*: Further Integration of the Positive Obligations under Article 4 of the ECHR and the CoE Convention on Action against Human Trafficking' (Strasbourg Observers blog, 28 April 2017): <https://strasbourgobservers.com/2017/04/28/chowdury-and-others-v-greece-further-integration-of-the-positive-obligations-under-article-4-of-the-echr-and-the-coe-convention-on-action-against-human-trafficking/> accessed 17 September 2018.

Overall, while Ireland has undertaken distinct obligations, at both an international level and a European level, to promptly identify victims of human trafficking, the specific form and content of the identification and investigation procedures is not prescribed. Similar to other human rights provisions of this nature, States are effectively left to decide how best to implement the relevant duties in their national system.

1.2 Ireland's approach to identifying victims of trafficking

Although international instruments outline the duty of States parties to act expeditiously to identify victims of human trafficking, the UN Special Rapporteur on trafficking in persons, especially women and children, has expressed concern that 'States are not paying adequate attention to issues related to the proper identification and protection of and assistance to victims'.[28] This issue is therefore not unique to Ireland: successful prosecutions of human trafficking offences elsewhere are 'still very low relative to the agreed size of the problem'[29] and conviction rates 'have remained remarkably low in many parts of the world'.[30] Ireland may be criticised for failing to provide a legislative basis for the identification of victims which may result in the exclusion of 'a large number of victims from the possibility of being identified',[31] particularly given the missed opportunity to do so through the recently enacted Criminal Law (Human Trafficking) (Amendment) Act 2013.[32] Currently there is no 'uniform way of identifying victims of trafficking'[33] and this uncertainty is reflected in low detection rates. In 2016, for example, only 95 victims were identified.[34]

Ireland's identification procedure is outlined in the Administrative Immigration Arrangements (AIA), which apply to 'a foreign national who is identified as a suspected victim of human trafficking' under s 2 or s 4 of the Criminal Law (Human Trafficking) Act 2008.[35] At present, EU and asylum-seeking victims are excluded from the identification process as the 'hopelessly outdated' AIA currently apply to trafficking victims solely from non-European Economic

---

28 UN Secretary-General, *Trafficking in persons, especially women and children: Note by the Secretary General* (United Nations, 12 August 2009) 10.

29 Anne Gallagher and Paul Holmes, 'Developing an Effective Criminal Justice Response to Human Trafficking: Lessons From the Front Line' (2008) 18(3) *International Criminal Justice Review* 318-343, 320.

30 United Nations Office on Drugs and Crime, *Global Report on Trafficking in Persons* (UNODC 2016) 48.

31 Immigrant Council of Ireland, *Submission to the US State Department Trafficking in Persons Report 2017* (ICI, January 2017) 4.

32 This may be contrasted with the Hungarian Government Decree No. 354/2012. (XII.13) on the identification order of victims of trafficking in human beings.

33 Patricia Stapleton, *Human Trafficking in Ireland: Identifying Victims of Trafficking* (Annual Critical Social Thinking Conference, January 2011) 199.

34 Department of Justice and Equality, *Trafficking in Human Beings in Ireland: Annual Report 2016* (2017).

35 Administrative Immigration Arrangements for the Protection of Victims of Human Trafficking (March 2011) <http://www.inis.gov.ie/en/INIS/Pages/PB08000021> accessed 16 January 2018.

Area countries.[36] The initial process results in the identification of a victim as a suspected victim of human trafficking. Such a determination is made 'by a member of An Garda Síochána not below the rank of Superintendent in the Garda National Immigration Bureau'[37] and 'the standard of proof used to identify a victim is the same as for a decision on whether there was sufficient evidence to prosecute an offender'.[38] Reasonable grounds for suspicion that an individual may be a victim of trafficking include indicators that the individual lacks freedom of movement, shows signs that their movements are being controlled, distrust of authorities and are not in possession of their passport. This presumed victim is then referred to the National Referral Mechanism.[39] The power to identify human trafficking victims in Ireland is thus placed within the power of law enforcement, in the form of An Garda Síochána.[40] This practice is also endorsed in countries such as Spain, Austria and the Netherlands.[41] In the United Kingdom, the UK Visa and Immigration Bureau and the UK Human Trafficking Centre, which is part of the UK National Crime Agency, are the two bodies which may formally identify these victims.[42] In Member States such as Malta, Italy and Latvia, NGOs or social services may also identify these victims.[43]

The current Irish procedure has been criticised as 'no stand-alone, formal identification procedure for all victims of trafficking, irrespective of nationality and immigration status, exists'.[44] The inadequacy of victim identification mechanisms was highlighted in the case of *P v The Chief Superintendent of the Garda National Immigration Bureau & Ors*, where the Garda National Immigration Bureau had failed to identify a trafficked woman in the Dóchas Centre for over two years.[45] At a domestic level, the Immigrant Council of Ireland 'has a number of concerns regarding the identification and treatment of victims of trafficking within the Irish State's current system'.[46] In particular, the extended delay before an initial decision is delivered on identification, has been

---

36 *Submission to the US State Department Trafficking in Persons Report 2017* (n 31) 4.

37 Corona Joyce and Emma Quinn, *Identifying Victims of Trafficking in Human Beings in Asylum and Forced Return Procedures: Ireland* (European Migration Network, April 2014) 4.

38 Department of Justice and Equality, *Roundtable on Identification of Victims of Human Trafficking* (December 2015) 3.

39 *Trafficking in Human Beings in Ireland: Annual Report 2016* (n 34) 4.

40 The Group of Experts on Action against Trafficking in Human Beings, *Report Concerning the Implementation of the Council of Europe Convention on Action against Trafficking in Human Beings in Ireland: First Evaluation Round* (GRETA, 2015) 43.

41 Stoyanova (n 23) 94.

42 Kirsty Thomson, 'International and European Standards in Relation to Victims and Survivors of Human Trafficking' in Margaret Malloch and Paul Rigby (eds), *Human Trafficking: The Complexities of Exploitation* (Edinburgh University Press 2016) 77.

43 European Migration Network, *Identification of victims of trafficking in human beings in international protection and forced return procedures* (EMN, 2014) 21.

44 Joyce and Quinn, (n 37) 2.

45 [2015] IEHC 222.

46 Immigrant Council of Ireland, *Asylum seeking victims of human trafficking in Ireland: Legal and practical challenges* (ICI, November 2011) 3.

highlighted as an issue that must be improved.[47] International anti-trafficking experts have also urged the Irish authorities to 'increase efforts to identify and protect victims of labor trafficking'.[48] In response Ireland, in its *Second National Action Plan to Prevent and Combat Human Trafficking*, stated that a main priority is to 'carry out a fundamental review of our formal identification process for victims of human trafficking to ensure that we have in place a process that meets international best practice'.[49] However, neither the AIA nor the identification process more generally have been formally revised as of yet.

Having briefly outlined the legal and policy context, the following sections draw on our findings from a qualitative 'victim-centred' study of labour trafficking in Ireland based on the premise that 'top down' approaches to analysing severe labour exploitation should be complemented by 'bottom up' analysis rooted in the experiences of victims.[50] Semi-structured interviews were conducted with fifteen individuals (13 female and two male) who were identified by the Migrant Rights Centre Ireland (MRCI) case workers as victims of trafficking for the purposes of labour exploitation. Although trafficking indicators were identified in all of these cases, only seven of the participants had been granted official victim of trafficking status. The interviews were arranged by MRCI and conducted on their premises, or at an alternative location nominated by the participant. The interviewees – who came from India, Kenya, Malawi, Nigeria, Pakistan, the Philippines, South Africa, and Zimbabwe – had left their trafficking situation by the time these interviews were conducted. The age range of the victims varied from 19 to 55 years when they accessed the services of MRCI. Thirteen participants were trafficked to Ireland either by a relative, a former employer, an acquaintance or a person known to the victim's family, friends or previous employers. The duration of the interviews ranged from 31 minutes to 97 minutes. These experiences, *derived from the victims themselves*, shed light on some of the factors that hamper the prompt and effective identification of victims.

2. Barriers to Investigation and Identification

2.1 Trafficker control techniques

Although States are often criticised for an absence of adequate identification procedures, it must be acknowledged that the identification of trafficking

47 The Group of Experts on Action against Trafficking in Human Beings, *Report Concerning the Implementation of the Council of Europe Convention on Action against Trafficking in Human Beings by Ireland: Second Evaluation Round* (GRETA, 2017) 30.

48 US Department of State, *Trafficking in Persons Report* (June 2017) 217.

49 Department of Justice and Equality, *Second National Action Plan to Prevent and Combat Human Trafficking in Ireland* (October 2016) 47.

50 For more details on this study see David M. Doyle, Cliodhna Murphy, Muiread Murphy, Pablo Rojas-Coppari, Rachel Wechsler, '"I Felt Like She Owned Me": Exploitation and Uncertainty in the Lives of Labour Trafficking Victims in Ireland' (2018) 59(1) *British Journal of Criminology* 231-51.

victims is a challenging process 'in most OSCE participating States as well as in Ireland'.[51] Traffickers employ 'numerous strategies to ensure that their activities remain hidden'[52] and to 'restrict victims' ability to seek help'.[53] These include, *inter alia*, limiting victims 'exposure to and understanding of the outside world as a means of controlling them'.[54] One interviewee recalled that her employer did not 'allow me to go out',[55] while another participant stated that 'my movements were controlled. Even on my day off'.[56] Moreover, victims of labour trafficking are frequently exploited in private households, agricultural or entertainment sectors,[57] environments which render detection by law enforcement authorities very difficult. The context and the nature of this activity hinder the detection and prompt identification of victims, resulting in it being 'difficult to gain an accurate picture of its true scale and nature'.[58]

The identification of victims may also be hampered due to the coercive behaviour of traffickers. Such acts of coercion include death threats addressed to the victim or his or her family. In certain circumstances, victims 'may be terrified, not only about what could happen to them, but also about what could be done to their families back home'.[59] In one instance, such threats were continuous: 'they keep threatening my parents back home'.[60] Another interviewee was also concerned about the well-being of their family in their country of origin: 'the mother of my employer, she lives in, in South Africa and I, she knows my family like, my sister when I was sending things, she was the one going and collect it from there. So, I was scared maybe she will do something bad to them'.[61] Threats of violence were also directed at the victims themselves. In one case, an interviewee was threatened with lethal violence:

---

51 Office of the Special Representative and Co-ordinator for Combating Trafficking in Human Beings, *Policy and legislative recommendations towards the effective implementation of the non-punishment provision with regard to victims of trafficking* (Organization for Security and Co-operation in Europe, 2013) 4.

52 David R Hodge, 'Assisting Victims of Human Trafficking: Strategies to Facilitate Identification, Exit from Trafficking and the Restoration of Wellness' (2014) 59(2) *Social Work* 111-118, 112.

53 Amy Farrell, Jack McDevitt, Rebecca Pfeffer, Stephanie Fahy, Colleen Owens, Meredith Dank and William Adams, *Identifying Challenges to Improve the Investigation and Prosecution of State and Local Human Trafficking Cases* (Final Report submitted to the National Institute of Justice, Office of Justice Programs, US Department of Justice, April 2012) 81.

54 Susie B Baldwin, Anne E Fehrenbacher and David P Eisenman, 'Psychological Coercion in Human Trafficking: An Application of Biderman's Framework' (2015) 25(9) *Qualitative Health Research* 1171-1181, 1174.

55 Female, Philippines, T8.

56 Female, South Africa, T2.

57 Kadriye Bakirci, 'Human trafficking and forced labour: A criticism of the International Labour Organisation' (2009) 16(2) *Journal of Financial Crime* 160-165, 163.

58 *Second National Action Plan to Prevent and Combat Human Trafficking in Ireland* (n 49) 4.

59 David Nelken, 'Human Trafficking and Legal Culture' (2010) 43 *Israel Review* 479-513, 483.

60 Female, South Africa, T4.

61 Female, South Africa, T15.

'if we want to kill you . . . we can just do that'.[62] These threats may prevent victims from seeking help or revealing their status as a human trafficking victim.

Research conducted elsewhere has found that 'traffickers commonly tell victims that if they talk to law enforcement, not only will the trafficker ensure that the victim's family is harmed in their home country, but they threaten that the victims will be deported as soon as they go to the police'.[63] One interviewee explained that although they managed to escape their exploitative situation, they were 'afraid of course, because they said I'm going to be deported and I don't have any idea about Ireland, about how everything works'.[64] Victims often fear 'retaliation by traffickers' and that ultimately they will be deported for attempting to leave their exploitative situation.[65] Such threats 'of denunciation and deportation can lead to a situation where the migrant is not physically constrained to leave the worksite but subjectively perceives a lack of freedom of movement'.[66] As one interviewee articulated, 'if they bring in the country they have already put fear in you that if you talk to people about your situation, they are going to deport you. They put that fear in you, you can't talk to anybody'.[67]

Other control techniques employed by traffickers to hinder the identification of trafficking victims, include 'deprivation of basic human needs such as food, sleep, and health care'[68] and 'manipulation of residency status, ambiguous documentation, control over accommodation and movement, utilization of language barriers'.[69] In one instance, an interviewee described the presence of CCTV cameras both inside and outside of their place of employment: '[e]very time the boss is watching for the camera, so I think what I can do'.[70] Methods such as the confiscation of travel documents were also regularly employed.[71] One participant stated that upon their arrival in Ireland their employer 'took my passport'.[72]

---

62 Female, Philippines, T13.

63 Farrell, McDevitt, Pfeffer, Fahy, Owens, Dank and Adams, (n 53) 85.

64 Female, Philippines, T13.

65 Amy Farrell, Jack McDevitt and Stephanie Fahy, 'Where are all the victims? Understanding the determinants of official identification of human trafficking incidents' (2010) 9(2) *Criminology & Public Policy* 201-233, 206.

66 Beate Andrees, *Forced Labour and Trafficking in Europe: How People are Trapped in, Live Through and Come Out* (International Labour Organization Working Paper 57, 2008) 25.

67 Female, Nigeria, T1.

68 Baldwin, Fehrenbacher and Eisenman, (n54) 1174.

69 Michael Potter and Jennifer Hamilton, 'Picking on vulnerable migrants: precarity and the mushroom industry in Northern Ireland' (2014) 28(3) *Work, employment and society* 390-406, 397.

70 Male, India, T10.

71 Donna M Hughes, 'The "Natasha" Trade: The Transnational Shadow Market of Trafficking in Women' (2000) 53(2) *Journal of International Affairs* 625-651, 636. Alexis A Aronowitz, 'Smuggling and Trafficking in Human Beings: The Phenomenon, the Markets that Drive it and the Organisations that Promote it' (2001) 9 *European Journal on Criminal Policy and Research* 163-195, 177.

72 Female, South Africa, T2.

2.2 Perceptions and distrust

Victims of human trafficking may fear disclosing their status to the authorities for numerous reasons.[73] In certain circumstances, 'victims do not see themselves as victims'[74] and 'struggle to define their experiences as human trafficking'.[75] Furthermore, the identification and investigation procedure is often 'based on the assumption that trafficked victims want to be identified as victims and rescued', but such assumptions may not be reflective of the victims own perception of their situation.[76] Indeed, some individuals hold the view that their current exploitative situation is preferable 'to the situation they came from'.[77] One interviewee, for example, stated, 'I was happy with the salary that they gave me, compared to the salary that I got back home',[78] while another remarked that 'at home things will be worse'.[79]

Difficulties also arise when victims 'only come to the realization that they have been trafficked after they have reached their destination'.[80] This was echoed by one interviewee who stated that they 'didn't know about the human trafficking'.[81] These victims often fail to come forward to identify themselves because they are 'unaware of their rights and of the existence of protections',[82] while 'not knowing the language of the country of destination' creates a situation of extreme dependency.[83] Such difficulties are further compounded by the unfamiliarity of their surroundings. One interviewee observed that 'I didn't know Ireland very well' and this contributed to the uncertainty and fear experienced.[84]

Victims may also be reluctant to approach 'the police and subsequently testify in court'.[85] This appears to be particularly pertinent in instances where the

---

73 Uwe P Gielen and Jaipaul L Roopnarine (eds), *Childhood and Adolescence: Cross-cultural Perspectives and Applications* (Prager 2004) 393.

74 Carolina Villacampa and Núria Torres, 'Human Trafficking for Criminal Exploitation: The Failure to Identify Victims' (2017) 23 *European Journal on Criminal Policy and Research* 393-408, 405.

75 Amy Farrell and Rebecca Pfeffer, 'Policing Human Trafficking: Cultural Blinders and Organizational Barriers' (2014) *The Annals of the American Academy of Political and Social Science*, Vol 653, 46-64, 50.

76 Maggy Lee, *Trafficking and Global Crime Control* (Sage Publications 2011) 59.

77 Monika Smit, 'Trafficking in human beings for labour exploitation. The Case of the Netherlands' (2011) 14 *Trends in Organized Crime* 184-197, 187.

78 Female, South Africa, T2.

79 Female, South Africa, T12.

80 Diego Hernandez and Alexandra Rudolph, 'Modern day slavery: What drives human trafficking in Europe?' (2015) 38 *European Journal of Political Economy* 118-139, 131.

81 Female, South Africa, T12.

82 Luis CdeBaca and Jane Nady Sigmon, 'Combating trafficking in persons: a call to action for global health professionals' (2014) 2(3) *Global Health: Science and Practice* 261-267, 263.

83 Mariyana Radeva Berket, 'Labour exploitation and trafficking for labour exploitation-trends and challenges for policy-making' (2015) 16 *ERA Forum* 359-377, 366.

84 Female, Kenya, T6.

85 Olga Pyshchulina, 'An Evaluation of Ukrainian Legislation to Counter and Criminalize Human Trafficking' (2003) 11(3) *Demokratizatsiya* 403-411, 407.

victims lack the relevant documentation required in the destination State. One interviewee stated that 'there are so many people who are in exploitation but they are scared to come out . . . Some of them are illegal and they think that if they maybe come out they are going to be deported'.[86] This fear may be based on their previous experiences with the authorities in their countries of origin. Such distrust in law enforcement may hamper identification opportunities, as victims may not believe that approaching the authorities will help them escape their trafficking situation. One participant recalled that, 'at first I was scared because I thought maybe they will arrest me or take me back home',[87] which is a fear that has been identified in other studies of victims of human trafficking. Victims may feel as though they have no other viable option but to remain in their exploitative environment.

2.3 Training, knowledge and collaboration

A lack of adequate training of frontline staff has been recognised as a problem surrounding the detection and identification of victims of human trafficking. This is not solely an Irish phenomenon. US studies have consistently found that 'lawmakers and law enforcers struggle to identify and combat human trafficking', resulting in low detection rates and prosecutions.[88] Studies have also found instances in which law enforcement officials have identified human trafficking cases as 'illegal employment and illegal migration'.[89] In this regard, a Tasmanian study found that 'poor victim identification or misclassification of victims' occurs in instances where law enforcement lack the required knowledge and training in understanding the concept of human trafficking.[90] This was also a criticism raised by an interviewee who noted that 'the [Irish] police sometimes, some of them don't know their work'.[91] As human trafficking is frequently equated with trafficking for the purposes of sexual exploitation, police officials 'tend to have limited experience with the identification of trafficking victims who have been exposed to other forms of exploitation, such as domestic servitude or forced labour in the construction, agriculture or garment industries'.[92] An absence of sufficient training inevitably impacts on the ability of law enforcement agencies to detect and identify cases of labour exploitation.

---

86 Female, Malawi, T7.

87 Female, South Africa, T14.

88 Amy Farrell, Colleen Owens and Jack McDevitt, 'New laws but few cases: understanding the challenges to the investigation and prosecution of human trafficking cases' (2014) 61 *Crime, Law and Social Change* 139-168, 139.

89 Deanna Davy, 'Justice for victims of human trafficking in Australia? Issues associated with Australia's criminal justice response to trafficking in persons' (2017) 20(1) *Contemporary Justice Review* 115-131, 125.

90 Nathan Irwin, 'Police officer understandings of human trafficking and awareness of anti-trafficking measures' (2017) *Policing: An International Journal of Police Strategies and Management* 291-305, 293.

91 Female, Nigeria, T3.

92 Organization for Security and Co-Operation in Europe, *Trafficking in Human Beings: Identification of Potential and Presumed Victims: A Community Policing Approach* (SPMU Publications Series Vol 10, June 2011) 18.

Efforts have been made in Ireland to improve practices among officials who are likely to interact with potential and suspected victims of human trafficking and to ensure that appropriate assistance is provided. During the reporting period for the US Department of State's *Trafficking in Persons Report* 2017, '69 police officers and 300 new probationer police officers received a three-day training course on trafficking awareness and 68 national police who work as immigration officers received trafficking awareness training. An additional 18 senior investigating officers received trafficking training'.[93] This increased focus on providing training in victim identification is welcome and the Department of Justice and Equality has reaffirmed its commitment to improving the victim identification procedure in Ireland, stating that they will extend 'this training beyond traditional sectors'.[94] This emphasis on training provisions is particularly important in the context of human trafficking as 'for those on the front line, the science of locating and identifying trafficked persons is frustratingly complex and inexact'.[95]

Furthermore, there is currently a 'lack of knowledge and blurred distinctions' between human smuggling and human trafficking which may result in confusion on the part of law enforcement authorities and a subsequent failure to accurately identify victims of human trafficking.[96] The absence of precise legal definitions at national level, renders the identification of victims a complex and potentially inaccurate process. This lack of clarity may also hamper victims in seeking assistance, as one interviewee recommended creating 'awareness about exploitation because like when I was there, I don't know what is exploitation'.[97] Indicators have been developed to help avoid such confusion and to aid organisations in detecting human trafficking and labour exploitation cases.[98] These include excessive working days or hours, bad living conditions, low or no salary and wage manipulation.[99] Although these indicators are a positive development, there is still an absence of a 'consensus on the tools available to identify victims'.[100] A uniform definitional approach would create certainty among the relevant authorities.

Finally, NGOs play a crucial role in raising awareness of human trafficking, lobbying for change in legislation and policy, and assisting victims. They are frequently the first point of contact for trafficking victims. One interviewee noted

---

93 *Trafficking in Persons Report* (n 48).

94 *Second National Action Plan to Prevent and Combat Human Trafficking in Ireland* (n 49) 35.

95 Gallagher and Holmes (n 29) 329.

96 International Organization for Migration, *Addressing Human Trafficking and Exploitation in Times of Crisis: Evidence and Recommendations for Further Action to Protect Vulnerable and Mobile Populations* (IOM December 2015) 8.

97 Female, Malawi, T7.

98 International Labour Organization, *Indicators of Forced Labour* (ILO 2012).

99 International Labour Organization, *Labour Exploitation Indicators* (ILO September 2009).

100 Nadejda Bespalova, Juliet Morgan and John Coverdale, 'A Pathway to Freedom: An Evaluation of Screening Tools for the Identification of Trafficking Victims' (2016) 40 *Academic Psychiatry* 124-128, 125.

that on leaving her trafficking situation, 'I get the support more from MRCI than I did from Government because when I left there I was really stranded, like I didn't know where to go'.[101] The Council of Europe Group of Experts against Trafficking in Human Beings (GRETA) has urged Ireland to 'promote multi-agency involvement in victim identification by formalising the role and input of specialised NGOs' and other relevant actors.[102] Such strengthening of 'inter-agency collaborations' would be in line with international best practice as outlined in the ETC and would contribute to the aim of eradicating human trafficking.[103] In Norway, for instance, 'the identification of potential victims is carried out by a number of different parties, such as the police, safe houses, immigration authorities and child protection services'.[104] A similar anti-trafficking strategy must be adopted in Ireland and formally include a range of stakeholders and specialist NGOs who are 'geared to respond to the needs of victims/potential victims'.[105]

3. Conclusion

This chapter has shown that there are clear obligations on States parties to accurately and expeditiously identify victims of human trafficking under both international and European law. These obligations have largely been developed in the twenty first century as a response to the phenomenon of human trafficking and have their legal roots in the broadly-drawn Art 4 UDHR provision. In particular, Art 4's framing of the issue as primarily one of *individual* protection against 'slavery-like practices', rather than a State duty to stamp out vestiges of a legal slave trade, was a necessary pre-requisite for the subsequent shift towards requiring States to prevent deeply hidden forms of 'modern slavery'. However, despite the advances in the legal framework, this chapter has outlined the difficulties which, in practice, hamper successful detection of this 'underidentified crime'.[106] The importance of establishing a comprehensive identification procedure at national and international level is paramount, as 'trafficking victims, despite their numbers, can be hard to identify, hard to

[101] Female, Nigeria, T3.

[102] *Report Concerning the Implementation of the Council of Europe Convention on Action against Trafficking in Human Beings by Ireland: Second Evaluation Round* (n 47) 28.

[103] David Okech, Whitney Morreau and Kathleen Benson, 'Human Trafficking: Improving victim identification and service provision' (2011) 55(4) *International Social Work* 488-503, 498.

[104] Heidi F Bjelland, 'Identifying human trafficking in Norway: A register-based study of cases, outcomes and police practices' (2017) 14(5) *European Journal of Criminology* 522-542, 525.

[105] Asian Development Bank, *The Significance of Referral Systems as a Response to Human Trafficking and Unsafe Migration* (Asian Development Bank 2009) 1.

[106] Kelle Barrick, Pamela K Lattimore, Wayne J Pitts, Sheldon X Zhang, 'Labor Trafficking Victimization among Farmworkers in North Carolina: Role of Demographic Characteristics and Acculturation' (2014) 2(2) *International Journal of Rural Criminology* 225-243, 235.

locate, hard to convince to leave their situation, and hard to provide services for in order to help them escape from bondage'.[107]

In the Irish context, the domestic legal and policy framework regarding victim identification has been criticised and calls for reform have been made. It has been remarked that 'the low numbers of such cases could just reflect the difficulty in getting this crime into the open and the fact that most countries have not yet geared up to applying the Protocol'.[108] Nonetheless, a more effective process of human trafficking victim identification and investigation must be established to enable both law enforcement and NGOs to provide victims with the support and assistance prescribed under national and international law. Any reform of law and policy in this area would also benefit from considering victims' perspectives.[109]

In conclusion, the broad prohibition of slavery and servitude in Art 4 UDHR has been influential and subsequent human rights norms have developed useful and more refined positive obligations of protection. However, it is imperative that the practical and effective enjoyment of this right by individuals is ensured. To date, the deficiencies of the non-statutory and piecemeal Irish system have meant that access to protection is out of reach for many victims. It is the responsibility of States to address these shortcomings and ensure that the necessary procedures are put in place to serve the needs of trafficking victims.

4. Bibliography

Administrative Immigration Arrangements for the Protection of Victims of Human Trafficking (March 2011): <http://www.inis.gov.ie/en/INIS/Pages/PB08000021> accessed 16 January 2018

Aronowitz, AA, 'Smuggling and Trafficking in Human Beings: The Phenomenon, the Markets that Drive it and the Organisations that Promote it' (2001) 9 *European Journal on Criminal Policy and Research* 163-195

Allain J, *Slavery in International Law: Of Human Exploitation and Trafficking* (Brill 2012)

Andrees, B, *Forced Labour and Trafficking in Europe: How People are Trapped in, Live Through and Come Out* (International Labour Organization Working Paper 57, 2008)

Asian Development Bank, *The Significance of Referral Systems as a Response to Human Trafficking and Unsafe Migration* (Asian Development Bank 2009)

Bakirci, K, 'Human trafficking and forced labour: A criticism of the International Labour Organisation' (2009) 16(2) *Journal of Financial Crime* 160-165

Baldwin, SB, Fehrenbacher, AE and Eisenman, DP, 'Psychological Coercion in Human Trafficking: An Application of Biderman's Framework' (2015) 25(9) *Qualitative Health Research* 1171-1181

---

[107] Frances P Bernat and Heather C Winkeller, 'Human Sex Trafficking: The Global Becomes Local' (2010) 20(1) *Women and Criminal Justice* 186-192, 187.

[108] Nelken (n 59) 485.

[109] Doyle, Murphy, Murphy, Rojas-Coppari, Wechsler, (n 50).

Barrick, K, Lattimore, PK, Pitts, WJ, Zhang, SX, 'Labor Trafficking Victimization among Farmworkers in North Carolina: Role of Demographic Characteristics and Acculturation' (2014) 2(2) *International Journal of Rural Criminology* 225-243

Bjelland, HF, 'Identifying human trafficking in Norway: A register-based study of cases, outcomes and police practices' (2017) 14(5) *European Journal of Criminology* 522-542

Berket, MR, 'Labour exploitation and trafficking for labour exploitation-trends and challenges for policy-making' (2015) 16 *ERA Forum* 359-377

Bernat, FP and Winkeller, HC, 'Human Sex Trafficking: The Global Becomes Local' (2010) 20(1) *Women and Criminal Justice* 186-192

Bespalova, N, Morgan, J and Coverdale, J, 'A Pathway to Freedom: An Evaluation of Screening Tools for the Identification of Trafficking Victims' (2016) 40 *Academic Psychiatry* 124-128

CdeBaca, L, and Sigmon, JN, 'Combating trafficking in persons: a call to action for global health professionals' (2014) 2(3) *Global Health: Science and Practice* 261-267

Davy, D, 'Justice for victims of human trafficking in Australia? Issues associated with Australia's criminal justice response to trafficking in persons' (2017) 20(1) *Contemporary Justice Review* 115-131

Department of Justice and Equality, *Roundtable on Identification of Victims of Human Trafficking* (December 2015)

Department of Justice and Equality, *Second National Action Plan to Prevent and Combat Human Trafficking in Ireland* (October 2016)

Department of Justice and Equality, *Trafficking in Human Beings in Ireland: Annual Report 2016* (2018)

Doyle, DM, Murphy, C, Murphy, M, Rojas-Coppari, P and Wechsler, R, '"I Felt Like She Owned Me": Exploitation and Uncertainty in the Lives of Labour Trafficking Victims in Ireland' (2018) 59(1) *British Journal of Criminology* 231-51

European Migration Network, *Identification of victims of trafficking in human beings in international protection and forced return procedures* (EMN, 2014)

European Migration Network, *Trafficked Persons As Asylum-Seekers: The Process of Identification and Access to Residence Rights in Austria* (EMN, February 2014)

Farrell, A and Pfeffer, R., 'Policing Human Trafficking: Cultural Blinders and Organizational Barriers' (2014) *The Annals of the American Academy of Political and Social Science*, vol. 653, 46-64

Farrell, A, Owens, C and McDevitt, J, 'New laws but few cases: understanding the challenges to the investigation and prosecution of human trafficking cases' (2014) 61 *Crime, Law and Social Change* 139-168

Farrell, A, McDevitt, J and Fahy, S, 'Where are all the victims? Understanding the determinants of official identification of human trafficking incidents' (2010) 9(2) *Criminology & Public Policy* 201-233

Farrell, A, McDevitt, J, Pfeffer, R, Fahy, S, Owens, C, Dank, M and Adams, W, *Identifying Challenges to Improve the Investigation and Prosecution of State and Local Human Trafficking Cases* (Final Report submitted to the National Institute of Justice, Office of Justice Programs. US Department of Justice, April 2012)

Forced Labour Convention (adopted 28 June 1930, entered into force 1 May 1932) ILO C29

Gallagher, A and Holmes, P, 'Developing an Effective Criminal Justice Response to Human Trafficking: Lessons From the Front Line' (2008) 18(3) *International Criminal Justice Review* 318-343

Gielen, UP and Roopnarine, JL, (eds), *Childhood and Adolescence: Cross-cultural Perspectives and Applications* (Prager 2004)

Hodge, DR, 'Assisting Victims of Human Trafficking: Strategies to Facilitate Identification, Exit from Trafficking and the Restoration of Wellness' (2014) 59(2) *Social Work* 111-118

Hernandez, D and Rudolph, A, 'Modern day slavery: What drives human trafficking in Europe?' (2015) 38 *European Journal of Political Economy* 118-139

Hughes, DM, 'The "Natasha" Trade: The Transnational Shadow Market of Trafficking in Women (2000) 53(2) *Journal of International Affairs* 625-651

Hungarian Government Decree No. 354/2012. (XII.13) on the identification order of victims of trafficking in human beings

Immigrant Council of Ireland, *Asylum seeking victims of human trafficking in Ireland: Legal and practical challenges* (ICI, November 2011)

Immigrant Council of Ireland, *Submission to the US State Department Trafficking in Persons Report 2017* (ICI, January 2017)

International Labour Organization, *Indicators of Forced Labour* (ILO 2012)

International Labour Organization, *Labour Exploitation Indicators* (ILO September 2009)

International Organization for Migration, *Addressing Human Trafficking and Exploitation in Times of Crisis: Evidence and Recommendations for Further Action to Protect Vulnerable and Mobile Populations* (IOM, December 2015)

Irwin, N, 'Police officer understandings of human trafficking and awareness of anti-trafficking measures' (2017) *Policing: An International Journal of Police Strategies and Management* 291-305

Joyce, C and Quinn, E, *Identifying Victims of Trafficking in Human Beings in Asylum and Forced Return Procedures: Ireland* (European Migration Network, April 2014)

Lee, M, *Trafficking and Global Crime Control* (Sage Publications 2011)

McAdam, M, 'Who's Who at the Border? A rights-based approach to identifying human trafficking at international borders' (2013) 2 *Anti-Trafficking Review* 33-49

Mantouvalou, V, 'Servitude and Forced Labour in the 21st Century: The Human Rights of Domestic Workers' (2006) 35(4) *Industrial Law Journal* 395

Milano, V, 'The European Court of Human Rights' Case Law on Human Trafficking in Light of L.E. v Greece: A Disturbing Setback?' (2017) 17(4) *Human Rights Law Review* 710

Naidu, A, 'The Right to Be Free from Slavery, Servitude and Forced Labor' (1987) 20 *Comparative and International Law Journal of Southern Africa* 108-113

Nelken, D, 'Human Trafficking and Legal Culture' (2010) 43 *Israel Review* 479-513

Office of the Special Representative and Co-ordinator for Combating Trafficking in Human Beings, *Policy and legislative recommendations towards the effective implementation of the non-punishment provision with regard to victims of trafficking* (Organization for Security and Co-operation in Europe, 2013)

Okech, D, Morreau, W and Benson, K, 'Human Trafficking: Improving victim identification and service provision' (2011) 55(4) *International Social Work* 488-503

Organization for Security and Co-Operation in Europe, *Trafficking in Human Beings: Identification of Potential and Presumed Victims: A Community Policing Approach* (SPMU Publications Series, Vol 10, June 2011)

Potter, M and Hamilton, J, 'Picking on vulnerable migrants: precarity and the mushroom industry in Northern Ireland' (2014) 28(3) *Work, employment and society* 390-406

Pyshchulina, O., 'An Evaluation of Ukrainian Legislation to Counter and Criminalize Human Trafficking' (2003) 11(3) *Demokratizatsiya* 403-411

Smit, M, 'Trafficking in human beings for labour exploitation. The Case of the Netherlands' (2011) 14 *Trends in Organized Crime* 184-197

Ssenyonjo, M. and Baderin, M.A., (eds), *International human rights law: six decades after the UDHR and beyond* (Ashgate Publishing Ltd 2010)

Stapleton, P, *Human Trafficking in Ireland: Identifying Victims of Trafficking* (Annual Critical Social Thinking Conference, January 2011)

Stoyanova V, *Human Trafficking and Slavery Reconsidered: Conceptual Limits and State's Positive Obligations in European Law* (CUP 2017)

Stoyanova, V, '*Chowdury and Others v. Greece*: Further Integration of the Positive Obligations under Article 4 of the ECHR and the CoE Convention on Action against Human Trafficking' (*Strasbourg Observers blog*, 28 April 2017) <https://strasbourgobservers.com/2017/04/28/chowdury-and-others-v-greece-further-integration-of-the-positive-obligations-under-article-4-of-the-echr-and-the-coe-convention-on-action-against-human-trafficking/> accessed 17 September 2018

Stoyanova, V, 'Article 4 of the ECHR and the Obligation of Criminalising Slavery, Servitude, Forced Labour and Human Trafficking' (2014) 3(2) *Cambridge Journal of International and Comparative Law* 407

Thomson, K, 'International and European Standards in Relation to Victims and Survivors of Human Trafficking' in Malloch M and Rigby P (eds), *Human Trafficking: The Complexities of Exploitation* (Edinburgh University Press 2016)

The Group of Experts on Action against Trafficking in Human Beings, *Report Concerning the Implementation of the Council of Europe Convention on Action against Trafficking in Human Beings in Ireland: First Evaluation Round* (GRETA, 2015)

The Group of Experts on Action against Trafficking in Human Beings, *Report Concerning the Implementation of the Council of Europe Convention on Action against Trafficking in Human Beings by Ireland: Second Evaluation Round* (GRETA, 2017)

UN Secretary-General, *Trafficking in persons, especially women and children: Note by the Secretary General* (United Nations, 12 August 2009)

United Nations Office on Drugs and Crime, *Global Report on Trafficking in Persons* (UNODC 2016)

United Nations Office on Drugs and Crime, *Model Law against Trafficking in Persons* [2009 V.09-81990 (E)]

US Department of State, *Trafficking in Persons Report* (June 2017)

US Department of State, *Trafficking in Persons Report* (June 2018)

Villacampa, C and Torres, N, 'Human Trafficking for Criminal Exploitation: The Failure to Identify Victims' (2017) 23 *European Journal on Criminal Policy and Research* 393-408

Ward E and Wylie G, 'Introducing Neo-abolitionism: Definition, Drivers and Debates' in Ward E and Wylie G (eds), *Feminism, Prostitution and the State: The Politics of Neo-Abolitionism* (Routledge 2017)

Chapter 7

FUNDAMENTAL RIGHTS AND EVOLVING TECHNOLOGIES: CONSIDERING THE UNIVERSAL DECLARATION OF HUMAN RIGHTS AT 70

By Maria Helen Murphy

1. Introduction

The Universal Declaration of Human Rights (UDHR) is widely considered to be a visionary document that has had a transformative effect on how human rights are viewed and conceptualised globally. This chapter considers how, on the 70th anniversary of the document, the UDHR retains its pertinence in light of societal changes brought about by developments in technology. The manner in which technology is used and regulated has incredible implications for all aspects of life – from how people work, to how people communicate, to how democracy operates. Accordingly, it is necessary to continually address the ways in which technology may be influencing individual lives and the operation of society more widely. As technology can be used in ways both beneficial and detrimental to human rights, it is not only important to consider the consequences of technological developments at the outset but also to continue to evaluate the human rights impact of existing technologies on an ongoing basis. It has been argued that human rights law has not, to date, 'proven itself especially adept at digital translation',[1] yet this chapter maintains that the human rights framework has the potential to play a vital role in the protection of human rights in a world of ever-increasing technology infiltration.

New technologies can, of course, facilitate both the exercise and the protection of human rights. This has been true from long before the modern concept of 'human rights' was developed. One illustration is provided by the classic example of the printing press, which exponentially increased capacity for free expression and access to information. More recently, the internet connects individuals to wider communities that enable the exchange of views and foster assemblies and associations (both virtual and physical) that facilitate the type of debate essential in democratic societies. Indeed, the United Nations Human Rights Council has passed a non-binding resolution condemning measures

---

1 Daniel Joyce, 'Privacy in the Digital Era: Human Rights Online' (2015) 16 *Melbourne Journal of International Law* 270.

that 'prevent or disrupt access to or dissemination of information online in violation of international human rights law', calling 'on all States to refrain from and cease such measures'.[2] A right to access the internet was not, of course, contained within the text of the UDHR, but it is clear that 'the same rights that people have offline must also be protected online'.[3] This chapter considers the central role of human rights in democratic societies and examines the case study of encryption in order to assess the continued importance of the UDHR in the face of technological development.

2. The Foundations of Democracy

Two, sometimes complementary and sometimes competing, rights have a particularly important role to play in the protection of human rights in the information age. These fundamental rights — as provided for in Arts 12 and 19 of the UDHR — still hold crucial relevance today. Article 12 of the UDHR provides protection for the right to privacy, stating:

> No one shall be subjected to arbitrary interference with his privacy, family, home or correspondence, nor to attacks upon his honour and reputation. Everyone has the right to the protection of the law against such interference or attacks.

Article 19 UDHR protects the right to free expression, stating:

> Everyone has the right to freedom of opinion and expression; this right includes freedom to hold opinions without interference and to seek, receive and impart information and ideas through any media and regardless of frontiers.

These rights were, of course, later incorporated into the text of the International Covenant on Civil and Political Rights.[4] Even though it is often claimed that the law struggles to keep up with developments in technology, human rights documents, such as the UDHR, are in effect technology neutral standards. As human rights documents tend to be comprised of broad statements of generally applicable principles, they are flexible and responsive to societal evolutions. Article 19 of the UDHR, for example, is clearly designed with technology

---

2 Human Rights Council 'The Promotion, Protection and Enjoyment of Human Rights on the Internet' (27 June 2016) UN Doc A/HRC/32/L.20, 3.

3 ibid.

4 International Covenant on Civil and Political Rights (adopted 16 December 1966, entered into force 23 March 1976) 999 UNTS 171 (ICCPR). Art 17 ICCPR states that '[n]o one shall be subjected to arbitrary or unlawful interference with his privacy, family, home or correspondence, nor to unlawful attacks on his honour and reputation' and Art 19 ICCPR states that '[e]veryone shall have the right to 'hold opinions without interference' and 'the right to freedom of expression; this right shall include freedom to seek, receive and impart information and ideas of all kinds, regardless of frontiers, either orally, in writing or in print, in the form of art, or through any other media of his choice'.

neutrality in mind. The decision to phrase the right to receive and impart information and ideas through 'any media' indicates an intention for broad application and effectively future-proofs the right against restriction on the grounds of formalist interpretations. The right to privacy also 'allows for new manifestations of the scope of protection'.[5] For example, even though Art 12 of the UDHR was drafted before 'the rise of networked communications', the concept of 'correspondence' 'logically covers the integrity and confidentiality of new forms of private electronic communications, such as e-mails and direct messages on platforms like Twitter'.[6]

Technology evangelists may argue that existing human rights standards are anachronistic in an information-driven world and champions of surveillance and censorship may contend that human rights are secondary to security, yet it is important to remember that human rights standards were not created in a vacuum.[7] Human rights were developed in order to protect fundamental democratic values deemed necessary to protect essential freedoms.[8] Both the right to privacy and the right to free expression are constitutive elements of modern democracy and each right is mutually supportive of the other.[9] Just as freedom of expression is a necessary precondition for the enjoyment of the right to vote, for the protection of press freedom, and for the rights to assemble and associate freely; so is privacy. A free vote must be a private vote. Where journalists cannot assure the privacy of communications with sources, the ability to hold power to account is undermined. Moreover, the rights to freedom of assembly and association are liable to be chilled where such activities are recorded and stored in government files. While the surveillance of individuals has clear implications for the protection of privacy, it also has the potential to inhibit freedom of expression by encouraging individuals to self-censor.[10] Without the protection of privacy and the accompanying ability to prepare and internally rationalise views, individuals and groups are prevented from fulfilling the independent role assigned to them in a pluralistic, democratic society.[11]

---

5 Wolfgang Schulz and Joris van Hoboken, 'Human Rights and Encryption' in *UNESCO Series on Internet Freedom* (UNESCO 2016) 52 <unesdoc.unesco.org/images/0024/002465/246527E.pdf> accessed 4 November 2018.

6 ibid.

7 Jim Plouffe, 'Privacy is Dead, Tech Evangelist Tells Entrepreneurs' (*InDaily*, 14 June 2016) <https://indaily.com.au/news/business/2016/06/14/privacy-is-dead-tech-evangelist-tells-entrepreneurs/> accessed 4 November 2018; Bruce Schneier, 'Terrorists, Data Mining, and the Base Rate Fallacy' (*Schneier on Security*, 10 July 2006) <www.schneier.com/blog/archives/2006/07/terrorists_data.html> accessed 4 November 2018.

8 Gordon Weil, *The European Convention on Human Rights: Background, Development and Prospects* (AW Styhoff 1963).

9 Emily Howie, 'Protecting the Human Right to Freedom of Expression in International Law' (2018) 20(1) *International Journal of Speech-Language Pathology* 12.

10 Daniel Solove, 'A Taxonomy of Privacy' (2006) 154(3) *University of Pennsylvania Law Review* 477, 481.

11 Alan Westin, *Privacy and Freedom* (Atheneum 1967) 368.

3. The Development of the International Rights to Privacy and Expression

A mandate for the Special Rapporteur on the promotion and protection of the right to freedom of opinion and expression has existed since 1993.[12] The mandate has been repeatedly renewed in subsequent years and David Kaye currently serves as the Special Rapporteur.[13] The growing relevance of the internet for human rights protection is evidenced in these short documents. While the internet was not mentioned in the 1993 resolution, in 2008, the resolution explicitly stated that the Special Rapporteur should:

> ...[C]ontinue to provide his/her views, when appropriate, on the advantages and challenges of new information and communication technologies, including the Internet and mobile technologies, for the exercise of the right to freedom of opinion and expression, including the right to seek, receive and impart information and the relevance of a wide diversity of sources, as well as access to the information society for all.[14]

Other resolutions adopted in this period continued the trend. For example, the 2009 resolution on the promotion and protection of all human rights recognised 'the importance of all forms of the media, including the printed media, radio, television and the Internet, in the exercise, promotion and protection of the right to freedom of opinion and expression.'[15] While the right to privacy has resulted in significant European Court of Human Rights case law and surveillance law reform across Europe, the right — at least in the context of information privacy — had been somewhat sidelined in the international human rights discourse.[16] The Snowden revelations renewed the global focus on privacy and, in 2013, a UN General Assembly resolution entitled 'The Right to Privacy in the Digital Age' was adopted.[17] In addition to affirming 'that the same rights that people have offline must also be protected online, including the right to privacy', the resolution expressed deep concern at the negative impact that surveillance and mass collection of personal data can have on the exercise and enjoyment

---

12 UNCHR Res 45 (1993).

13 HRC Res 7/36 (2008); HRC Res 16/4 (2011) HRC Res 25/2 (2014).

14 HRC Res 7/36 (2008). The 2011 and 2014 resolutions were very concise documents simply recalling previous resolutions and extending the mandate of the Special Rapporteur.

15 HRC 'Promotion and Protection of all Human Rights, Civil, Political, Economic, Social and Cultural Rights, including the Right to Development' (2 October 2009) UN Doc A/HRC/12/L.14, 2.

16 Notable cases (among many) include: *Klass v Germany* (1979-80) 2 EHRR 214; *Malone v The United Kingdom* [1984] ECHR 10; *Huvig v France* (1990) 12 EHRR 528; *Kruslin v France* (1990)12 EHRR 547; *Liberty v The United Kingdom* [2008] ECHR 568; *Roman Zakharov v Russia* [2015] ECHR 1065. Maria Helen Murphy, 'A Shift in the Approach of the European Court of Human Rights in Surveillance Cases: A Rejuvenation of Necessity' (2014) 5 *European Human Rights Law Review* 507.

17 UNGA Res 68/167 (18 December 2013) UN Doc A/RES/68/167.

of human rights.[18] The relevance of technological change for the protection of fundamental rights is captured by the resolution's acknowledgement that:

> ...[T]he rapid pace of technological development enables individuals all over the world to use new information and communication technologies and at the same time enhances the capacity of governments, companies and individuals to undertake surveillance, interception and data collection, which may violate or abuse human rights, in particular the right to privacy, as set out in article 12 of the Universal Declaration of Human Rights.[19]

Moreover, the resolution recognised the right to privacy as one of the foundations of a democratic society and an important tool 'for the realization of the right to freedom of expression'.[20] Since then, numerous resolutions have been adopted on the issue.[21] Notably, in 2015, the Human Rights Council made the decision to appoint a Special Rapporteur on the right to privacy and Joseph Cannataci was subsequently appointed to that role.[22] The debate regarding encryption encapsulates the modern challenge to human rights very well and both Special Rapporteurs have examined the issue in detail as discussed in the following section.

4. A Case Study: Encryption

To take the example of public key encryption, which allows the secure sharing and storing of information on the internet and on electronic devices, it is clear that the UDHR still has relevance in the modern context. It is contended that, at its core, encryption protects the sanctity of an individual's thoughts and communications. As individuals in a democratic society need to be able to 'meet, discuss, and develop without fear of undue government interference', encryption has a crucial structural role to play in modern democratic societies by safeguarding an individual zone of privacy for secure communication.[23] Threats to this right can originate from both State and private actors. As Art 12 of the UDHR guarantees respect for correspondence and privacy, government interference with encryption — a key tool used by many to shield their data from scrutiny by unauthorised third parties — clearly requires consideration of the Article. Article 19 of the UDHR is equally, if not more, relevant as encryption is an important tool to prevent the chilling of speech. Without secure means of communication and information storage, individuals are likely to self-censor and limit their communications and information access. Notably,

---

18 ibid 2.

19 ibid.

20 ibid 1.

21 For example, UNGA Res 69/166 (18 December 2014) UN Doc A/RES/69/166.

22 HRC Res 28/16 (2015).

23 Maria Helen Murphy, *Surveillance and the Law: Language, Power, and Privacy* (Routledge 2019) 24.

in addition to protecting the content of communications, Art 19 protects the mode of transmission or reception of communications.

A defining challenge of regulation in the internet age is the international nature of modern communication and the blurring of territorial boundaries on the internet. The Snowden revelations exposed how the surveillance network of the modern Nation State is now global and unhindered by the practical territorial limitations of the past.[24] What is more, data sharing agreements between surveillance allies have the potential to facilitate the surveillance of citizens while circumventing domestic legal requirements.[25] This reality is one of the reasons why international human rights instruments, such as the UDHR, have the potential to play such an important role in this area. Marko Milanovic points to the benefits of using international human rights instruments as a regulatory framework in light of 'the fact that surveillance measures are now deployed against masses of ordinary people both at home and abroad, rather than simply against the agents of foreign governments.'[26] The expansiveness of Art 19 of the UDHR, which recognises the importance of receiving and imparting information and ideas 'regardless of frontier', further illustrates the potential role of an international system of rights protection in the internet age.

When considering the importance of international human rights at the domestic level, Australia provides an interesting subject. The Australian Constitution provides for limited rights protection in comparison to comparable documents, such as the Irish or United States Constitution.[27] Moreover, Australia is not, of course, a European State and so neither the European Convention on Human Rights nor the Charter of Fundamental Rights applies. Interestingly, it has been posited that Australia's high level of acceptance of international human rights can be largely explained by the absence of a written bill of rights and the concern of Australian citizens about the reputation of the country.[28] Relevant to the question under consideration here is the fact that Australia established

[24] Edward Snowden, a former US government security contractor, leaked classified National Security Agency documents that exposed the details of several global surveillance programmes. Glenn Greenwald, *No Place to Hide* (Metropolitan Books 2014).

[25] Privacy International, 'Human Rights Implications of Intelligence Sharing: Briefing to National Intelligence Oversight Bodies' (September 2017) <https://privacyinternational.org/advocacy-briefing/739/briefing-national-intelligence-oversight-bodies-human-rights-implications> accessed 4 November 2018.

[26] Marko Milanovic, 'Human Rights Treaties and Foreign Surveillance: Privacy in the Digital Age' (2015) 56(1) *Harvard International Law Journal* 81, 140. For a discussion on the extraterritorial application of international rights in the context of foreign surveillance, see ibid.

[27] The Australian Constitution protects five rights explicitly: the right to vote; some limited property rights; the right to trial by jury; freedom of religion; and prohibition of discrimination on the basis of State of residency. See ss 41, 51, 80, 116, 117. See also the role of the court in expanding the rights provided, *Australian Capital Television Pty Ltd v Commonwealth* (1992) 177 CLR 106.

[28] Dana Zartner, 'The (Un)common Law: Legal Tradition and the Diverging Policies of the USA and Australia toward International Human Rights Law' (2013) 34(4) *International Political Science Review* 411, 421.

the Australian Human Rights Commission to increase the acceptance and observance of human rights in the State according to the provisions of the ICCPR. Moreover, Australia has implemented decisions of the Human Rights Committee and Australian courts have delivered judgments citing the UDHR.[29]

In spite of this acceptance of international human rights, the Australian government is currently facing criticism regarding encryption restricting proposals contained in the Telecommunications and Other Legislation Amendment (Assistance and Access) Bill 2018. The Bill provides a framework for enhanced cooperation between communications providers and law enforcement. Under the Bill, law enforcement are empowered to ask or compel service providers to share information about their network infrastructure. Of particular relevance to this chapter, service providers may be required to remove electronic protection from communications and be required to ensure that they have the capability to comply with law enforcement requests.[30] Such provisions infringe on the 'zone of privacy created by encryption and anonymity to protect freedom of expression' and privacy.[31]

In discussions of technology regulation, the metaphor of the law being in a race with technology is ever-pervasive, with the law depicted as 'always lagging behind the swift progress of technological development'.[32] Accordingly, legislation that enhances surveillance powers is very often explained as the simple 'catching-up' of the law with technology. In this context, it is not surprising that the Australian Cyber Security Minister, Angus Taylor, asserts that the Assistance and Access Bill will 'modernise' existing laws 'developed during an analogue era decades ago'.[33] While the Bill explicitly states that service providers cannot be required 'to implement or build a systemic weakness, or a systemic vulnerability, into a form of electronic protection',[34] the 'cramped' definition of the term 'systemic', which is interpreted to exclude 'actions that weaken methods of encryption or authentication on a particular device/s', undermines the protection provided by this statement.[35] As pointed out by Riana Pfefferkorn, the Bill:

---

29 *The King v Wallis* (1949) 48 CLR 529; *Mabo v Queensland* (1989) 166 CLR 186, 217; *Re Minister for Immigrations and Multicultural and Indigenous Affairs* (2003) 211 CLR 441, 454.

30 Telecommunications and Other Legislation Amendment (Assistance and Access) Bill 2018, s 317.

31 Mandate of the Special Rapporteur on the Promotion and Protection of the Right to Freedom of Opinion and Expression Ref OL AUS 5/2018 (11 September 2018) 6 <www.ohchr.org/Documents/Issues/Opinion/Legislation/OL-AUS-5-2018.pdf> accessed 4 November 2018.

32 Murphy (n 23) 76.

33 Michael McGowan, 'Australia Drafts Laws Forcing Facebook and Google to Reveal Encrypted Data' *The Guardian* (London, 6 June 2018) <https://www.theguardian.com/technology/2018/jun/06/planned-laws-to-force-tech-firms-to-reveal-encrypted-data>.

34 Telecommunications and Other Legislation Amendment (Assistance and Access) Bill 2018, s 317ZG.

35 Riana Pfefferkorn, 'Comments on Exposure Draft of Assistance and Access Bill 2018' (29 September 2018) <cyberlaw.stanford.edu/files/publication/files/2018-09-09%20

> ...[R]isks forcing technology companies to create insecure versions of their products and services that, while ostensibly limited to a single incidence, in fact open the door to the very systemic vulnerabilities the Bill professes to avoid.[36]

A key human rights difficulty of encryption restricting actions is that such measures undermine the rights to privacy and expression of everyone who uses the internet and not just targeted individuals.[37] Accordingly, it is difficult to envision how government interference with encryption could be justified under a proportionality analysis, certainly without extensive safeguards. The conflict of the proposed legislation with the UDHR and the ICCPR has been central in the public debate in Australia.[38] For example, in a submission on the Bill by Australian Lawyers for Human Rights, the Joint Committee on Intelligence and Security were reminded that:

> Australia had a significant role in drafting the UDHR and in its adoption by the United Nations General Assembly on 10 December 1948. This is a proud history that Australia has in upholding basic human rights and we should be vigilant to guard against their infringement by the government of the day.[39]

In an illustration of how encryption is central to the protection of privacy and free expression, both the UN Special Rapporteurs on the right to privacy and freedom of expression wrote to the Australian government on the matter.[40] The global implications of the proposals further highlight the importance of

---

Pfefferkorn%20Comments%20to%20Australian%20Govt%20on%20Assistance%20%26%20Access%20Bill.pdf> accessed 4 November 2018.

36 ibid 2.

37 Moreover, the appropriate targets of such action, namely terrorists and organised criminals, are the individuals 'most likely to circumvent weak encryption'. Maria Helen Murphy, 'Technological Solutions to Privacy Questions: What is the Role of Law?' (2016) 25(1) *Information & Communications Technology Law* 3, 29. For more on the international principles on the application of human rights in this area see: Necessary and Proportionate Coalition, 'Necessary & Proportionate: International Principles on the Application of Human Rights to Communications Surveillance' (May 2014) <https://necessaryandproportionate.org/principles> accessed 4 November 2018.

38 Australian Lawyers for Human Rights, 'Australia's Proposed Encryption Legislation Disastrous for Right to Privacy and Global Communications Security' (28 September 2018) <https://alhr.org.au/consultation-relation-telecommunications-legislation-amendment-assistance-access-bill-2018/>.

39 Australian Lawyers for Human Rights, 'Consultation in Relation to the Telecommunications and Other Legislation Amendment (Assistance and Access) Bill 2018' (10 September 2018) 5 <https://alhr.org.au/wp/wp-content/uploads/2018/09/2018-09-10-ALHR-Submission-Encryption-etc.pdf> accessed 4 November 2018.

40 Mandate of the Special Rapporteur on the Right to Privacy Ref OL AUS 6/2018 (12 October 2018) www.ohchr.org/Documents/Issues/privacy/O_LAUS_6.2018.pdf; Mandate of the Special Rapporteur on the Promotion and Protection of the Right to Freedom of Opinion and Expression Ref OL AUS 5/2018 (11 September 2018) <www.ohchr.org/Documents/Issues/Opinion/Legislation/OL-AUS-5-2018.pdf>.

considering international human rights law. As pointed out by the Special Rapporteur on the right to privacy:

> The legislation established in Australia is important internationally due to the risk of malware introduced into one device, spreading laterally throughout IT environments – a risk that is growing with the convergence of cyber and electronics and of major concern to technical and cyber security communities.[41]

The Special Rapporteur on the promotion and protection of the right to freedom of opinion and expression wrote that as aspects of the proposed Bill 'would severely impinge on the rights to privacy and freedom of expression', any limitations of those rights must be 'prescribed by law' and must abide by the 'strict requirements of necessity and proportionality'.[42]

5. Conclusion

This chapter considered the value of the UDHR in addressing the human rights challenges posed by the use of new technologies. In particular, the importance of the rights to privacy and free expression in the encryption context were highlighted. Setting aside the legal force of the UDHR, it is also a powerful symbol that has shaped the development of international norms and influenced the actions of domestic policymakers worldwide.[43] If new policies cannot work within the boundaries of human rights, society should first re-evaluate the use of the technology before reformulating fundamental ideals. As pointed out by the Australian Human Rights Commission:

> Since the advent of the Universal Declaration of Human Rights 70 years ago, the modern human rights framework has proven adaptable to changing external events. And so our task is not to develop new human rights standards, but rather to apply the existing standards to address the technological challenges that confront us.[44]

---

[41] Mandate of the Special Rapporteur on the Right to Privacy Ref OL AUS 6/2018 (12 October 2018) 16 <www.ohchr.org/Documents/Issues/privacy/O_LAUS_6.2018.pdf>.

[42] Mandate of the Special Rapporteur on the Promotion and Protection of the Right to Freedom of Opinion and Expression Ref OL AUS 5/2018 (11 September 2018) 1 <www.ohchr.org/Documents/Issues/Opinion/Legislation/OL-AUS-5-2018.pdf>.

[43] The UDHR can, of course, be said to be part of customary international law. Louis Henkin, *The Age Of Rights* (Columbia University Press 1990) 19; Hurst Hannum, 'The Status of the Universal Declaration of Human Rights in National and International law' (1995/1996) 25 *Georgia Journal of International & Comparative Law* 287, 322; see also Jack Goldsmith, 'International Human Rights Law and the United States Double Standard' (1998) 1 *Green Bag* 365 and Amina M Adanan, 'The Universal Declaration as Customary International Law' in this volume.

[44] Australian Human Rights Commission, 'Human Rights and Technology Issues Paper' (July 2018) 11 <www.humanrights.gov.au/sites/default/files/document/publication/AHRC-Human-Rights-Tech-IP.pdf> accessed 4 November 2018.

As human rights bodies continue to reckon with the risks of technology-enabled and rights-restricting practices (such as undermining internet security, mass data collection, and algorithmic processing), the response should not be a rushed search for a work-around or an attempt to shoehorn new controls into traditional categories.[45] Human rights instruments, like the UDHR, provide useful language and a framework to present coherent opposition to government overreach.[46] Crucially, the dialogue of rights provides 'a space for contestation' where rights 'can be rationally discussed'.[47]

6. Bibliography

Australian Human Rights Commission, 'Human Rights and Technology Issues Paper' (July 2018) <https://www.humanrights.gov.au/sites/default/files/document/publication/AHRC-Human-Rights-Tech-IP.pdf>

Australian Lawyers for Human Rights, 'Australia's Proposed Encryption Legislation Disastrous for Right to Privacy and Global Communications Security' (28 September 2018) <https://alhr.org.au/consultation-relation-telecommunications-legislation-amendment-assistance-access-bill-2018/>

Australian Lawyers for Human Rights, 'Consultation in Relation to the Telecommunications and Other Legislation Amendment (Assistance and Access) Bill 2018' (10 September 2018) <https://alhr.org.au/wp/wp-content/uploads/2018/09/2018-09-10-ALHR-Submission-Encryption-etc.pdf>

Goldsmith, J, 'International Human Rights Law and the United States Double Standard' (1998) 1 *Green Bag* 365

Hannum, H, 'The Status of the Universal Declaration of Human Rights in National and International law' (1995/1996) 25 Georgia Journal of International & Comparative Law 287

Henkin, L, *The Age Of Rights* (Columbia University Press 1990)

Howie, E, 'Protecting the Human Right to Freedom of Expression in International Law' (2018) 20(1) *International Journal of Speech-Language Pathology* 12

Joyce, D, 'Privacy in the Digital Era: Human Rights Online' (2015) 16 *Melbourne Journal of International Law* 270

McGowan, M, 'Australia Drafts Laws Forcing Facebook and Google to Reveal Encrypted Data' *The Guardian* (6 June 2018) <https://www.theguardian.com/technology/2018/jun/06/planned-laws-to-force-tech-firms-to-reveal-encrypted-data>

Murphy, MH, 'Algorithmic Surveillance: The Collection Conundrum' (2017) 31(2) *International Review of Law, Computers & Technology* 225

Murphy, MH, 'Technological Solutions to Privacy Questions: What is the Role of Law?' (2016) 25(1) *Information & Communications Technology Law* 3

Murphy, MH, 'A Shift in the Approach of the European Court of Human Rights in Surveillance Cases: A Rejuvenation of Necessity' (2014) 5 *European Human Rights Law Review* 507

Murphy, MH, *Surveillance and the Law: Language, Power, and Privacy* (Routledge 2019)

[45] Maria Helen Murphy, 'Algorithmic Surveillance: The Collection Conundrum' (2017) 31(2) *International Review of Law, Computers & Technology* 225.

[46] ibid.

[47] Milanovic (n 26) 81.

Necessary and Proportionate Coalition, 'Necessary & Proportionate: International Principles on the Application of Human Rights to Communications Surveillance' (May 2014) <https://necessaryandproportionate.org/principles>

Pfefferkorn R, 'Comments on Exposure Draft of Assistance and Access Bill 2018' (29 September 2018) <cyberlaw.stanford.edu/files/publication/files/2018-09-

Milanovic, M, 'Human Rights Treaties and Foreign Surveillance: Privacy in the Digital Age' (2015) 56(1) *Harvard International Law Journal* 81

Plouffe, J, 'Privacy is Dead, Tech Evangelist Tells Entrepreneurs' (*InDaily*, 14 June 2016) <http://indaily.com.au/business/2016/06/14/privacy-is-dead-tech-evangelist-tells-entrepreneurs/>

Privacy International, 'Human Rights Implications of Intelligence Sharing: Briefing to National Intelligence Oversight Bodies' (September 2017) <https://privacyinternational.org/advocacy-briefing/739/briefing-national-intelligence-oversight-bodies-human-rights-implications>

Schneier, B, 'Terrorists, Data Mining, and the Base Rate Fallacy' (*Schneier on Security*, 10 July 2006) <https://www.schneier.com/blog/archives/2006/07/terrorists_data.html>

Schulz W and J van Hoboken, 'Human Rights and Encryption' in *UNESCO Series on Internet Freedom* (UNESCO 2016) <unesdoc.unesco.org/images/0024/002465/246527E.pdf>

Solove, D, 'A Taxonomy of Privacy' (2006) 154(3) *University of Pennsylvania Law Review* 477

Weil, G, *The European Convention on Human Rights: Background, Development and Prospects* (AW Styhoff 1963)

Westin, A, *Privacy and Freedom* (Atheneum 1967)

Zartner, D, 'The (Un)common Law: Legal Tradition and the Diverging Policies of the USA and Australia toward International Human Rights Law' (2013) 34(4) *International Political Science Review* 411

Chapter 8

POLICY DEVELOPMENTS IN IRELAND: IMPLEMENTING THE UN CONVENTION ON THE RIGHTS OF PERSONS WITH DISABILITIES

By Siobhan Barron

1. Introduction: The UDHR and UNCRPD

This chapter presents an outline of disability policy developments in Ireland over many years, particularly over the past 25 years to 2018, and looks at these in the context of international conventions. It recognises that continued progress is evident, but also that some issues are at early stages of development. It presents the potential of national frameworks and structures to drive and measure progress, particularly in relation to the UN Convention on the Rights of Persons with Disabilities (UNCRPD).[1]

Many international conventions and instruments provide a framework of human rights that each State must adhere to in respect of its citizens. The Universal Declaration on Human Rights (UDHR), adopted by the General Assembly of the United Nations on 10 December 1948, is a statement of human rights agreed by countries for the first time. It gave rise to a range of other international agreements, which are legally binding for the countries who ratify them, including in particular the International Covenant on Civil and Political Rights and the International Covenant on Economic, Social and Cultural Rights in the 1960s.[2]

Whereas these instruments cover all citizens including those with disabilities, it was recognised that because there are specific actions required to ensure that those rights are realised for persons with disabilities, that a specific Convention was required. This realisation became a reality in 2006 with the adoption of the UNCRPD. The creation of the UNCRPD was unique among human rights

[1] Convention on the Rights of Persons with Disabilities (adopted 13 December 2006, entered into force 3 May 2008) 2515 UNTS 3.

[2] International Covenant on Civil and Political Rights (adopted 16 December 1966, entered into force 23 March 1976) 999 UNTS 171 (ICCPR); International Convention on Economic, Social and Cultural Rights (adopted 16 December 1966, entered into force 3 January 1976) 993 UNTS 3.

conventions because of the inclusion of organisations concerning people with disabilities in the negotiations and drawing up of the Convention.[3]

It is recognised that the Convention itself does not contain new rights. However, it reinforces the rights of previous instruments by defining them and directing how they can be achieved. The intention is to promote, protect and ensure the full and equal enjoyment of all human rights and fundamental freedoms by all persons with disabilities. These principles must underpin all legislation, policy, practice and services.

2. Data

Data on the numbers of persons with disabilities in Ireland is supported by the national census conducted by the Central Statistics Office, in which questions have been built on the International Classification of Functioning since 2006. Since then, the portion of the population with disabilities has continuously increased, in particular rising by 8.1% to 13.5% in the most recent Census of 2016,[4] compared to 2011 with slightly higher numbers of women with disabilities. In the 2016 Census, it is notable that there have been significant increases in those declaring themselves as having emotional and mental health difficulties.[5]

Approximately 70% of people who acquire a disability will do so while of working age, i.e. 20-64, which highlights the importance of inclusive and supportive workplaces.[6] The Health Service Executive (HSE) advised that over 8,000 persons with disabilities are in supported residential services, either congregated settings or supported living arrangements in the community with a further 18,000 (approximately) also accessing day services. The numbers of persons recorded with disabilities in any survey is sensitive to what information is used and how it is measured. The outcomes of Census 2011 and Census 2016 for example, showed 13% and 13.5% of population recorded with a disability respectively, and is based on those who self-report as having a disability of some kind. HSE data is based on those who present for, and access disability services.[7]

---

[3] Irish Human Rights and Equality Commission, 'Statement on the UN Convention on the Rights of Persons with Disabilities' (2018) <www.ihrec.ie/statement-un-convention-rights-persons-disabilities> accessed 21 December 2018.

[4] 'Census of Population 2016 – Profile 9 Health, Disability and Carers' <www.cso.ie/en/releasesandpublications/ep/p-cp9hdc/p8hdc/p9d/> accessed 21 December 2018.

[5] 'Press Statement Census 2016 Results Profile 9 – Health, Disability and Carers' <www.cso.ie/en/csolatestnews/pressreleases/2017pressreleases/pressstatementcensus2016resultsprofile9-healthdisabilityandcarers/> accessed 21 December 2018.

[6] National Disability Authority, 'Research on good practice in the employment of people with disabilities in the public sector' <http://nda.ie/Publications/Employment/Employment-Publications/Good-practice-in-employment-of-people-with-disabilities-in-the-public-sector1.pdf> accessed 21 December 2018.

[7] 'Transforming Lives Programme to implement the recommendations of the 'Value for money and policy review of disability services in Ireland – Report on future needs for

3. History of Disability Policy in Ireland

In common with many other countries, for many years, the history of how disability was considered and dealt with in Ireland was based on a medical model, and services were largely dependent on the voluntary sector.[8] It was primarily dealt with and located in the health policy area. However, developments in the 1980s saw a change in language and understanding emerge, and in the 1990s, there was a move to focus on disability from an equality perspective. One of the key developments included the establishment of a government department with responsibility for equality and law reform in 1993, following which the Minister for the Department of Equality and Law Reform established an independent Commission on the Status of Persons with Disabilities on 29 November 1993. The majority of members, 60%, were people with disabilities, carers or family members. The Report of the Commission on Status of Persons with Disabilities was published in October 1996.[9]

The Commission was tasked to review the situation for persons with disabilities in Ireland, and to advise the government on practical measures as to how persons with disabilities could exercise their rights to participate to the fullest extent of their potential in economic, social and cultural life. Further to extensive consultation and deliberations, the Commission reported to government in 1996 setting out over 400 recommendations covering all areas of life and outlined the legislation, policy and structural changes it considered would be necessary. Its findings included the need to develop equality legislation on protection from discrimination, rights based disability legislation, the establishment of a National Disability Authority (NDA), the need to address access to mainstream services and accessibility of the environment.

In 1997, the Department of Equality and Law Reform merged with the Department of Justice to become the Department of Justice, Equality and Law Reform (DJELR). Equality legislation was enacted in 1998 and 2000 to protect persons with disabilities, and others, against discrimination in relation to training, employment and access to goods, services and facilities, respectively.[10] This provided the basis for new equality infrastructure, for example the Equality Authority and the Equality Tribunal were established in 1999, the latter with responsibility to deal with individual cases of discrimination. The Equality Acts were subsequently amended in the Equality Act 2004.

On 12 June 2000, the government established the National Disability Authority (NDA) on the dissolution of the National Rehabilitation Board (NRB) whose

---

disability services' <http://nda.ie/Publications/Disability-Supports/Transforming-Lives.pdf> accessed 21 December 2018.

8 Suzanne Quin & Bairbre Redmond (eds), *Disability and Social Policy in Ireland,* (University College Dublin Press 2003).

9 'A strategy for equality – Report of the Commission on the Status of People with Disabilities' <http://nda.ie/nda-files/Strategy-for-Equality-Overview-and-Commissions-Recommendations11.pdf> accessed 21 December 2018.

10 Employment Equality Act 1998 and Equal Status Act 2000.

functions were transferred to mainstream national bodies dealing with training, employment services and information supports for citizens generally. The NDA's functions, on the other hand, were designed to ensure independent, objective and evidence informed advice on matters relevant to persons with disabilities and to guide mainstream policy and practice in particular.[11] In announcing the establishment of the NDA, the Taoiseach also launched the government's commitment to disability mainstreaming.[12]

The Irish Human Rights Commission was also established in 2000, but was later merged with the Equality Authority in 2014 to become the Irish Human Rights and Equality Commission (IHREC), with functions to protect and promote human rights and equality in Ireland and build a culture of respect for human rights, equality and intercultural understanding in the State.[13] The functions of the Equality Tribunal were transferred to the mainstream body dealing with employment rights, the Work Relations Commission.

Against this backdrop of changes in Ireland, work was progressing at international level towards a UN Convention on disability rights. At the same time, the disability sector sought the introduction of national disability rights legislation and a Bill was developed but withdrawn in 2001. The government formalised a consultation mechanism, establishing a Disability Legislation Consultation Group comprised of disability stakeholders representing mainly umbrella disability groups, providing a forum for engagement with government department officials as relevant to the legislation.[14]

The Disability Bill 2004 was produced by DJELR, and as it applied to all government departments, was developed through a process of co-ordinated working by the relevant officials facilitated by the Department of An Taoiseach. The Bill was further advanced as the core element of the National Disability Strategy launched by the government in 2004. The Strategy also included the Education for Persons with Special Education Needs Act 2004,[15] legislation to

---

[11] National Disability Authority Act 1999, s 8.

[12] Department of An Taoiseach, 'Launch of the National Disability Authority' <www.taoiseach.gov.ie/eng/News/Archives/2000/Taoiseach's_Speeches_Archive_2000/13-06-2000_Speaking_at_the_launch_of_the_National_Disability_Authority.html> accessed 21 December 2018.

[13] Irish Human Rights and Equality Commission Act 2014, s 10.

[14] In March 2002, following the withdrawal of the Disability Bill, 2001, the DJELR set up an Expert Consultation Team with the task to consult with stakeholders and report to government. At the same time, the Minister of State invited the Chairperson of the National Disability Authority to 'facilitate meaningful dialogue at the national level with people with disabilities, their families, carers and service providers'. This led to the formation of the Disability Legislation Consultation Group (DLCG), made up of persons with disabilities and national umbrella groups and organisations in the disability sector. The NDA provided secretariat to the group. DLCG, 'Equal Citizen's – Proposals for core elements of Disability Legislation (2003)' <www.fedvol.ie/_fileupload/File/equal_citizens.pdf> accessed 21 December 2018.

[15] The Act provides that children are to be educated in an inclusive setting unless this would not be in the best interests of the child or the effective provision of education for

advance personal advocacy supports, and commitments to a five-year multi-annual investment programme to address waiting lists for disability supports and the introduction of disability proofing for memoranda for government consideration.

The Disability Act 2005[16] was enacted the following year, and provides for the progressive development of health and personal social services to meet an individual's needs informed by an assessment of needs, and places extensive obligations on the public sector with regard to the accessibility of services, facilities and buildings. It also places obligations on those bodies to ensure a minimum employment target for persons with disabilities is achieved. A key element entails requirements for specific government departments to produce disability action plans (called sectoral plans) in consultation with persons with disabilities, to set out how they would work with other relevant departments for their delivery and to report progress to the Oireachtas (the Irish Parliament) at specific intervals. The Act also provided for the establishment of a Centre of Excellence in Universal Design in the NDA. This centre was established to promote the adoption of universal design in relation to the built environment, products, services and Information Communication Technology (ICT) through awareness raising, standards and development of curricula for the relevant professions.

A range of structures and procedures were subsequently established alongside the National Disability Strategy to support the implementation of the legislation and policies involved, and to monitor progress in delivery. This included a national steering group to oversee progress under the Strategy, comprising officials from the various government departments, also to include the NDA and a newly formed Disability Stakeholder Group (DSG),[17] which replaced the DLCG. The DSG originally comprised a similar structure to the DLCG but over the years, the composition was revised to comprise individuals with disabilities, parents or family members and those from disability organisations,

---

other children in mainstream education. Furthermore, the Act was brought into law to assist children with special educational needs to leave school with the skills necessary to participate, to the level of their capacity, in an inclusive way in the social and economic activities of society and to live independent and fulfilled lives; and to provide for the greater involvement of parents of children with special educational needs in the education of their children. See: <http://www.irishstatutebook.ie/eli/2004/act/30/enacted/en/html>.

16 The Disability Act 2005 <www.irishstatutebook.ie/eli/2005/act/14/enacted/en/html> accessed 21 December 2018.

17 The DSG comprises both disability service providers and persons with a disability who will bring their lived experience to bear on the work of the group. The purpose of the DSG is to provide a forum within which disability stakeholders can work together to present one forum within which disability stakeholders can work together to present one voice to Government through the Disability Strategy Implementation Group (NDSIG) on strategic issues in relation to the National Disability Strategy. The DSG members are, in turn, nominated to sit on other Departments' consultative committees. The Group has an independent Chairperson and Secretariat. Services are provided by the NDA. Department of Justice and Equality, 'Minister McGrath appoints new Disability Stakeholder Group' <www.justice.ie/en/JELR/Pages/PR18000269> accessed 21 December 2018.

with a view to ensuring the strategy would be informed by the lived experience of disability.

At departmental level, consultative committees were established to coincide with the production of sectoral plans in six government departments.[18] These committees review progress by the Department in delivering on its commitments in the strategy, and are comprised of officials, representatives of the DSG, other disability stakeholders and the NDA.

The era in which the Disability Strategy was launched in 2004, including the years that followed, saw other important developments in the disability landscape including the establishment of the National Council of Special Education (NSCE) in 2003[19] and the Health Information and Quality Authority (HIQA) in 2007.[20] A national strategy for mental health service development and quality for persons with mental health was published in 2006, entitled 'A Vision for Change'.[21] A comprehensive review of disability services policy and value for money was conducted by the Department of Health in relation to HSE funded services and published in 2012,[22] which informed an implementation plan for transforming traditional services to individualised supports for persons with disabilities. The implementation of the review's recommendations took

---

18 The six government departments were the Department of Health & Children; the Department of Social & Family Affairs; the Department of Transport; the Department of Communications, Marine & Natural Resources; the Department of the Environment, Heritage & Local Government; and the Department of Enterprise, Trade & Employment. A number of these departments have been renamed or reconfigured since the time of the Act.

19 The NCSE was first established as an independent statutory body by order of the Minister for Education and Science in December 2003 and was formally established under the Effective Provision for Special Education Needs (EPSEN) Act 2005.

20 HIQA was established under the Health Act 2007. HIQA is the independent Authority established to drive continuous improvement in Ireland's health and social care services.

21 'A Vision for Change' is a strategy document published in 2006 by the Department of Health setting out direction for Mental Health Services in Ireland. The Department of Health describes the strategy as "A Vision for Change" details a comprehensive model of mental health service provision for Ireland. It describes a framework for building and fostering positive mental health across the entire community and for providing accessible, community-based, specialist services for people with mental illness. The expert group which developed the strategy combined the expertise of different professional disciplines, health service managers, researchers, representatives of voluntary organisations, and service user groups. The Department of Health established a steering group to monitor its implementation. Department of Health, 'A Vision for Change' <https://health.gov.ie/future-health/mental-health-a-vision-for-change/a-vision-for-change/> accessed 21 December 2018.

22 This Value for Money and Disability Policy Review is an evaluation of the efficiency and effectiveness of the HSE-funded statutory and non-statutory disability services in Ireland. It was conducted by the Department of Health and the HSE under the auspices of the Government's programme of Value for Money Reviews for 2009-2011 and makes a range of recommendations about how these services should be structured. The follow on action to implement the findings come under the banner entitled 'Transforming Lives'. Department of Health, 'Value for Money and Disability Policy Review' <https://health.gov.ie/blog/publications/value-for-money-and-policy-review-of-disability-services-in-ireland/> accessed 21 December 2018.

on the title of the Transforming Lives Programme in subsequent years. The changes to policy and practice required under this programme are significant.

4. International Policy and Ireland's Response

The role of international law and policy is important in shaping Irish disability law, policy and practice, which is founded on respecting the rights of persons with disabilities. How society itself is changing in terms of education, culture, attitudes and expectations can also drive change and priorities. National law, policy and practice continues to evolve from the historic medical model – segregation and paternalistic approaches – to a human rights model, which respects each individual's rights to choose how they want to live their lives and to achieve their goals. Services, which grew from charitable and institutional arrangements often provided by the voluntary sector focused on incapacity rather than ability, are transforming to a community based supports model. It is recognised that disability must be a focus of all policy areas to ensure equality and human rights are realised.

Ireland signed the UNCRPD in 2006 and ratified it in March 2018, but has delayed ratification of the Optional Protocol.[23] The protocol provides for the Committee on the Rights of Persons with Disabilities (the UNCRPD Monitoring Committee) to receive and consider complaints from or on behalf of individuals or groups.[24] It is noted that complaints should only be made under the Protocol when national mechanisms for dealing with such complaints have been exhausted.

The Irish Government adopted a phased approach towards ratification of the Convention and the Optional Protocol. This is based on its intention to identify and address specific actions to ensure the highest possible level of compliance with the Convention. In 2018, the government's stated position is that it intends to ratify the Optional Protocol as soon as possible, at the latest following completion of Ireland's first reporting cycle to the UN Committee. It is recognised that this first reporting cycle will also guide on any further actions which may be needed to enhance Ireland's compliance with the Convention.[25]

---

23 Optional Protocol to the Convention on the Rights of Persons with Disabilities (adopted 13 December 2006, entered into force 3 May 2008) 2518 UNTS 283 (Optional Protocol). Irish Government had not yet ratified the Convention as of May 2019.

24 The Optional Protocol provides that 'A State Party to the present Protocol ("State Party") recognizes the competence of the Committee on the Rights of Persons with Disabilities ("the Committee") to receive and consider communications from or on behalf of individuals or groups of individuals subject to its jurisdiction who claim to be victims of a violation by that State Party of the provisions of the Convention. No communication shall be received by the Committee if it concerns a State Party to the Convention that is not a party to the present Protocol', < www.ohchr.org/en/hrbodies/crpd/pages/optionalprotocolrightspersonswithdisabilities.aspx > accessed 21 December 2018.

25 Seanad Éireann debate, 21 March 2018, 'Ratification of UN Convention on the Rights

Ireland has a history of only ratifying international conventions when work is advanced towards the implementation of their provisions, to ensure that necessary legislation is in place. It is recognised that the civil and political rights provided in the Convention required immediate attention, while action was also necessary to progressively realise the economic, social and cultural rights of the Convention. Prior to signing the Convention in 2006, Ireland had enacted a range of legislation providing a legal basis for many of the Convention's provisions, particularly through equality legislation protecting against discrimination in employment and access to goods and services. Upon ratification of the Convention, national legislation had also been enacted in relation to Art 12, namely the Assisted Decision Making (Capacity) Act 2015 and legislation is being developed to address deprivation of liberty as appropriate for persons in institutions and nursing homes, recognising these as particularly important areas for attention.[26]

Given the breadth of the policy and service areas covered by the Convention, a considered and planned approach to its implementation is required. The following sections provide an overview of some of key developments in Ireland to progress equality for persons with disabilities over the years as relevant in terms of supporting Ireland to deliver on its obligations under the Convention.

5. Delivering on the UNCRPD

While through ratification of the UNCRPD, Ireland has signalled its commitment to the vision of the Convention, practical realisation of each of the articles requires a programmatic approach through clear action plans with targets for continued progress and resource planning. This can be in turn integrated into each department and organisation's corporate business plan, with cross-sectoral links as appropriate and thereafter integrated into work programmes of their divisions and units.

There are a range of government strategies and programmes already in progress that continue to be active in 2019 which have the potential to support the implementation of many of the Convention's provisions. As living strategies evolving over time, they provide a framework for continuous improvement and progress through focused, joined up working, by government departments and relevant bodies.

The structures in place to support and oversee their implementation can enable

of Persons with Disabilities: Statements' <https://www.oireachtas.ie/en/debates/debate/seanad/2018-03-21/21/> accessed 21 December 2018.

26 The Assisted Decision-Making (Capacity) Act 2015 provides a statutory framework for individuals to make legally-binding agreements to be assisted and supported in making decisions about their welfare, their property and their affairs where the person lacks, or may lack, the capacity to make individual decisions unaided. The legislation requires presumption of capacity as one of its guiding principles.

regular review of progress by disability stakeholders and also the co-design of solutions to address areas of delay. They also provide a means of escalating issues where Ministerial intervention is required. Co-ordinated reporting is supported by the Department of Justice and Equality (DJE, formerly DJELR), within its equality remit, and it is also the focal point for Ireland's reports on the UNCRPD.

6. Role of the National Disability Authority

The NDA's work has evolved since it was established in light of various developments, so that it is built on supporting implementation of the strategies, programmes and the Convention through its research, advice and technical guidance. Its work includes facilitated workshops and consultation with stakeholders. In more recent years, this work has been focused on guiding transformation of community supports to supports for persons with disabilities to live lives of their choosing in the community and also on evaluating outcomes achieved. It has also included development of 11 codes of practice to support the implementation of assisted decision-making legislation.

The NDA also has a role to independently assess how national strategies are being implemented, to examine the reasons for any blockages and to advise on how they can be addressed. It has developed indicators to support the long-term measurement of progress and impact of these strategies, helping identify trends and issues while informing ongoing priority setting and improvements.

What is more, the NDA's Centre for Excellence in Universal Design has a remit to promote the Universal Design of the built environment, products, services, and information and communications technology, so that they can be accessed, understood and used independently to the greatest extent possible by everyone including persons with disabilities.[27] Its work with national standards bodies, professional bodies and educational bodies supports the achievement of the goals of Art 4 of the Convention to progress awareness and adoption of universal design in practice.[28]

7. National Disability Inclusion Strategy

The National Disability Strategy has transformed over the years as it was

---

27 Disability Act 2005, s 6.

28 Art 4 of the UNCRPD refers explicitly to Universal Design in terms of requiring State to promote and to undertake activities to advance its application in good, services, equipment and facilities. It states: 'f) To undertake or promote research and development of universally designed goods, services, equipment and facilities, as defined in Art 2 of the present Convention, which should require the minimum possible adaptation and the least cost to meet the specific needs of a person with disabilities, to promote their availability and use, and to promote universal design in the development of standards and guidelines'.

reshaped and focused in consultation with disability stakeholders. The current National Disability Inclusion Strategy 2017–2021 sets out actions committed by government departments and agencies to address many of the areas covered by the Convention, which should inform their annual business planning and activities.[29] The Strategy's goals are focused on removing barriers to equality and reaching potential, accessing housing, education, employment, transport and services. It incorporates the commitment to ratify the Optional Protocol to the Convention, as well as commitments to deliver on national strategies and programmes covering actions to enhance employment opportunities and transformation of disability services, specific actions to make websites and services accessible, and to enhance access to education, employment, health services, housing and transport.

The strategic priorities are focused on:

- Equality and choice: This includes actions to ensure persons with disabilities are treated equally before the law, make their own choices and decisions, are treated with dignity and respect and free from all forms of abuse, enjoy improved participation in political and public life, accessible and that public services and information, public services are universally designed.
- Joined up policies and public services are key to progressing equality and access to services as relevant to children, and to facilitate their transition within and out of education. Engaging persons with disabilities in planning, design, delivery and evaluation of public services is recognised as good practice.
- Education: Actions to support children and adults to reach their full potential are included.
- Employment: The strategy recognises that person with disabilities should be encouraged and motivated to develop to the maximum of their potential in further education and employment, to have the opportunity to work and have a career, to be able to access support so that they can remain in or return to work, and that they are financially better off in work. Employer needs are also recognised e.g. that they can easily access information on employing persons with disabilities.
- Health and well-being actions include those to support persons with disabilities to achieve and maintain best possible physical, mental and emotional well-being.
- A person–centred approach is recognised as key to transforming disability services so that they can support individuals to live a fulfilled life of their choosing, to achieve maximum independence, to participate in everyday life and community activities, and to be

---

[29] The National Disability Inclusion Strategy is a whole of government approach to improving the lives of persons with disabilities. Department of Justice and Equality, 'National Disability Inclusion Strategy 2017-2021' <www.justice.ie/en/JELR/dept-justice-ndi-inclusion-stratgey-booklet.pdf/Files/dept-justice-ndi-inclusion-stratgey-booklet.pdf> accessed 24 February 2019.

active citizens. This includes having timely access to assessments, early intervention and services, that disability services are delivered to high quality standards, that person with disabilities are involved in planning, design and evaluation of public services, and the introduction of individualised funding.

- Living in the community is a key focus of policy supporting transformation from historical models to support individuals to live an independent life in a home of their choosing in the community. It is also important that new homes are universally designed.
- Transport and accessible places are key to enabling independence and choice so that persons can get to and from their chosen destination independently using accessible transport, and that buildings and facilities are accessible whereby planning and design is informed by engagement with persons with disabilities and others.

A steering group chaired by the Minister of State with Special Responsibility for Disability Issues, and comprising senior government department officials, the HSE, the DSG and the NDA monitors the implementation of the Strategy. Given the cross-departmental nature of the Strategy and the Steering Group, any challenges or obstacles arising can be identified early in order to focus on solutions. The Minister's involvement can ensure on-going issues can be highlighted at Cabinet level as appropriate. The NDA independently assesses and measures progress and the outcomes for persons with disabilities. Stakeholder engagement is key, and supported by the consultative committees in government departments where detailed work programmes can be reviewed. As a living strategy, to further develop over the years, it can enable continued enhancement and momentum to achieve the intent of the UNCRPD.

8. National Comprehensive Employment Strategy for Persons with Disabilities

Persons with disabilities in Ireland are only half as likely to be in work than those without disabilities. Most recent figures show that only 36.2% of persons with disabilities are in employment, compared to 72.8% of the population without disabilities aged 20-64 years old.[30] This gap has remained consistent over time, and is one of the more pronounced gaps in the European region. Factors influencing lower employment outcomes for persons with disabilities include typically lower levels of educational achievement, lower expectations and ambitions with regard to employment, and challenges in expanding employer engagement. Recognising the integrated nature of these challenges, the Comprehensive Employment Strategy for People with Disabilities (CES)[31]

---

30 Central Statistics Office, Census 2016, Profile 11 – Employment, Occupations and Industry.

31 Department of Justice and Equality, 'The Comprehensive Employment Strategy for People with Disabilities' < www.justice.ie/en/JELR/Comprehensive%20 Employment%20Strategy%20for%20People%20with%20Disabilities%20-%20FINAL.

was launched at the end of 2015 as a whole-of-government commitment to achieving better employment outcomes for those with disabilities. The shape of the CES was informed by research carried out by the NDA on the core pillars for a strategic approach to addressing the various barriers to employment for persons with disabilities. The CES covers the period to 2024 and comprises six strategic priorities as follows:

- To build skills, capacity and independence;
- To provide bridges and supports into work;
- To make work pay;
- To promote job retention and re-entry to work;
- To provide co-ordinated and seamless support;
- To engage employers.

In addition, it recognises the various pathways to work, diversity of ability, range of support needs and the role of different actors, such as government departments, state agencies, employers and unions to address barriers to accessing, retaining and returning employment. The Strategy will support the progressive implementation of Arts 24, 26 and 27 of the Convention in particular, but it also recognises the importance of transport access as a means of getting to education, training and work.

By focusing on mainstream policy and services, as well as specialist supports, the Strategy is founded on the pathway to work from the early stages in school onto further and higher education, training and employment. It also recognises the different starting points for individuals on their journey, their means of getting there and that it is not a one-size fits all approach in terms of the nature and breadth of the work but also the degree of support, if any, that is required. Delivery of the 10-year strategy is enabled via three yearly action plans, requiring joined up working by departments, to ensure effective links between education, training and employment, support for transitions, access to supports for work and actions by employers to support future job opportunities, including for those with high support needs.

The first three years of the strategy, known as the foundation stage, included actions to examine financial disincentives to work, the commencement of a pilot of pre-activation, testing an employer information service and agreement of an approach to supported employment. The next three year-action plan will take the learning forward to implementation with a view to increasing numbers of persons with disabilities in work. Implementation is guided by a national implementation group with an independent chair and comprising government departments, the NDA and disability stakeholders. Annual independent assessments of progress are conducted by the chair and reports are published. The NDA also conducts an assessment and advises on actions necessary.

---

pdf/Files/Comprehensive%20Employment%20Strategy%20for%20People%20with%20 Disabilities%20-%20FINAL.pdf> accessed 24 February 2019.

9. Transforming Lives Programme

Articles 19 and 20 of the Convention are especially important as they are about the right of persons with disabilities to live in the community with choices equal to others, full inclusion and participation in the community, and supported to live as independently as possible. Realising the ambition of these Articles requires continued efforts to transform traditional services, many of which are delivered in the health and social care space, but which also cross over to other policy areas including, for example, housing.

Unlike other jurisdictions, social care supports in Ireland are delivered through the national HSE and the voluntary sector bodies that it funds. Annual funding in the region of over €1.7bn is provided in this regard. The national Transforming Lives programme is designed to support the transition from the traditional means of services and segregation, toward enabling people to live lives of their choosing in the community, and so comprises actions, which include for example:

- Transitioning from institutional living arrangements in large residential centres to supported living arrangements of choice as part of the community;
- A move away from segregated day care service arrangements to supports for inclusion in the mainstream community, training and employment informed by each person's goals and choices;
- A major transformation from the old models of providing services to groups to tailored supports decided by the individual;
- Individualised funding development;
- The development of frameworks to guide those in providing services on implementation of person centred planning and ensuring that supports provided are tailored to achieving an individual's quality of life outcome goals;
- Enhanced data systems to enable consistent monitoring of investment and the outcomes achieved.

It is noteworthy that the first set of national standards for disability services and related regulations were adopted in 2013.[32] Services are inspected against the standards by HIQA, and this has been significant in driving continuous improvement in residential settings, where HIQA has powers to de-register services where standards are consistently not achieved.

---

32 The National Standards for Residential Services for Children and Adults with Disabilities were launched in January 2013 and provide a framework for HIQA to assess whether residential services are providing high quality, safe and effective services and supports to adults and children who live there in line with the requirements of the Health Act 2007 HIQA, 'National Standards for Residential Services for Children and Adults with Disabilities' <www.hiqa.ie/sites/default/files/2017-02/Standards-Disabilities-Children-Adults.pdf> accessed 24 February 2019.

The progressive delivery of the Transforming Lives programme and its constituent parts will be important to complying with a range of Articles in the Convention, but also in how they dovetail with other relevant strategies, such as the National Disability Inclusion Strategy and the CES. With any significant change programme, effective transition planning is required ensuring persons with disabilities are central and involved in decision making in particular. There are other actors who need to be engaged as appropriate such as families, staff, the local community and others. However, the pace of progress can prove challenging, noting that Ireland has started a programme of deinstitionalisation later than other jurisdictions for example, and given historical models of funding and model services. The pace of change can be challenging requiring adequate resources, wider cultural changes, effective local networks, use of tools and frameworks (e.g. person centred planning framework) and that other elements outside of disability funded supported are operating effectively. For example, availability of suitable housing is important as is access to mainstream services in the community. The progress by Ireland in decongregation, i.e. deinstitutionalisation is raised for attention in a report of the European Fundamental Rights Agency, which was published December 2018.[33]

10. Legislation

Compliance with the UNCRPD has required amendments to national legislation and the development of new legislation. This includes in particular the enactment of the Assisted Decision Making (Capacity) Act 2015, as relevant to Art 12 on equal recognition before the law to be supported by an independent Decision Support Service.[34] At the time of writing this chapter, the development of a large suite of Codes of Practice to support its implementation is at an advanced stage. Work is also underway by the Department of Health to finalise legislation to address deprivation of liberty, in line with Art 14 of the

[33] The Fundamental Rights Agency chose five countries to conduct case studies on, as part of their review of the decongregation process across Europe, identifying barriers and drivers in the process. 'The right to independent living of persons with disabilities' <http://fra.europa.eu/en/project/2014/right-independent-living-persons-disabilities> accessed 21 December 2018. The final report, which presents the main insights gained as part of the case studies on the drivers and barriers to deinstitutionalisation was published in December 2018. 'From institutions to community living for persons with disabilities: perspectives from the ground' <https://fra.europa.eu/sites/default/files/fra_uploads/fra-2018-from-institutions-to-community-living-ground-perspectives_en.pdf> accessed 13 May 2019.

[34] As stated by the Fundamental Rights Agency (FRA) in relation to Art 12 of the UNCRPD, it 'addresses the right to equality before the law and the issue of legal capacity, which is the law's recognition of the decisions a person makes. It lies at the heart of a human rights based approach to disability and underpins the exercise of many other rights'.< www.un.org/development/desa/disabilities/convention-on-the-rights-of-persons-with-disabilities/article-12-equal-recognition-before-the-law.html> accessed 21 December 2018.

Convention.[35] The legislation will be significant in terms of the implications for organisations and individuals, and the change in mindset required in society (e.g. requiring a presumption of capacity in the first instance). The Bill will establish a legal framework with appropriate protections and safeguards for people who may lack capacity to consent to admission to or discharge from a designated facility.

11. Empowering Persons with Disabilities

The Convention highlights the importance of persons with disabilities being empowered to participate fully in all aspects of life, including socio-economic, civic and political activities. This includes ensuring that individuals are enabled to receive and understand relevant information, which is presented in a format and method suitable to their requirements, but also ensuring that they can advocate for themselves and their own needs, be this in the work place, in an educational or social care setting, or in any other area of life. In recognition of this, there has been work undertaken in the voluntary sector to support self-advocacy on the part of persons with disabilities. An Advisory Group has been established under new legislation by the IHREC to advise it in relation to the fulfilment of IHREC's independent monitoring role under Article 33 of the UNCRPD.

Work is underway to consider structures to ensure effective participation of individuals with disabilities in the design and delivery of relevant services, while there has also been an increased emphasis on the co-design and co-production of actions across a range of departments. The National Advocacy Service is resourced to provide advocacy supports to persons with disabilities who choose them across the country, assisting them in ensuring their will and preferences are heard in situations where issues have arisen with those providing services and supports, either in traditional disability services, or in mainstream community settings. These developments are important in ensuring persons with disabilities are central to supporting cultural change and having a voice in society.

---

[35] Art 14 of the UNCRPD provides that persons with disabilities 'are not deprived of their liberty unlawfully or arbitrarily, and that any deprivation of liberty is in conformity with the law, and that the existence of a disability shall in no case justify a deprivation of liberty'. It requires that States Parties 'ensure that if persons with disabilities are deprived of their liberty through any process, they are, on an equal basis with others, entitled to guarantees in accordance with international human rights law and shall be treated in compliance with the objectives and principles of this Convention, including by provision of reasonable accommodation'. Committee on the Rights of Persons with Disabilities, 'Guidelines on Article 14 of the Convention on the Rights of Persons with Disabilities' <www.ohchr.org/Documents/HRBodies/CRPD/GC/GuidelinesArticle14.doc> accessed 21 December 2018.

12. Monitoring Implementation of the UNCRPD

As set out above there are various strategies and programmes in place that cover many areas encompassed in the Articles of the UNCRPD and their implementation is supported by a network of steering groups and committees involving disability stakeholders.

In light of the cross-agency nature of many of the issues involved these structures have the potential to assist achievement of co-ordinated working, and joined up working to deliver on the goals of the Convention. They can also provide a mechanism for ongoing and regular review of progress actions, problem solving and proactive development of further action plans, working with stakeholders in this regard. The framework and processes involved could therefore support a systematic approach to meeting the goals of the Convention.

The national independent monitoring body for the UNCRPD is the IHREC, and this role is recognised further in the Disability (Miscellaneous Provisions) Bill 2016. Under the legislation, it will be the role of the IHREC to review the adequacy of law and practice with regard to the implementation of the Convention.[36] This independent monitoring framework will scrutinise the State's progress in implementing the Convention's obligations to protect, respect and uphold the human rights of persons with disabilities.

Engagement with civil society, in particular persons with disabilities and their representative organisations, will be key to understanding the lived experience and will guide areas for priority attention. The Disability (Miscellaneous Provisions) Bill 2016 provides for the establishment, by the IHREC, of an Advisory Group (referenced above) comprising a majority persons with disabilities, which will support monitoring activities through offering advice and assistance to the Commission in the fulfilment of its independent monitoring role.[37]

The means of assessing and measuring progress will be critical to informing Ireland's reports to the UN Committee but also to guiding areas to target within available resources. The NDA has also been assigned a statutory duty to provide information and advice to the IHREC, including the development and provision of statistical information if required, as relevant to the UNCRPD.

---

[36] At the time of writing this Chapter in 2018, the Disability Miscellaneous Provisions Bill has yet to complete all stages of the legislative process. It provides amendment to the Irish Human Rights and Equality Commission Act 2014, to include a duty 'to keep under review the adequacy and effectiveness of law and practice in the State relating to the protection of persons with disabilities' and 'to appoint an advisory committee to assist and advise it on matters relating' to this function, while stating that at least half of the committee's members will be persons with disabilities.

[37] IHREC, 'Disability Advisory Committee Applicant Information Booklet' (October 2018) <www.ihrec.ie/app/uploads/2018/09/IHREC_Information-Booklet_Disability-Advisory-Committee.pdf> accessed 21 December 2018.

The NDA already has functions to monitor the implementation of codes of practice for public services in terms of their accessibility, which can be helpful in establishing how services are performing over time. As mentioned above, the NDA is also monitoring the delivery and impact of national strategies and programmes, which in turn informs continued improvement. Access to robust data and learning from persons with disabilities and others on the lived experience will be critical in guiding on how Ireland is progressively delivering on the Convention, not just in terms of outputs, but especially in terms of establishing outcomes for persons with disabilities over time.

13. Conclusion

As a Convention that highlights the equal rights of persons with disabilities in common with all citizens, the UNCRPD provides a mechanism to ensuring human rights can be realised for all. While not conferring new rights, it places the onus on States Parties to realise these rights for persons with disabilities. Ireland only ratified the Convention in 2018 but a range of the policies and strategies at national level have been in place for a number of years supporting the gradual change of culture and practice required to realise many of the aims and objectives of UNCRPD. Expectations of significant change on foot of ratification of the Convention are high, but it is important to reflect on the extent to which change and improvement has been underway over the course of the last number of decades, and that progressive realisation continues.

This work is on-going, although in many cases, implementation is dependent on resources and on achieving new ways of working. A number of strategies and programmes outlined earlier in this chapter were scheduled for implementation at the same time as the recent economic downturn and global recession. During this period, budgets for delivery of services and supports were severely curtailed, and it is only in recent years that there have been some signs of economic improvement. The Convention's articles rightly speak to every aspect of the individual's life, and in keeping with this, many of Ireland's strategies and policies adopt a 'whole of government' approach, tying in the full range of actors required to realise change, and devising mechanisms for cross-departmental cooperation. This has not been without its challenges, but it is welcome that traditional siloes have begun to break down.

By leveraging the progress and developments to date, Ireland has the potential to ensure that existing strategies and programmes can serve as frameworks to continuously advance necessary actions relevant to UNCRPD, while also supporting continued involvement by persons with disabilities. The programmes in question have evolved over many years and require ongoing review to ensure continuous progress and measurement. There are opportunities to ensure their clear alignment with the overarching aims of the Convention itself, and build on learning from experiences and developments in other jurisdictions.

The Convention's provisions cover all policy areas and the focus on mainstreaming should ensure that they are integrated into all legislative and policy considerations as well as practice. Successful implementation will be evident in increased participation in work, in the community, in social and cultural activities; in increased individual choice, control, autonomy, and in quality of life. Effective data can enhance the richness of evidence, knowledge and experience to inform and drive the continued progressive implementation of the Convention as will the involvement of persons with disabilities themselves, which in turn will ensure full alignment with the vision of the UDHR.

14. Bibliography

Central Statistics Office, *Profile 9–Health, Disability and Carers* (2016)

Central Statistics Office, *Press Statement: Census 2016 Results Profile 9 – Health, Disability and Carers* (2 November 2017)

Commission on the Status of People with Disabilities, *A Strategy for Equality Report of the Commission on the Status of People with Disabilities* (1996)

Department of Health, *The Report of the Expert Group on Mental Health Policy – A Vision for Change* (2006)

Department of Health, *Value for Money and Policy Review of Disability Services in Ireland* (2012)

Health Services Executive, Working Group 3, *Transforming Lives Programme to implement the recommendations of the "Value for Money and Policy Review of Disability Services in Ireland"– Report on Future Needs for Disability Services* (September 2018)

Irish Human Rights and Equality Commission, *Statement on the UN Convention on the Rights of Persons with Disabilities* (2018)

Irish Human Rights and Equality Commission, *Disability Advisory Committee Applicant Information Booklet* (2018)

National Disability Authority, *Research on good practice in the employment of people with disabilities in the public sector* (2018)

Quin S and Redmond B (trs), *Disability and Social Policy in Ireland* (University College Dublin Press 2003)

CHAPTER 9

UNITED NATIONS TARGETED SANCTIONS AND HUMAN RIGHTS: CHALLENGING THE NARRATIVE

By Déirdre Clancy

1. INTRODUCTION[1]

The Universal Declaration of Human Rights (UDHR) was drafted against the background of the pledge of Member States to 'achieve, in cooperation with the United Nations (UN), the promotion of universal respect for and observance of human rights and fundamental freedoms'.[2] The seven decades since the adoption of the UDHR have seen a multiplication of human rights tools, mechanisms and range of duty bearers, all charged with delivering on that potential. As the principal organ of international governance charged with countering threats to international peace and security, the UN Security Council has, however, been a reluctant human rights duty bearer.[3] The Council's authorisation of use of force on human rights and humanitarian grounds under Art 42 of the UN Charter has been much debated.[4] Less examined is the relationship between the Council's authority to impose sanctions under Art 41 and the protection of fundamental human rights—particularly where positive correlations might be found.[5]

1 The analysis takes a practitioner's approach: the author served as the humanitarian expert on the UN Somalia Eritrea Monitoring Group (UNSEMG), the group of experts appointed by the Secretary General to assist the Security Council Committee pursuant to resolution 751 (1992) concerning Somalia, between October 2013 and December 2017.

2 *Universal Declaration of Human Rights*, GA Res 217A (III), UN GAOR 3rd sess, 183rd, UN Doc A/810 (10 December 1948) (UDHR), preamble.

3 The Council has constantly vacillated in its interpretation of Art 2 (7) of the UN Charter, 1945— 'the United Nations has no authority to intervene in matters which are within the domestic jurisdiction of any State'—notwithstanding the clear Chapter VII exception: 'this principle shall not prejudice the application of enforcement measures under Chapter VII of the Charter'. See also Art 1 (3) and Art 24 (1), UN Charter 1945.

4 See, for example, Christine Gray, 'The use of force for humanitarian purposes' in Henderson C, and White ND, (eds.), *Research Handbook on International Conflict and Security Law, Jus ad Bellum, Jus in Bello and Jus post Bellum* (Edward Elgar 2013).

5 Pursuant to Art 41 of the UN Charter, the Council can take measures 'not involving the use of armed force' to give effect to its decisions including 'complete or partial interruption of economic relations and of rail, sea, air, postal, telegraphic, radio, and other means of communication, and the severance of diplomatic relations'.

Initially sanctions were used sparingly. Between 1965 and 1990, only two sanctions regimes were imposed by the Council.[6] The end of the Cold War saw an escalation in the popularity of the mechanism, with 12 mandates commenced in the nineties alone.[7] As the Council's enthusiasm for sanctions grew, however, so did criticism of the impact, culminating in grave allegations about the humanitarian toll in Iraq.[8] As a result, since the mid-1990s the Council has exclusively imposed 'targeted' or 'smart' sanctions, regimes designed to discriminate—at least in theory—between intended and unintended targets. Under the new architecture, sanctions have also evolved to specifically address violations of human rights and humanitarian law. Since 2004, the Council has explicitly designated these violations as prohibited conduct which triggers the imposition of the individualised sanctions mechanism (e.g. asset freeze and travel ban). Today, the Council oversees eight out of 14 such sanctions regimes.[9] With the International Criminal Court (ICC) facing challenges of legitimacy and efficacy in a polarised global political climate,[10] the chapter explores to what extent UN targeted sanction regimes have the potential to bolster the protection of populations in countries under sanction through checking the power of those who commit grave violations.

Recent developments in the norms and practice surrounding UN targeted sanctions suggest the potential for positive human rights outcomes. Much of the focus of public discussion, however, has been on the negative impact of sanctions, in particular on the humanitarian situation of vulnerable populations and on enjoyment of the right to a fair hearing.[11] The chapter acknowledges that UN sanctions practice—from design to implementation—is politicised and frequently inconsistent, including when it comes to actions to promote and protect human rights. Not only is human rights protection rarely the primary purpose of sanctions, but the Council generally avoids deliberation on the broader consequences of sanctions measures, particularly in terms of social, economic and cultural rights.[12] Compounding the issue, the effectiveness of

---

6 With respect to the-then Rhodesia, and South Africa. See discussion below at n 25.

7 See, for example, David Cortright and George A Lopez, *The Sanctions Decade, Assessing UN sanctions in the 1990s* (Lynne Rienner 2000).

8 See, for example, M M Ali and I H Shah, 'Sanctions and Childhood Mortality in Iraq' (2000) 335 *The Lancet* 1851-1857. A major pillar of this evidence has recently been challenged: see, for example, Tim Dyson and Valeria Cetorelli, 'Changing views on child mortality and economic sanctions in Iraq: a history of lies, damned lies and statistics' (2017) 2 *British Medical Journal Global Health* 1.

9 See discussion below at section 2.1.

10 See, for example, statements made by Judge Christoph Flugg, inter alia, reported at Daniel Boffey, 'UN court judge quits The Hague citing political interference' (*The Guardian*, 28 January 2018) available at <www.theguardian.com/law/2019/jan/28/international-criminal-court-icc-judge-christoph-flugge-quits-citing-political-interference-trump-administration-turkey> accessed 17 April 2019. See also discussion below on the interaction of ICC and sanctions investigations.

11 See discussion below.

12 As Mikael Erikson notes, 'contemporary UN sanctions policies suffer from a general lack of early and credible policy analysis, deficiencies in institutional coordination and information dissemination, weak implementation and a lack of evaluation/assessment'. Mikael Erikson, 'Unintended consequences of UN sanctions', in TJ Biersteker, Sue E.

sanctions continues to be questioned. A recent study of UN targeted sanctions by the Targeted Sanctions Consortium (TSC) determined that they were effective in achieving at least one of the three identified purposes of sanctions—coercion, constraint and signalling—only 22% of the time.[13]

Nevertheless, enthusiasm for sanctions as a tool of peace and security remains undimmed, and in the last seven years alone, the Council has established five new mandates.[14] The chapter posits that there is scope to leverage UN sanctions processes in support of the promotion and protection of human rights, particularly when understood as part of a dynamic system of international intervention. In calling for a broader framework of analysis, the chapter suggests a number of areas where human rights outcomes—both positive and negative—might be more effectively studied and pursued in order to contribute to fulfilling the Council's role in delivering on the vision in Art 28 UDHR of a 'social and international order in which the rights and freedoms set forth in this Declaration can be fully realized'.

2. Targeted Sanctions and Human Rights: Norms and Practice

Since 1966, the Security Council has established 30 sanctions regimes with widely different purposes. These have ranged from efforts to push conflict parties to the negotiating table, to counterterrorism, nuclear non-proliferation, and supporting criminal accountability mechanisms such as the Lebanon-focussed UN International Independent Investigation Commission.[15] To advance these purposes, the Council has deployed various types of sanctions measures, from diplomatic (e.g. withdrawal or expulsion of missions), sectoral (e.g. restriction on the fuel trade), commodity (e.g. prohibition on the export of charcoal), transport (restriction of movement by air or sea), to arms embargoes (prohibition on import of military material) and restrictions on the banking/financial sector. Increasingly, the Council also directly imposes asset freezes

Eckert and Marcos Tourinho (eds.), *Targeted Sanctions, The Impacts and Effectiveness of United Nations Action* (CUP 2016) 271.

13 Drawing on the work of 50 scholars and policy practitioners, the Targeted Sanctions Consortium (TSC) studied 23 targeted sanctions regimes between 1991 and 2014, through detailed analysis of 63 sanctions episodes. In assessing the effectiveness of sanctions, the TSC categorised the purpose of sanctions in three ways: to coerce a change in target's behaviour; to constrain access to resources needed to engage in proscribed activity; and to signal a violation of an international norm, stigmatizing targets. For a narrative presentation of the Consortium's framework of analysis and findings, as described by its principal researchers, see Biersteker and others, ibid.

14 Sanctions regimes have been imposed on the Central African Republic (CAR), Libya, Mali, South Sudan, and Yemen. It is notable, however, that Council agreement has been impossible around the Syrian conflict.

15 The Commission was charged with investigating the assassination of the former Prime Minister of Lebanon. Resolution 1636 mandated and established a Security Council Committee to register individuals designated by the Commission and the Government of Lebanon.

or travel bans on particular individuals and entities associated with prohibited conduct, an approach known as 'individualised sanctions'.[16]

At time of writing there were 14 targeted sanctions regimes in force. Each regime is governed by a sanctions committee comprised of members of the Council, chaired by a non-permanent member.[17] Since 1999, most committees have been supported by groups of technical experts (variably termed expert groups, panels or monitoring groups) performing a variety of functions, from collecting and coordinating exchange of information, to monitoring and analysing trends in peace and security, and conducting investigations. Until recently, each sanctions regime was geographically focused on a particular State or sub-region.[18] The ISIL (Da'esh) and Al-Qaida sanctions regime was the first mandate to have transnational scope.[19]

There are generally four elements within the country or situation-based sanctions cycle—all of which interact dynamically.

- *Determination of a threat to peace and security and establishment of the mandate:* This is the normative and signalling stage of the process where the Council sets out the challenge in peace and security terms, imposes general measures (e.g. arms embargo) and/or describes the types of future conduct ('listing' or 'designation' criteria), which will attract individualised sanctions measures (travel bans or asset freeze).
- *Investigation and/or monitoring*: During this period, Member States and expert panels collect and process information to assist the committee in tracking violations, analysing the context, and developing recommendations for the Council.
- *Independent reporting by expert groups (where mandated):* Depending on the particular mandate, reports drafted by expert groups contain (a) an overall analysis of the situation (b) details of investigations undertaken by the group (including narrative, documentary, testimony or forensic evidence and conclusions); recommendations (relating to the mandate itself or the context), and

---

16 States, international organisations, private and public entities, in addition to natural persons, all have an obligation to comply with these proscriptions. States have additional obligations to enforce sanctions, and in some cases, to take active measures to prevent sanctions violations.

17 For an overview of current sanctions regimes see < www.un.org/securitycouncil/sanctions/information> accessed 30 December 2018.

18 The sanctions regime applying to Sudan focuses on the situation in the three States in the region of Darfur. See resolution 1591 (2005).

19 Security Council Committee pursuant to resolutions 1267 (1999), 1989 (2011) and 2253 (2015) concerning ISIL (Da'esh), Al-Qaida, and associated individuals, groups, undertakings and entities.

statements of case setting out the information which the Council might wish to consider in making decisions on designations.[20]

- *Decision-making*: There are two types of Council sanctions decisions: those designating individuals and entities, and those addressing the regime as a whole. The latter generally contains the Council's view of the improvement or deterioration of the situation under focus and appropriate modification of the mandate; an indication of the roadmap towards lifting sanctions; and requests or directions to Member States, UN agencies or other actors with respect to the broader context within which sanctions are unfolding.

2.1. Human rights and the normative framework

The history of UN sanctions mandates reflects the Council's struggle with embracing its human rights responsibilities.[21] For example, in the same year as the Council was authorising Chapter VII action on humanitarian grounds in Somalia, some Member States were still insisting that the Council could not 'discuss human rights situations per se or make recommendations on matters outside its competence'.[22] The fortunes of human rights in Council politics have continued to fluctuate since then, rippling through various phases of sanctions law-making. The newest iteration of big-power Council fault lines around human rights were on display again recently in October 2018 when Russia succeeded in preventing a formal Council briefing on human rights in Syria by the UN High Commissioner for Human Rights.[23]

The protection of human rights is therefore rarely an explicit purpose of sanctions, notwithstanding the preambular language on the wellbeing of populations, which often frames Council sanctions resolutions. Human rights have tended to be an implicit component, sometimes expressed in terms of a secondary humanitarian goal or linked to attenuating civilian harm. The TSC

---

20 The reports of expert groups are published as documents of the Council. Parts of the report may strictly confidential and not released beyond the members of the UNSC. Statements of case are always strictly confidential.

21 For an overview of the history of the approach of the Council to human rights and Art 2 (7) of the UN Charter, see Security Council Report, *Human Rights and the Security Council—An Evolving Role* (Security Council Report 2016).

22 Permanent Representative of India, Provisional verbatim record of the three thousand one hundred and fifth meeting of the UN Security Council, 11 August 1992, S/PV.3105. The statement was delivered during a heated exchange on a request to permit the then Special Rapporteur on Iraq, Max van der Stoel to address the Council on the human rights situation in Iraq, a country under UN sanctions.

23 The International Committee of the Red Cross declared in April 2017 that an international armed conflict existed in Syria. See also, Amnesty International, statement, 'New low for the UN Security Council as Russia takes Syrian human rights off the table', 23 March 2018. The briefing ultimately took place in Arria formula. Arria formula Council meetings are informal meetings convened upon the initiative of a member to hear the views of entities or individuals with information on matters within the competence of the UN Security Council.

found, for example, that the protection of human rights could be identified as a general objective underlying 24 of the sanctions episodes they studied.[24]

Unfolding in the context of decolonisation struggles in Africa at the height of the Cold War, the first two comprehensive sanctions regimes imposed by the Council essentially addressed issues of fundamental human rights. Rights relating to the exercise of the right of self-determination and the constellation of violations connected to the crime of apartheid were at the heart of the first decision to impose economic and trade sanctions on Southern Rhodesia (now Zimbabwe) and later, an arms embargo on South Africa. In the resolutions establishing the mandates, the Council even made explicit reference to the UDHR and to the rights set out in the UN Charter.[25] The rhetoric of solidarity was, however, undermined by the subsequent widespread evasion and flouting of the measures, including by Council members, rendering sanctions minimally effective.[26] The appetite for sanctions waned.

In the 1990s, as large-scale violations of international humanitarian law came to characterise civil strife and internationalised conflicts in Somalia, Haiti, Rwanda, Iraq and the Former Yugoslavia, the Council once again opened up its Chapter VII sanctions toolbox. Citing the 'the heavy loss of human life and widespread material damage resulting from the conflict', in 1992 the Council imposed a general and complete arms embargo on Somalia.[27] Almost a year later, when the Council moved beyond sanctions to authorise the use of force in Somalia under Art 42 of the UN Charter it referenced the escalating 'magnitude of the human tragedy' and the 'obstacles being created

---

24 The TSC defines 'episodes' as periods in which sanctions regimes remain stable in terms of 'purposes, types, targets and contexts', TSC (n 13).

25 The Southern Rhodesian embargo was imposed further to the unilateral declaration of independence by the white minority regime; the South African embargo came in response to the increasing violence of the apartheid system. Security Council resolution 217 (1965) condemned the 'usurpation of power by a racist settler minority in Southern Rhodesia' (paragraph 3), and invited States to apply diplomatic, economic and military sanctions and an embargo on oil and petroleum products. Resolution 232 (1966) made the embargo mandatory and reaffirmed the 'the inalienable rights of the people of Southern Rhodesia to freedom and independence [...] and the legitimacy of their struggle to secure the enjoyment of their rights as set forth in the Charter of the United Nations' (paragraph 4). With respect to South Africa, resolution 418 (1977) condemned the government's 'resort to massive violence against and killings of the African people, including schoolchildren and students and others opposing racial discrimination' and 'for its acts of repression' (preamble). A later resolution reaffirmed 'the legitimacy of the struggle of the South African people for the elimination of apartheid and the establishment of a democratic society in accordance with their inalienable human and political rights as set forth in the Charter of the United Nations and the Universal Declaration of Human Rights', resolution 591 (1986), preamble.

26 See, for example, George W Shepherd, 'The Failure of the Sanctions against Rhodesia and the Effect on African States: A Growing Racial Crisis' (1968) 15 (1) *Africa Today* 8-12 and Bronwen Manby, 'South Africa: The Impact of Sanctions' (1992) 46 (1) *Journal of International Affairs* 193-217.

27 Resolution 733 (1992), preamble.

to the distribution of humanitarian assistance'.[28] The Council demanded that all 'parties movements and factions' facilitate humanitarian access and desist from breaches of humanitarian law.[29] The intimation that those who committed such acts would be 'held individually accountable', however, had little teeth: neither the sanctions instrument, nor the mandate authorising use of force, encompassed any measures to give effect to the Council's threat.[30]

The Council's flurry of sanctions-making during the 1990s coincided with intensified international efforts to hold individual perpetrators of international crimes to account. The Council's own activities included the establishment of *ad hoc* international criminal law mechanisms with respect to Rwanda, the former Yugoslavia and a hybrid Court in Sierra Leone—all countries the locus of UN sanctions at the time.[31] Nevertheless, the Council still remained reluctant to cite violations of 'human rights' or protection of civilians as a basis for sanctions action. It would also take another decade for concerns about impunity for violations of international humanitarian law to find expression in sanctions designation criteria.

As noted above, in 1999 the Council began to deploy a more discriminate, 'targeted' or 'smart' sanctions model. The multi-layered purposes and wide-ranging targets of this new sanctions' architecture gradually allowed the Council to embed protection of human rights objectives in sanctions mandates. This has been primarily achieved through the individualised sanctions mechanism, which has become the cornerstone of targeted sanctions. The first individualised sanctions listing criteria referencing human rights and international humanitarian law were broadly worded. In Resolution 1572 (2004) the Council mandated the imposition of sanctions on individuals threatening peace and national reconciliation in Côte d'Ivoire, in addition to, 'any other person determined as responsible for serious violations of human rights and international humanitarian law [...] [and] any other person who incites publicly hatred and violence'.[32] Later when the-then President Gbagbo refused to accept the results of the December 2010 election, the Council imposed individual targeted sanctions on Gbagbo, his wife, and three key supporters, determining that the 'attacks currently taking place in Côte d'Ivoire against the civilian population could amount to crimes against humanity.[33]

[28] Resolution 794 (1992), preamble.

[29] ibid, paras 2-4.

[30] ibid, para 5.

[31] The Council authorised the creation of the International Criminal Tribunal for the Former Yugoslavia (ICTY) in resolution 827 (1991) and the International Criminal Tribunal for Rwanda (ICTR) in resolution 955 (1994). Establishment of the Special Court for Sierra Leone was agreed by the UN and Sierra Leone further to a direction by the Council in resolution 1315 (2002).

[32] Resolution 1572 (2004), para 9.

[33] Resolution 1975 (2011), preamble. In January the UN Secretary-General's special advisers on the prevention of genocide and the responsibility to protect (R2P) had issued a joint statement calling for the Council to act. United Nations, Statement attributed to the UN Secretary-General's Special Advisers on the Prevention of Genocide and the Responsibility to Protect on the Situation in Côte d'Ivoire, 19 January 2011.

Since then the Council has issued progressively precise messages about the human rights and international humanitarian law violations of concern in each country context, from obstruction of humanitarian aid to the recruitment of children. In 2017, for example, the Council listed a range of conduct which could attract sanction in Mali, including 'the commission of acts of violence (including killing, maiming, torture, or rape or other sexual violence), abduction, enforced disappearance, forced displacement, or attacks on schools, hospitals, religious sites, or locations where civilians are seeking refuge'.[34] Profiting from trafficking in persons and smuggling of migrants and trafficking in cultural property in certain circumstances, was also declared a criterion for listing.[35] The Council has also expanded how it articulates the scope of its designation criteria to include not only those directly engaged in the prohibited conduct, but also other forms of responsibility, such as planning or participation. In the Libya regime, for example, the listing criteria include 'individuals and entities involved in or complicit in ordering, controlling, or otherwise directing, the commission of serious human rights abuses against persons'.[36] Individuals 'acting for or on behalf of or at the direction of' such individuals or entities are also potentially subject to designation.[37]

These recent human rights-related developments in sanctions law-making reflect advances in the treatment by the Council of three conflict-related themes which it has progressively placed at the centre of its agenda since the mid-nineties: children in armed conflict (CAC)—initially focussed on recruitment and use of children,[38] women peace and security—particularly sexual violence in conflict,[39] and protection of civilians in conflict.[40]

In resolution 1539 (2004) the Council first expressed its intention to impose sanctions on military and political leaders who did not sign and implement action plans to end violations against children in the context of the Council's annual reporting process.[41] Fifteen years later, recruitment and use of children is an explicit designation criterion in five sanctions regimes—Central African Republic (CAR), Democratic Republic of Congo (DRC), Mali, Somalia,

---

34 Resolution 2374 (2017), para 8 (f).

35 Resolution 2374 (2017), para 8 (c). An association with engagement in hostilities or obstructing the 2015 Mali peace agreement is required for application of the criterion.

36 Resolution 1970 (2011), para 22 (a).

37 ibid, para 22 (b).

38 The Council established its Council Working Group on Children in Armed Conflict in resolution 1612 (2005).

39 Resolution 1325 (2000).

40 The first Council resolution on the protection of civilians in armed conflict was adopted in 1995 (resolution 1265). In resolution 1296 (2000) the Council declared that 'the deliberate targeting of civilian populations or other protected persons and the committing of systematic, flagrant and widespread violations of international humanitarian and human rights law in situations of armed conflict may constitute a threat to international peace and security' (para 5).

41 Para 5 (c).

South Sudan.[42] Commission of sexual and gender-based violence (SGBV) is also a designation criterion in the same mandates, drafted on a 'stand-alone' basis for the first time in the CAR and South Sudan regimes in 2017 and 2018 respectively.[43] Three country regimes—Libya, Sudan and Yemen—also contain broad human rights, humanitarian law and atrocity designation criteria, which encompass these violations. It is not clear, however, that this emphasis on SGBV will continue. In November 2018, Russia and China objected to, and ultimately abstained in the vote on Resolution 2441 (2018) which introduced a specific designation criteria on SGBV into the Libya regime.[44]

It has only been in one sanctions regime, however, where protection of civilians from harm has found direct expression in the *objective* of the mandate from the outset, as articulated through the international responsibility to protect principle.[45] In Resolution 1970 (2011) on Libya the Council cited the commission of human rights and humanitarian law violations and the 'Libyan authorities' responsibility to protect its population' as the basis both for imposition of sanctions and a referral to the ICC.[46] In addition to a two-way arms embargo, the Council drafted the principal individual sanction designation to encompass involvement in 'the commission of serious human rights abuses [...] including by being involved in or complicit in planning, commanding, ordering or conducting attacks, in violation of international law, including aerial bombardments, on civilian populations and facilities'.[47] The package of measures adopted by the Council in response to attacks by the Libyan State on its own population reflected the convergence of an unusual set of interests. These are unlikely to be repeated, not least as a result of the chaos created by the broader international intervention in Libya which followed the resolution.[48]

---

42 CAR: resolution 2134 (2014) at para 37(c); DRC: Resolution 1807 (2008) at para 13; Mali: resolution 2374 (2017) at para 8 (g); Somalia: resolution 2002 (2011) at para 1(d); and South Sudan: resolution 2206 (2015) at para 7 (e). The conduct is also targeted implicitly in broader formulations relation to international humanitarian law.

43 In the past SGBV had been encompassed within broader criteria, masking its priority and potentially limiting the scope of conduct, which could found designations. The same formulation was used in the two regimes: '[p]lanning, directing, or committing acts involving sexual and gender-based violence' Resolution 2339 (2017), para 17 (c) and resolution 2428 (2018), para 14 (e).

44 Para 11.

45 This was the second sanctions regime imposed on Libya. The first lasted from 31 March 1992–12 September 2003. See, inter alia, George A Lopez, *Tools, tasks and tough thinking: Sanctions and R2P, A policy brief* (Global Centre for the Responsibility to Protect 2013).

46 Preamble.

47 Paragraph 22(a), Resolution 1970 (2011).

48 See, for example, remarks by Russia in the course of a discussion in the Sudan Sanctions Committee on large scale violations perpetrated against civilians participating in anti-government protests in Sudan in December 2018/January 2019: "raising the issue of anti-Government protests in Khartoum, which in itself constitutes interference in the country's internal affairs, comes under the rubric of geopolitical engineering and the West's well-known policies aimed at replacing regimes that it does not like. We all know what that led to in Libya, South Sudan and various other countries." UN Security Council, Seventy-fourth year, 8446th meeting, 17 January 2019 S/PV.8446.

3. Negative Unintended Consequences

Notwithstanding the normative developments outlined above, discussion of the positive interaction between human rights and targeted sanctions in the literature is scant, with most of the focus of human rights analysis on the negative impact of sanctions on individual human rights.[49] As noted above, the shift towards use of targeted measures in the mid-1990s was intended to avoid criticism that the Council's sanctions decisions were undermining basic human rights.[50] These charges have persisted. The TSC assessed, for example, that between 1999 and 2016 there were 'negative humanitarian consequences' in 44% of the targeted sanctions episodes they studied. They also observed 'increases in human rights violations' in 26%, and a 'strengthening of authoritarian rule' in 34%, of those episodes.[51] Erikson suggests that the latter two findings correlate with the assumption that 'the more pressure a target regime experience[s], the more internal repression it [will] exert'.[52]

The most significant public criticism of sanctions, however, continues to relate to their humanitarian assistance-related human rights toll, particularly in countries which are the subject of multiple sanctions regimes, and where less discriminating, sectoral sanctions are in place.[53] The Democratic People's Republic of Korea (DPKR), for example, is subject to broad UN sectoral and trade sanctions in addition to a variety of bilateral and regional sanctions regimes, all operating in parallel.[54] In late 2017, the then UN High Commissioner for Human Rights warned that tighter controls on bank transfers had 'caused a slowdown in UN ground operations, affecting the delivery of food rations, health kits and other humanitarian aid' to over 13 million people.[55] He urged the Council to adopt measures, which would mitigate the impact of sanctions on humanitarian access. Notwithstanding this and other calls, in 2017, and again in 2018, the Council expanded the scope of items and activities

---

49 See discussion below.

50 Art 1(3) and Art 55 of the UN Charter indicate that the UN, including the UNSC, is bound to respect 'human rights and fundamental freedoms for all' and that any derogation must comply inter alia with the principle of proportionality.

51 See Biersteker and others (n 12) 28.

52 Erikson (n 12) 205.

53 See, for example, Press release, Office of the High Commission on Human Rights, UN expert warns against harsh effects of sanctions and blockades on civilians, Geneva, 13 September 2018, with particular reference to Gaza, Iran, Syria, and Venezuela. UN sanctions against Iran were terminated in 2016 further to resolution 2231 (2015).

54 Including from the European Union, Japan, South Korea and the United States (US).

55 See, Statement by UN High Commissioner for Human Rights Zeid Ra'ad Al Hussein, Security Council briefing on the situation in the Democratic People's Republic of Korea, 8 December 2017. See, Press release, Office of the High Commission on Human Rights, 'UN expert warns against harsh effects of sanctions and blockades on civilians' Geneva, 13 September 2018.

covered by sanctions.[56] By 1 October 2018, the 2018 UN humanitarian 'Needs and Priorities Plan' for DPKR was only eleven per cent funded.[57]

Another challenge from the humanitarian perspective has been the development of sanctions regimes which target entities and individuals engaged in acts defined as 'terrorist'. In countries with acute humanitarian need—such as in Afghanistan and Somalia—encounters with these non-state actors can trigger fear-driven over-compliance with sanctions by humanitarian workers, generating a chilling effect on humanitarian access. Paying a fee at a road block, for example, can be interpreted as a sanctions breach and attract criminal penalty in the State where a charity is registered.[58] On the other side of the conflict equation, the individuals who are potential targets of sanctions can perceive humanitarian workers as hostile agents of the international community, further paralysing humanitarian access. Meanwhile, members of the local community in exile are also subject to suspicion of involvement in terrorist financing when they make financial transfers home to bridge the humanitarian funding gap. In response to these concerns in the context of the Somalia sanctions regime, the Council created a modest 'carve out' for humanitarian operations in 2010. This provided that 'the payment of funds necessary to ensure the timely delivery of urgently needed humanitarian assistance' by the UN or specified partners would not be subject to the assets freeze imposed on designated entities.[59] This limited exemption, however, has not been incorporated into other unilateral sanctions regimes applicable in Somalia—such as the US—undermining the operation of the carve out. Neither has the Council adopted the Somalia carve out mechanism into other sanctions regimes: the cooperative political dynamics at play in the Council on Somalia are not as present elsewhere.

In 2014 the UN Human Rights Council appointed a Special Rapporteur on the negative impact of unilateral coercive measures on the enjoyment of human rights.[60] Although addressing unilateral measures and not multilateral sanctions, the decision reflected renewed concerns about human rights and sanctions in general. The International Court of Justice (ICJ) has also begun to address the matter. In July 2018, in a case dealing with unilateral sanctions imposed

---

56 S/2017/829, 2 October 2017 and S/2017/822, 29 September 2017. See, for example, International Federation of the Red Cross, Press release, 'DPRK: Deadly heatwave threatening lives of children and elderly' 10 August 2018.

57 For the latest information on UN humanitarian funding in DPKR see <https://fts.unocha.org> accessed 30 December 2018.

58 UN Security Council Resolution 2161 (2014) provides, for example, that payment of 'costs incurred with respect to transportation and lodging' can be considered as proscribed provision of economic resources in the context of al-Qaeda and its associates.

59 Resolution 1916 (2010) as renewed annually. In his most recent report to the Somalia Sanctions Committee, the Under-Secretary-General for Humanitarian Affairs and Emergency Relief Coordinator noted that if the 'carve out' was not renewed it would likely 'result in delays in the delivery of humanitarian assistance in areas controlled by non-State armed groups, which would put affected communities at risk of loss of lives and livelihoods and of exposure to suffering', S/2018/896.

60 Resolution adopted by the Human Rights Council, 27/21, Human Rights and Unilateral Coercive Measures, 26 September 2014.

by the United Arab Emirates (UAE) on Qatar the ICJ granted a number of provisional measures sought by Qatar. The Court noted that 'at least some of the rights asserted by Qatar under Art 5 of CERD [International Convention on the Elimination of All Forms of Racial Discrimination] are plausible'.[61] Later, on 3 October 2018, in a case addressing US sanctions on Iran, the Court ordered the US to remove impediments to the free export to Iran of medicines, foodstuffs, agricultural commodities and specified civil aviation equipment.[62]

As the ICJ cases move forward for substantive consideration there is potential for the Council to be encouraged to weigh analogous human rights considerations in its own sanctions practice, particularly those relating to social, economic and cultural rights. Article 22 UDHR makes clear that everyone 'is entitled to realization, through national effort and international co-operation and in accordance with the organization and resources of each State, of the economic, social and cultural rights indispensable for his dignity and the free development of his personality'. In 2015 the High-Level Review of Sanctions recommended that the Council should conduct regular sanctions impact assessments and 'commission pre-assessments of the humanitarian and socio-economic effects when contemplating imposition of broad sectoral or financial sanctions'.[63] These proposals have not yet been formally endorsed by the Council.

3.1 The human rights of individuals' subject to designation or mentioned in connection with potential sanctions violations

A second area of criticism of sanctions relates to considerations underpinning Articles 8 and 10 of the UDHR—the right to an effective remedy and the right to a fair hearing. As will be discussed below, these have been at the centre of the debate on sanctions conducted by human rights lawyers during the last decade.

Sanctions designations are rarely the product of fully reasoned, transparent decision making, involving due process considerations—they are primarily political decisions made in a political context. Particularly when conduct related to 'terrorism' is under scrutiny, designation decisions are often based on confidential information. As a result, until recently, the subject of a designation was rarely able to ascertain details of the reason for listing or have an opportunity to address the allegations. It was European human rights litigation which finally forced the Council to begin to address the matter, triggered by a case brought

---

61 International Court of Justice, *Application of the International Convention on the Elimination of All Forms of Racial Discrimination* (Qatar v. United Arab Emirates) Request for indication of provisions measures, Order 23 July 2018. The orders made related to the question of family separation, the impact of sanctions on education, and access to justice, for Qataris in the UAE.

62 International Court of Justice, Alleged violations of the 1955 Treaty of Amity, Economic Relations and Consular Rights, Islamic Republic of Iran v United States of America, Request for the Indication of Provisional Measures, Order, 3 October 2018.

63 Compendium of the High-level Review of United Nations Sanctions, June 2015, A/69/941 S/2015/432, paras 135 and 136.

by Yassin Abdullah Kadi citing European human rights legal protections. Mr Kadi had been subject to a worldwide asset-freeze and travel ban under the-then Al Qaeda UN sanctions regime—all without being informed of the reasons for his listing or being given an opportunity to challenge the measure, including at the point when the European Union issued its implementing regulation. In September 2008, the European Court of Justice (ECJ), as it was then known, found in favour of Mr Kadi, declaring *inter alia*, that the guarantee of effective judicial protection within the EU legal order required that grounds for listing must be communicated to the designated entity.[64]

The *Kadi* case and a subsequent deluge of litigation by individuals similarly situated had huge implications for sanctions practice.[65] First, in 2006, the Council created the Office of the Focal Point for De-listing (FPD) to which individuals and entities could apply to trigger a review of their designation.[66] A few years later, the Office of the Ombudsperson to the ISIL (Da'esh) & Al-Qaida Sanctions Committee came into being.[67] The Ombudsperson is an independent and impartial office with the capacity to substantively review requests from individuals, groups or entities seeking to be removed from the ISIL/Al Qaida list. The Office has the mandate to gather and analyse information, compile a report and present arguments supporting a recommendation to the request to the Committee. Unless challenged by a consensus in the Committee or a unanimous vote in the Council—scenarios, which have not yet arisen—the Ombudsperson's decisions are considered final.[68] In contrast to the Ombudsperson, however, the FPD, the equivalent entity for all other sanctions regimes has no substantive review function, acting only as a 'post box' and liaison between Member States and the petitioner.[69] Although these two developments are significant, particularly in terms of how the UN Security Council felt constrained to respond

---

64 Joined Cases C-402/05 P and C-415/05 P, *Yassin Abdullah Kadi and Al Barakaat International Foundation v. Council of the European Union and Commission of the European Communities* [2008] ECR I–6351.

65 According to an EU study, by 2017, 'cases regarding restrictive measures had [become] the second most frequent issue heard by the [ECJ]'. European Union, Directorate General for External Policies of the Union, *Targeted sanctions against individuals on grounds of grave human rights violations – impact, trends and prospects at EU level* (Policy Department for External Relations, 2018).

66 Resolution 1730 (2006).

67 The Office of the Ombudsperson was established by Security Council resolution 1904 (2009) and extended by subsequent mandates. For an independent assessment of the effectiveness of the work of the Ombudsperson as of 2017 see Saura-EStapà J, 'The UN Security Council Ombudsperson: an original institution still under construction' (2017) 54 *Revista Catalana de Dret Públic* 185-195.

68 See also Office of the Ombudsperson to the Security Council, *Historical Guide of the Ombudsperson Process through Security Council resolutions and Reports of the Office of the Ombudsperson to the Security Council* (updated March 2018) available at <www.un.org/securitycouncil/sites/www.un.org.securitycouncil/files/historical_guide_ombudsperson_process_march_2018.pdf> accessed 30 December 2018.

69 For an overview of current procedures before, and jurisdictional scope of, the FPD, see <https://www.un.org/sc/suborg/en/sanctions/delisting> accessed 1 December 2018. Although the FPD is the only recourse for those designated under regimes outside ISIL (Da'esh) & Al-Qaida, it also has limited functions with respect to the latter list.

to the human rights-related findings of a body to which it did not strictly owe compliance, the challenges identified in *Kadi* remain. As a result, only one of the 14 sanctions regimes currently in force—the ISIL (Da'esh) & Al-Qaida regime—offers listees recourse to an impartial review.[70] Despite calls by non-permanent members of the Council for an extension of the Ombudsperson's remit in order to erode this effectively two-tier sanctions practice, permanent members continue to resist the development.[71]

UN sanctions framework and practice have responded in other ways to developments in EU human rights litigation. These include the publication of 'narrative summaries of reasons' for listing—including with respect to past decisions,[72]and the incorporation of explicit humanitarian and other exemptions in how travel ban and asset freeze measures are contoured.[73] Meanwhile the courts continue to expand their scrutiny and challenge Council practice. In March 2017, for example, the General Court of the European Union found that the reason given in the Council's narrative summary for the listing of Aisha Qaddafi—'Daughter of Muammar Qadhafi, Closeness of association with regime'—was a 'general, stereotypical formulation' and not sufficiently 'individual, specific and concrete'.[74] This resulted in the annulment of the EU implementing regulation giving force to the Security Council decision on Qaddafi.

At a more granular level, the jurisprudence has also affected the way in which sanctions expert panels operate. In particular it has altered the approach taken by panels to the development of statements of case, how they rely on open source material, and how material presented to the Council is classified. Whereas in the past, for example, information presented confidentially to the Council could be relied upon as a basis for designation recommendations, the need for greater transparency has forced new calculations around the safety of interlocutors and the confidentiality of lines of investigation.

Additional issues of procedural fairness remain.[75] One area which has not yet

70 The Council's ability to reject the Ombudsperson's recommendation undermines the independence of the function. For example, on the same day that Ali Ahmed Nur Jim'ale was delisted by ISIL/Daesh Committee further to a recommendation of the Ombudsperson he was listed under the Somalia Eritrea sanctions' regime. Mr Jimale was ultimately delisted from the latter regime in March 2014.

71 See, for example, H.E. Ambassador Geir O Pedersen, Permanent Representative of Norway, 'Security Council working methods–targeted sanctions', Statement on behalf of the group of Like-Minded States on targeted sanctions, delivered before the President of the Security Council on 23 October 2014. For other proposals relating to improving due process see High-Level Review Compendium (n 61) 30.

72 See <https://www.un.org/sc/suborg/en/sanctions/narrative-summaries> accessed 1 December 2018.

73 See, for example, resolution 2399 (2018), paras 14–19.

74 T-681/14, *Aisha Muammer Mohamed El-Qaddafi v. Council of the European Union*, 28 March 2017, ECLI: EU: T:2017:227, 58.

75 For a detailed discussion of recent jurisprudence, including decisions with respect to non-terrorism related listings, and detailed recommendations for reform, see Rebecca

been litigated—and is unlikely to be due to absence of potential jurisdiction—are the human rights implications of mention in an expert panel report, without subsequent designation. Mere mention of a name in a report in association with an alleged violation can have a significant impact on the reputation and finances of an individual or entity—even if sanctions do not immediately result, the threat remains. The only currently available recourse is for an expert panel to ensure that an opportunity to comment on the allegations is given and taken into consideration in the text presented to the Council. Expert panels generally provide an 'opportunity to reply' to individuals and entities who are likely to be identified as responsible for violations in a report to the Council.[76] There also appears to be some scope for correction of fact after publication of the report: in one instance in 2016, for example, the Council took the unusual step of issuing a statement clarifying that a person named in a Somalia expert panel report was not involved in a suicide bombing.[77]

Ensuring experts adhere to the highest standards of evidence collection and analysis is critical in preventing instances in which sanctions or de facto sanctions are improperly imposed. The standard used by the Ombudsperson in assessing requests for delisting, for example, is 'sufficient information to provide a reasonable and credible basis for the listing presently'. This is intended 'to balance the individual rights to privacy, freedom of movement and property with the right to life and security and the obligation on the Security Council to protect'.[78] It would be useful to encourage the adoption of this standard for all expert panels across the board—practice is not uniform.

3.2 The human rights of individuals engaged within the sanctions process more broadly

Individuals who assist expert panels do so at their own cost and risk and there are instances in which those who have engaged have been killed—although issues of causation are unclear.[79] The Council is now more aware of the consequences of cooperation, including with respect to the human rights of interlocutors who participate in sanctions processes. In 2009, the Council added 'obstruction of the work of the Monitoring Group' as a basis for designation after an attack on an individual who had provided information to the UN Somalia Eritrea Monitoring

Brubaker, James Cockayne, and Nadeshda Jayakody, *Fairly clear risks, Protecting UN sanctions' legitimacy and effectiveness through fair and clear procedures* (United Nations University 2008).

76 See, for example, detailed 'Opportunity to Reply' and 'Investigative' methodologies set out in Annexes to the 2017 Final Report of the Panel of Experts on Yemen S/2017/18.

77 UN Security Council statement, 'Security Council Sanctions Committee on Somalia and Eritrea Communicates Additional Information from Monitoring Group on 2014 Final Report', 14 April 2016, TSC/12322.

78 See, Kimberly Prost, 'The Office of the Ombudsperson; a Case for Fair Process' (2012) Working Paper No 4.3 presented at the United Nations Security Council, Sanctions and the Rule of Law Workshop held at the Australian Mission to the United Nations, New York on 31 May 2012. Judge Kimberly Prost held the position of Ombudsperson between July 2010 and July 2015.

79 Confidential information known to the author.

Group (UNSEMG).[80] Related to this, the question of how informed consent is communicated and managed with respect to witnesses and interlocutors in different contexts has critical human rights and protection implications. There is more to be done. Use of confidential sourcing is one of the few tools available to expert groups to secure the safety of interlocutors. Classification of material as confidential, however, can undermine perceptions of the report's credibility, and—although rarely in practice—the ability of targets to respond to accusations. Expert panels also do their best to liaise with relevant UN protection mandates, such as the UN High Commissioner for Refugees, but there are no formal referral procedures.[81] The killing of two expert panel members in the DRC's Kasai region in 2017 was an acute reminder of the danger to which those involved in sanctions investigations can be exposed. No one has yet been held responsible, although a trial of two dozen militia members, a number of whom are suspected State agents, recommenced in August 2018.[82] The Council has now begun to include attacks on members of expert groups as a listing criterion in new and renewed mandates.[83]

4. Protection of Human Rights and Sanctions Measures in Practice

Occasions where the effectiveness of sanctions has been assessed in positive human rights terms are few. The scholars of the TSC found that where protection of human rights was a general objective of a sanctions episode, effective coercion was only identifiable in two episodes of the regimes they studied (Cote d'Ivoire and DRC). Where target constraint was the intent, and human rights among the objectives, only two episodes were classified as effective (Libya and DRC). Signalling was a more successful purpose where human rights was a sanctions objective—there were three episodes in Libya, Cote d'Ivoire, and DRC which were identified as effective. It is indicative of the overall perception of the general impact of sanctions with respect to human rights, however, that the TSC's framework of assessment for unintended consequences does not contemplate unexpected *positive* human rights outcomes.[84]

One of the difficulties in approaching this question is the challenge of assessing

---

80 Resolution 1907 (2009), para 15 (e).

81 An Assistant Secretary-General for human rights has been designated to lead UN efforts to put an end to intimidation and reprisals against those cooperating with the UN on human rights. The methods available to the ASG, however, are rarely appropriate to the sanctions' context. See <www.ohchr.org/EN/Issues/Reprisals/Pages/ReprisalsIndex.aspx> accessed 30 December 2018.

82 Initial UN investigations were inconclusive. See Aaron Ross, 'Who killed U.N. experts in Congo? Confidential prosecutor's file offers clues', *Reuters*, 17 December 2017.

83 See for example, Resolution 2441 (2018), para 11.

84 The TSC *Sanctions APP* identifies them as: strengthening one faction, strengthening authoritarian rule, rally round the flag, corruption, legacy of criminalisation, burdens on neighbouring States, humanitarian consequences, increase in human rights violations and increase in state enforcement capacity. The TSC sanctions app is available on Google Play, https://play.google.com/store/apps/details?id=air.com.fcolaco.sanctions&hl=en.

causality between the sanctions purpose attained—coercion, constraint or signalling—and the objectives of, and actions taken pursuant to, the sanctions measure. This is compounded where, as is increasingly the case, other international interventions are deployed in parallel—whether unliteral or multilateral actions. As Eriksson points out, '[t]here is seldom a linear relation between a dependent and an independent variable in the sanctions policy practice, and coding social events more generally can rarely catch or perfectly mirror reality'.[85] In particular, there may be a gap between how primary and secondary human rights objectives of Council intervention are identified, tending to constrain the scope of the analysis. For example, while the TSC analysis classifies human rights as a general purpose of the first three episodes of the Somalia sanctions regime, it does not do so for the fourth or fifth episodes: it was during these latter periods, however, when the Council explicitly added the commission of human rights and international humanitarian law violations to the designation criteria.

Another factor complicating assessment of the human rights impact of sanctions is the fact that the human rights elements of the evolving sanctions normative framework have been little, and inconsistently, activated by the Council. For example, it is difficult to discern a clear pattern in the approach by the Council to whether or not violations of human rights or humanitarian law are sufficient on their own to ground designations. At the level of the sanctions' framework itself, for example, the CAR, Libya, South Sudan and Yemen regimes require—or required when first drafted—a link to be found between the human rights or humanitarian law conduct at issue and a threat to the peace, security and stability of the country.[86] In 2016, the criteria were decoupled for the CAR but continue to be maintained in the other regimes.[87]

Beyond the question of the sanctions' framework, in terms of practice, it might be assumed that the Council would act and message consistently across sanctions regimes, drawing on evidence-based analysis of what works, close attention to context, and common standards. This not the case, however, whether between sanctions mandates, or with respect to the Council's broader activities in pursuit of international peace and security. For example, the Council regularly requests UN special mechanisms with mandates relating to SGBV to address sanctions committees, including inviting them to suggest individuals and entities for listing.[88] Nevertheless parties listed in the annex to the annual report of the Secretary-General on conflict-related sexual violence,

---

85 Erikson (n 12) 204.

86 The Yemen approach is a common formulation: 'individuals or entities [...] engaging in or providing support for acts that threaten the peace, security or stability of Yemen' which acts 'may include, but are not limited to [...] acts that violate applicable international human rights law or international humanitarian law, or acts that constitute human rights abuses'. Resolution (2140) 2014, paragraph 17–18.

87 Resolution 2262 (2016), paras 12–13.

88 During the High-Level Review of Sanctions, it was even recommended that the Council should 'include in the mandate and in existing mechanisms for the protection of women and girls an obligation to report perpetrators and their military and political

particularly those deemed "persistent violators" are rarely designated in country regimes.[89] The situation is the same with respect to child recruitment and use; it is only in the DRC where listings by the Council have reflected engagement with these mechanisms. The DRC Sanctions Committee Guidelines, in fact, explicitly provide for designations on the basis of information received from the Council Working Group or the Special Representative of the Secretary General on CAC.[90]

Similarly, between country mandates, the same conduct is often also treated differently, notwithstanding the fact that all sanctions committees have the same membership. While SGBV crimes have been the basis for listing in CAR, DRC, Libya, and South Sudan, for example, the Council has repeatedly ignored information provided by expert panels on the widespread use of sexual violence in the Libya, Sudan and Yemen conflicts.[91] One potential approach to tackling this disconnect in such a divided global order is the establishment of thematic, rather than polarising country-based, mandates. The transnational nature of enquiries on a theme such as human trafficking, for example, could soften political resistance to designations and increase the number of Member States assisting investigations.

Although at the outset the Council may agree on a robust mandate, it is often subsequently unable to muster the collective political will to activate the measures. The reality is that the particular political and economic interests of Council Member States are all the more at play when it comes to enforcing the mandate. In Somalia, for example, there is a broad swathe of State and non-State actors, both national and international, who are consistently identified as responsible for an extensive list of prohibited conduct, spanning the spectrum from corruption to unlawful export of charcoal to forced displacement. In the twenty-six years of the mandate, however, only a few individuals connected with Al-Shabaab or its affiliates have been designated. With State-building an underlying goal of the Somalia sanctions framework, the Council appears reluctant to target those connected either with the Somalia State apparatus or with the multiple Member States engaged in Somalia. Economic considerations are also pivotal. Despite repeated presentation of compelling evidence of horrific crimes connected with piracy, for example, the Council has left national

---

leaders to expert groups and to the relevant sanctions committees'. High-Level Review Compendium (n 63) para 143.

89 Pramila Patten, 'Moving from a Culture of Impunity to a Culture of Deterrence: The Use of Sanctions in Addressing Sexual Violence in Conflict' (2018) UN ECOSOC Chamber, 22 October 2018.

90 See the Guidelines of the Committee for the conduct of its work, as adopted by the Committee on 6 August 2010, available at <www.un.org/securitycouncil/sites/www.un.org.securitycouncil/files/1533_committee_guidelines.pdf> accessed 30 December 2018.

91 See reports of the expert panels on Libya, Sudan, and Yemen at https://www.un.org/securitycouncil/ accessed 30 December 2018.

jurisdictions to pursue the guilty: considerations relating to insurance and ransom payment take priority.[92]

One outcome of the Council's struggle with the contours of its human rights mandate is that its sanctions gaze is rarely focussed on the commission of human rights and humanitarian law violence by State actors. Although the Council's designation of Presidents (or former Presidents) in Cote D'Ivoire and Libya are clear exceptions, non-State actors with weak international constituencies have been the overweening focus of the Council where human rights, humanitarian law or humanitarian obstruction grounds are at issue. This is slowly changing. The South Sudan list now contains a number of army officers and members of the government who are cited, inter alia, for violations against civilians.[93] In the DRC the first designation of a government-ally was made in February 2018.[94] In June 2018, six individuals were listed for involvement in human trafficking in Libya including one government official.[95]

There is one common theme, however, across regimes when it comes to individual sanctions for human rights and humanitarian law violations. The Council is still reluctant to designate where they are the sole potential grounds for listing. As Happold notes, 'in practice participation in violations of human rights and humanitarian law does not, of itself, amount to conduct justifying the imposition of targeted sanctions: rather it seems to be an exacerbating factor'.[96] With respect to the crime of child recruitment and use, for example, individuals have been designated on this basis in the CAR, DRC and South Sudan regimes, but then only in the context of other violations.[97] The situation is the same with respect to reference to SGBV crimes in designations for those regimes—and Libya. It is clear therefore that there is a constantly oscillating

---

92 In 2013, authorities lured the then self-proclaimed 'retired' pirate network leader Mohamed Abdi Hassan (Afweyne) to Belgium where he was later tried and sentenced to 20 years in prison. Afweyne had been a consistent subject of investigation and reporting by the UNSEMG.

93 See <www.un.org/securitycouncil/sanctions/2206/materials/summaries> accessed 30 December 2018, for the narrative summaries for listing in the South Sudan regime. At time of writing both the South Sudan Deputy Minister for Defence and the Army Chief of Staff were subject to measures.

94 This listing came after multiple designations of DRC political and security officials by EU and US sanctions regimes. See narrative summary of reasons for listing at <www.un.org/securitycouncil/sanctions/1533/materials/summaries> accessed 30 December 2018.

95 See United Nations, 'Security Council Committee concerning Libya Adds Six Individuals to Its Sanctions List', Press Release, 7 June 2018, TSC/13371. The listing criteria cited included paragraph 4(a) of resolution 2174 (2014) viz., 'planning, directing, or committing, acts that violate applicable international human rights law or international humanitarian law, or acts that constitute human rights abuses'.

96 Mathew Happold, 'UN sanctions and human rights and humanitarian law devices' in Van Der Herick L (ed.), *Research Handbook on UN Sanctions and International Law* (Edward Elgar 2017) 143.

97 See, for example, David S Koller and Miriam Eckenfels-Garcia, 'Using targeted sanctions to end violations against children in armed conflict' (2015) 33 *Boston University International Law Journal* 1.

gap between the normative framework for sanctions, and the practice of the Council. It is also difficult to extrapolate a consistent Council theory of how sanctions measures are intended to impact the situation on the ground from its practice. Happold, for example, has challenged the containment value of sanctions when it comes to individual human rights violators in particular, noting that 'it is perhaps best to see the TSC's use of sanctions as human rights devices, and indeed the Council's activities in this area in general, as engaging in what has been called a signalling or stigmatising function'.[98] A more detailed assessment of the context for, and impact of, designations made on human rights, humanitarian law or related grounds would help highlight these disconnects and encourage more effective deployment of the emerging framework.

5. Areas for Exploration

In the context of an inconsistent Council practice where sanction measures themselves are unlikely to be wielded to advance human rights, how can the signalling effect of sanctions be leveraged? Three areas are discussed below: interaction of sanctions processes with other international human rights and accountability mechanisms, the operation of expert groups, and the role of third parties in reducing the likelihood of violations.

5.1 Interaction with other human rights/accountability interventions

Sanctions today are usually deployed as only one component of a range of international and regional interventions, from UN peacekeeping and political missions, to accountability mechanisms. ICC situation investigations, for example, are currently unfolding in five countries under UN sanction.[99] In two of these, the Council referred the situations to the ICC and imposed sanctions in the same resolution (Sudan and Libya). In CAR, the Council simultaneously imposed an arms embargo and established an international commission of enquiry—all while an ICC investigation was ongoing.[100]

There has been variable practice when it comes to interactions between the processes. In CAR, for example, the existence of ICC charges was later noted by the Council in its designation of Joseph Kony.[101] In the DRC, the trajectory was reversed, all six cases initiated by the Court have been in respect of individuals

98 Happold (n 96) 145.

99 Libya and Sudan were referred to the ICC by the Council in resolution 1970 (2011) and resolution 1593 (2005) respectively. The situations in CAR, DRC and Mali were referred by their own governments.

100 Resolution 2127 (2013), paragraph 24. The CAR case was unusual in that the Government of CAR had referred a previous situation of violence in 2002/2003 to the ICC in December 2004. It subsequently in May 2014 also referred the situation since 2012 to the Court.

101 See narrative summary of the listing for Joseph Kony available at <www.un.org/securitycouncil/sanctions/2127/materials/summaries/individual/joseph-kony> accessed 30 December 2018.

previously designated by the Council.[102] In the Libya case, ICC charges also followed particularly swiftly on designation for three key individuals.[103] In other situations, however, there has been no overlap between the individuals targeted by the two mechanisms. In the Sudan sanctions context, for example, a polarised Council has failed to reinforce the investigative direction of the Court, notwithstanding information received from the Sudan expert panel.[104] At the same time, on the ground, there has been significant interaction between some expert groups and the ICC in terms of sharing information, within respective mandate constraints.[105]

A more detailed analysis of how the two processes interact could improve sanctions practice. One of the findings of the TSC, for example, was that where international and hybrid international criminal mechanisms were used alongside sanctions, sanctions were deemed 'effective' in 60 per cent of such episodes, particularly with respect to constraining and signalling.[106] The recent decision by the ICC Assembly of States parties to activate the Court's jurisdiction over the crime of aggression creates additional impetus.[107] There is now a much larger intersection between the overall object of sanctions—restoring international peace and security—and conduct under ICC scrutiny. There are significant outstanding issues, however, around the optimal deployment of the two tools, from questions of impact and effectiveness, to procedure and sequencing, and how the various actors and organs involved in the process engage with each other.[108] What should be the implication of the acquittal by the ICC of a Council-listed individual, for example, where the underlying conduct was substantially the same as that cited in the narrative summary for listing?

One critical issue to be borne in mind is that although the realms of sanctions action and international accountability mechanisms overlap, they do not fully share the same objectives. While the former aims primarily to constrain *future* behaviour, the latter is fixated, at least in its procedural focus, on determining *past* responsibility. This can produce contradictory dynamics. Bentall is of the

---

[102] See <www.icc-cpi.int/drc> accessed 30 December 2018.

[103] For example, in June 2011, the ICC issued arrest warrants for three individuals who had been on the Libya list since 26 February of that year, Gaddafi himself, his son Saif Al-Islam and Abdullah Al-Sanussi. See <www.un.org/securitycouncil/sanctions/1970/materials/summaries> accessed 30 December 2018.

[104] For an overview of the progress of investigations see Prosecutor of the International Criminal Court, Twenty-Eighth Report of the Prosecutor of the International Criminal Court to the United Nations Security Council pursuant to UNSCR 1593 (2005).

[105] See, for example, the Relationship Agreement between the UN and ICC and the UN, 'Best Practices Manual for United Nations – International Criminal Court Cooperation', 26 September 2016.

[106] Paul Bentall, 'United Nations targeted sanctions and other policy tools: diplomacy, legal, use of force' in Biersteker et al (n 12) 97.

[107] International Criminal Court, press release, 'Assembly activates Court's jurisdiction over crime of aggression', 15 December 2017.

[108] See, for example, the discussion in Enrico Carisch, Sue Eckert, Loraine Rickard-Martin, Background Paper, High Level Review of UN Sanctions available at <www.hlr-unsanctions.org/main/background> accessed 30 December 2018.

view, for example, that an ICC referral triggers an inexorable legal process which forces the Council to cede 'control and agency', reducing the 'potential bargaining' power of the Council with the target and thus the effectiveness of the sanctions measure.[109] As Lopez notes, 'sanctions work when they not only enrage, but actually engage, their targets and imposers'.[110]

How sanction measures, and the sanctions process itself, interacts with human rights monitoring and reporting entities in the context of the UN's broader peace and security mandate is another area which would reward study.[111] Article 55 of the UN Charter sees 'universal respect for, and observance of, human rights' as integral to the 'creation of conditions of stability and well-being which are necessary for peaceful and friendly relations among nations'. The 2015 High Level Review of UN Sanctions found that the inclusion of human rights abuses as designation grounds had created a 'productive and growing relationship between the sanctions system and Council-mandated human rights actors'.[112] There are still challenges, however, both on the ground and in the Council Chamber.

As UN operations in the field become increasingly integrated across peace, political, humanitarian and human rights functions, the Council has begun to explicitly require sanctions expert panels and UN entities to cooperate.[113] For example, in January 2018, the Council extended the mandate of the expert panel in the CAR regime, instructing it to:

> ...[C]ollect, in cooperation with MINUSCA [United Nations Multidimensional Integrated Stabilization Mission in the Central African Republic], and report to the Committee acts of incitement to violence, in particular on an ethnic or religious basis, that undermine the peace, stability or security of the CAR and identify those perpetrators.[114]

The impact of intertwining mandates needs to be carefully assessed.

On the plus side, panel experts with their singular mandate can assume the

---

[109] Bentall (n 106) 99.

[110] Lopez (n 45).

[111] See for example, the request by the Council to the Secretary-General in conjunction with the High Commissioner on Human Rights (HCHR) 'to take appropriate steps to increase the number of human rights monitors deployed in the CAR' in the resolution commencing the sanctions regime. Resolution 2127 (2013), para 26. Nevertheless, there has been little exploration of the practicalities of this dimension: it is not mentioned at all, for example, in Cortright D, Lopez GA, and Gerber-Stellingwerf, L, *Integrating UN Sanctions for Peace and Security* (The Sanctions and Security Research Program University of Notre Dame 2010).

[112] High-Level Review Compendium (n 63) 46.

[113] An integrated mission is a strategic partnership between a multi-dimensional United Nations peacekeeping operation and the UN Country Team, under the leadership of the Special Representative of the Secretary General (SRSG) and the Deputy SRSG/Resident or Humanitarian Coordinator.

[114] Resolution 2399 (2018), para 32(g).

burden of investigation where it is too sensitive for UN entities and their partners to engage on the ground. They can highlight cases and situations in detail, including identifying responsible actors, and putting the experience of communities directly before the Council. Sanctions investigations can also generate pressure on targets to take steps which are being urged by other UN actors: sharing of information by sanctions investigators, for example, can buttress efforts under the UN's Human Rights Due Diligence policy to persuade State security forces to adopt mitigation measures which tend to reduce violations.[115] Thus the process of investigations itself can produce a modifying effect on the conduct of potential targets without requiring Council consensus on particular measures. This interaction can also, however, present challenges. At the field level, multiple entities may be seeking information on the same events and in relation to the same conduct. This can have implications in the short term for the handling and analysis of evidence, but also for the safety of UN staff, partners and communities if collaboration with sanctions investigators is assumed by hostile targets. Operational effectiveness may also be vulnerable to the investigative gaze of sanctions. Officials from the UN Office of the High Commissioner for Human Rights may be rightly concerned, for example, that association with sanctions could damage a capacity-building relationship with the police.

There may also be issues be relating to confidentiality and protection where an undertaking from a UN entity comes up against a contrary demand from a sanctions mandate. Operating under Chapter VII, the Council can, in theory, compel cooperation with its investigations. At one point in the Somalia context, for example, there was a standoff between the UN Children's Agency, UNICEF and the expert panel over the sharing of primary data on grave violations committed against children collected through the UN Monitoring and Reporting Mechanism (MRM).[116] In addition to concerns about the confidentiality undertakings embedded in the monitoring process itself, there was alarm at the implication that a humanitarian agency would be seen as an extension of the Council, undermining perceptions of its neutrality, impartiality and independence—and potentially putting staff in harm's way. The tensions in this case unfortunately spilled over into the Council, with the Council expressing 'concern' and 'urging enhanced information sharing and dialogue'.[117] The matter was eventually resolved but it illustrates some of the difficulties in managing interactions between entities which may seem to have similar objectives but where multiple other obligations must be honoured.

---

115 Human rights due diligence policy on United Nations support to non-United Nations security forces, available at <www.ohchr.org/Documents/HRBodies/SP/AMeetings/20thsession/IdenticalLetterSG25Feb2013_en.pdf> accessed 30 December 2018. If after engagement by the UN with the entity, the appropriate mitigation measures are not taken and violations persist, cooperation must be suspended.

116 The MRM was established by Resolution 1612 (2005).

117 Resolution 2111 (2013). The panel had told the Council, rather pointedly, that 'despite repeated requests, the Monitoring Group was unable to obtain monitoring and reporting mechanism data from UNICEF regarding perpetrators to assist in its investigations'. Report of the Somalia and Eritrea Monitoring Group on Somalia, S/2013/413, para 171.

5.2 Operations and approach of expert panels

First appointed in 1999, expert panels have become constant features of the sanctions' implementation and monitoring function. With increasingly broad and complex mandates, expert panels, at least theoretically, have a huge realm of freedom in terms of choice of focus, investigations and investigative method.[118] There is room therefore for expert panels to adopt a strategic approach to investigations which potentially enhances the human rights signalling or deterrence effect of a regime. The very fact of ongoing investigations, for example, can affect how targets view the permissiveness of the environment. Although most investigations are confidential, it will often become clear where a panel is looking well before any formal opportunity of reply is provided. Anecdotal evidence suggests that targets have taken evasive or temporary behaviour-modifying action in response to ongoing investigations: in some cases, targets have even approached panels to 'negotiate'. In the Somalian context, for example, potential targets particularly feared that mention in a panel report could impact ability to enter into business contracts with the international community.[119] One of the questions which arises, therefore, is the extent to which it would be beneficial in deterrence terms for the UN or other actors to engage in deliberate communications efforts around the scope and operation of the regime. In Somalia, for example, targets were very aware of—and sensitive to—the focus of sanctions on violations of the arms embargo, corruption, diversion of humanitarian aid, and on the charcoal ban. At the same time, there was little knowledge that attacks on civilians were also a subject of interest to the Council—except when conducted by Al-Shabaab.

Choice of investigations by a panel can also create a context in which the Council is encouraged to engage on an issue, even if it is not ready to address actors directly in sanctions terms. Over a number of years, for example, the UNSEMG pursued a number of investigations aimed at highlighting violations by the security forces in Somalia, a sector which received significant international support. Although no person or entity related to the security services has been sanctioned to date, through successive resolutions the Council emphasised the need for civilian oversight, investigation and prosecution, and latterly, human rights vetting of the security forces. [120] Large scale attacks by federal security forces reduced. Increasing pressure from the international community on State actors with respect to the operation of the security forces, including withdrawal of funding from some elements, can also be linked to UNSEMG reporting.

---

[118] As a matter of practise they will be constrained heavily by the feasibility of investigations—accessibility of evidence, safety of interlocutors etc. In addition, sometimes Council itself suggests a particular focus.

[119] The aid sector alone accounted for 27% of Somalia's GDP in 2017. Ministry of Planning, Investment and Economic Development of Somalia, *Analysis of Aid Flow Data,* March 2018, available at <https://s3.eu-central-1.amazonaws.com/somalia-aid-flows.so/Aid+Flows+in+Somalia+-+2018FINAL.pdf> accessed 30 December 2018.

[120] See <www.un.org/securitycouncil/sanctions/751/resolutions> accessed 30 December 2018.

5.3 Actions by third parties to reduce the likelihood of violations

Sanctions decisions are increasingly not only about restriction and prohibition. The Council often uses the sanctions context, to encourage, or direct, various actors to take positive actions, which affect the overall environment and tend to reduce the likelihood of violations. Increasingly, for example, sanction panel reports include detailed recommendations aimed at creating an enabling environment for adherence to sanctions; human rights protection is often the object of these. In the Somalian context, for example, a single Council sanctions resolution in 2014 addressed a range of human rights-related issues from the protection of supply routes for humanitarian access, to the creation of a civilian causality tracking mechanism, and the implementation of standard operating procedures for dealing with children separated from armed grounds.[121] This kind of engagement is particularly useful in contexts where the promise of modification of sanctions is part of an ongoing dialogue between the Council and the target member States (e.g. in Somalia it was around government recognition and the progressive lifting of the arms embargo).

Compliance is not only a matter for targets and Member States. In Somalia, for example, sanctions investigations into diversion of humanitarian assistance were clearly correlated with significant improvements in monitoring and risk management by the humanitarian community. The establishment of the UN Risk Management Unit, for example, came shortly after the UNSEMG's 2011 investigations into a network of aid diversion involving militia, NGOs and World Food Program contractors.[122] Although diversion continues to be endemic in Somalia, the challenges are now more openly acknowledged and systems are beginning to be put in place to challenge the business model which perpetuates the problem.

6. The Future of Sanctions as an Instrument of Human Rights Promotion and Protection

In 1995, at the height of the "decade of sanctions" and enthusiasm for international criminal law, the Appeals Chamber in the *Tadić* case declared that the UDHR had paved the way for 'a State-sovereignty-oriented approach' to be 'gradually supplanted by a human-being-oriented approach' in international law.[123] Normative evolutions in targeted sanctions instruments are increasingly placing the individual directly in the crosshairs of the Council, whether as

---

[121] Resolution 2182 (2014).

[122] See Jeffrey Gettleman and Neil MacFarquhar, 'Somalia Food Aid Bypasses Needy, U.N. Study Says' *New York Times* (New York 9 March 2010) available at <www.nytimes.com/2010/03/10/world/africa/10somalia.html> accessed 17 April 2019. For information on the Risk Management Unit (RMU) see <https://www.uninsomalia.org/risk-management-unit> accessed 28 April 2019.

[123] IT-94-1-AR72 *Prosecutor v Tadić*, Appeals Chamber, Decision on the Defence Motion for Interlocutory Appeal on Jurisdiction, 35 ILM (1996) 32, para 97.

duty bearer, target, or object of protection, complementing the development of international accountability mechanisms.[124]

Notwithstanding the fragility, inconsistency and complexity of sanctions as a political instrument, some human rights practitioners are optimistic about this potential. The Special Representative of the Secretary General (SRSG) on Sexual Violence in Conflict, for example, has described the willingness of the Council to consider SGBV grounded designations, as 'critical' in the context of the continuing national and international impunity gap for such crimes.[125] An analysis by former advocates at the Watchlist for Children in Armed Conflict concluded that 'highly tailored sanctions may prove to be an effective tool in combatting violations against children in armed conflict, even where the perpetrators are non-State actors.[126] In addition to the virtues of international signalling, the multiple processes triggered by the imposition of targeted sanctions—and their interaction with other human rights and accountability mechanisms—can play a role both in constraining conduct and creating an environment less likely to enable violation of human rights. There is also room for the operations of independent sanctions experts to be deployed more strategically to advance human rights outcomes.

There is still much to be done, however, in understanding the processes through which sanctions mandates with human rights and humanitarian law protective capacities are implemented in practice. Beyond the question as to whether specific sanctions targets, objectives and purposes have effectively coalesced, new kinds of analyses which provide insight into how sanctions can be leveraged in favour of human rights as part of a broader, dynamic system of international response to crises, are ripe for exploration.

7. Bibliography

Ali, MM, and Shah, IH, 'Sanctions and Childhood Mortality in Iraq' (2000) 355 *The Lancet* 1851

Amnesty International, Statement, 'New low for the UN Security Council as Russia takes Syrian human rights off the table', 23 March 2018

Bentall, P, 'United Nations targeted sanctions and other policy tools: diplomacy, legal, use

[124] Although States are responsible for adopting implementation measures to give effect to Council decisions, the establishment of a Council listing procedure bolsters the overall trend towards individualisation of responsibility for breaches of international law—including human rights. For a detailed discussion of this see Larissa Van Der Herick, 'The Individualization of Enforcement in International Law: Exploring the Interplay between United Nations Targeted Sanctions and International Criminal Proceedings' in Tiyanjana Maluwa, Max du Plessis and Dire Tladi (eds.), *The Pursuit of a Brave New World in International Law, Essays in Honour of John Dugard* (Brill 2017).

[125] Patten (n 89). See also Sophie Huve, *The Use of UN Sanctions to Address Conflict-Related Sexual Violence* (The Georgetown Institute for Women, Peace and Security 2018).

[126] Eckenfels-Garcia and Koller (n 97) 23.

of force' in Biersteker, TJ, Eckertand, SE, and Tourinho, M (eds), *Targeted Sanctions, The Impacts and Effectiveness of United Nations Action* (CUP 2016)

Brubaker, R, Cockayne, J, and Jayakody, N, *Fairly clear risks, Protecting UN sanctions' legitimacy and effectiveness through fair and clear procedures* (United Nations University 2008)

Carisch, E, Eckert, S, and Rickard-Martin, L, Background Paper, High Level Review of UN Sanctions available at http://www.hlr-unsanctions.org/main/background, accessed 30 December 2018

Cetorelli, V, and Dyson, T, 'Changing views on child mortality and economic sanctions in Iraq: a history of lies, damned lies and statistics' (2017) 2(2) *British Medical Journal Global Health* 1

Cortright, D, and Lopez, GA, *The Sanctions Decade, Assessing UN sanctions in the 1990s* (Lynne Rienner 2000)

Cortright D, Lopez, GA, and Gerber-Stellingwerf, L, *Integrating UN Sanctions for Peace and Security* (The Sanctions and Security Research Program University of Notre Dame 2010)

du Plessis, M, Maluwa, T, and Tladi, D, (eds), *The Pursuit of a Brave New World in International Law, Essays in Honour of John Dugard* (Brill 2017)

Eckenfels-Garcia, M, and Koller, DS, 'Using targeted sanctions to end violations against children in armed conflict' (2015) 33(1) *Boston University International Law Journal* 1

Erikson M, Unintended consequences of UN sanctions, in Biersteker, TJ, Eckertand SE, and Tourinho M (eds), *Targeted Sanctions, The Impacts and Effectiveness of United Nations Action* (CUP 2016)

European Union, Directorate General for External Policies of the Union, *Targeted sanctions against individuals on grounds of grave human rights violations – impact, trends and prospects at EU level* (Policy Department for External Relations 2018)

Franco C, *Coercive Diplomacy, Sanctions and International Law, Report of the international conference on "Coercive Diplomacy, Sanctions and International Law" organised in Rome on 13 February 2015* (Istituto Affari Internazionali 2015)

Gray, C, 'The use of force for humanitarian purposes' in Henderson C, and White ND, (eds), *Research Handbook on International Conflict and Security Law, Jus ad Bellum, Jus in Bello and Jus post Bellum* (Edward Elgar 2013)

H.E. Ambassador Geir O. Pedersen, Permanent Representative of Norway, 'Security Council working methods–targeted sanctions', Statement on behalf of the group of Like-Minded States on targeted sanctions, delivered before the President of the Security Council on 23 October 2014

Happold, M, 'Targeted Sanctions and Human Rights', in Happold M, and Eden, P, (eds), *Economic Sanctions and International Law* (Hart Publishing 2016)

Happold, M, 'UN sanctions and human rights and humanitarian law devices' in Van Der Herick L, *Research Handbook on UN Sanctions and International La,* (Edward Elgar 2017)

Huve, S, *The Use of UN Sanctions to Address Conflict-Related Sexual Violence* (The Georgetown Institute for Women, Peace and Security 2018)

International Criminal Court, *Press Release, 'Assembly activates Court's jurisdiction over crime of aggression'*, 15 December 2017

King, K, Modirzadeh, NK, and Lewis, DA, *Understanding Humanitarian Exemptions: UN Security Council Sanctions and Principled Humanitarian Action* (Harvard Law School Program on International Law and Armed Conflict, Counterterrorism and Humanitarian Engagement Project 2016)

Lopez, GA, *Tools, tasks and tough thinking: Sanctions and R2P, A Policy Brief* (Global Centre for the Responsibility to Protect 2013)

Manby, B, 'South Africa: The Impact of Sanctions' (1992) 46(1) *Journal of International Affairs* 193

Ministry of Planning, Investment and Economic Development of Somalia, *Analysis of Aid Flow Data,* March 2018, available at https://s3.eu-central-1.amazonaws.com/somalia-aid-flows.so/Aid+Flows+in+Somalia+-+2018FINAL.pdf, accessed 30 December 2018

New York Times, 'Somalia Food Aid Bypasses Needy, U.N. Study Says', 9 March 2010

Office of the Ombudsperson to the Security Council, Historical Guide of the Ombudsperson Process through Security Council resolutions and Reports of the Office of the Ombudsperson to the Security Council (updated March 2018) available at https://www.un.org/securitycouncil/sites/www.un.org.securitycouncil/files/historical_guide_ombudsperson_process_march_2018.pdf, accessed 30 December 2018

Patten, P, 'Moving from a Culture of Impunity to a Culture of Deterrence: The Use of Sanctions in Addressing Sexual Violence in Conflict' (2018) UN ECOSOC Chamber, 22 October 2018

Prosecutor of the International Criminal Court, Twenty-Eighth Report of the Prosecutor of the International Criminal Court to the United Nations Security Council pursuant to UNSCR 1593 (2005)

Prost, K, 'The Office of the Ombudsperson; a Case for Fair Process' (2012) Working Paper No 4.3 presented at the United Nations Security Council, Sanctions and the Rule of Law Workshop held at the Australian Mission to the United Nations, New York on 31 May 2012

Provisional verbatim record of the three thousand one hundred and fifth meeting of the UN Security Council, 11 August 1992, S/PV.3105

Ross, A, 'Who killed U.N. experts in Congo? Confidential prosecutor's file offers clues', Reuters, 17 December 2017

Saura-EStapà, J, 'The UN Security Council Ombudsperson: an original institution still under construction' (2017) 54 *Revista Catalana de Dret Públic* 185

Security Council Report, *Human Rights and the Security Council—An Evolving Role* (Security Council Report 2016)

Shepherd, GW, 'The Failure of the Sanctions against Rhodesia and the Effect on African States: A Growing Racial Crisis' (1968) 15(1) *Africa Today* 8

United Nations Office of the High Commission on Human Rights, "UN expert warns against harsh effects of sanctions and blockades on civilians' Geneva, 13 September 2018

United Nations Security Council statement, 'Security Council Sanctions Committee on Somalia and Eritrea Communicates Additional Information from Monitoring Group on 2014 Final Report', 14 April 2016, TSC/12322

United Nations Security Council, *Compendium of the High-level Review of United Nations Sanctions* (2015) A/69/941 S/2015/432

United Nations Security Council, Seventy-fourth year, 8446th meeting, Verbatim record, 17 January 2019 S/PV.8446

United Nations, 'Security Council Committee concerning Libya Adds Six Individuals to Its Sanctions List', Press Release, 7 June 2018, TSC/13371

United Nations, 'Statement attributed to the UN Secretary-General's Special Advisers on the Prevention of Genocide and the Responsibility to Protect on the Situation in Côte d'Ivoire', 19 January 2011

United Nations, Human rights due diligence policy on United Nations support to non-United Nations security forces, available at <https://www.ohchr.org/Documents/HRBodies/SP/AMeetings/20thsession/IdenticalLetterSG25Feb2013_en.pdf>, accessed 30 December 2018

Van Der Herick, L, 'The Individualization of Enforcement in International Law: Exploring the Interplay between United Nations Targeted Sanctions and International Criminal Proceedings' in du Plessis, M, Maluwa, T, and Tladi, D, (eds), *The Pursuit of a Brave New World in International Law, Essays in Honour of John Dugard* (Brill 2017)

Chapter 10

THE CONTEMPORARY THREAT TO CIVIL LIBERTIES AND HUMAN RIGHTS ACTIVISM

By Liam Herrick

1. Introduction

As we mark the seventieth anniversary of the Universal Declaration of Human Rights (UDHR), we are witnessing a moment of profound crisis for the international human rights movement. In his final remarks to the United Nations Human Rights Council in June 2018, outgoing High Commissioner for Human Rights, Zeid Ra'ad Al Hussein, posed the question:

> [W]hy is the Universal Declaration, and the whole body of human rights law that followed it, the object of so much attack now – not only from the violent extremists, like the *Takfiris*, but also from authoritarian leaders, populists, demagogues, cultural relativists, some Western academics, and even some UN officials?'[1]

2. Threats and Critiques

Indeed, the threats to human rights are coming from many sources. The Trump administration's attacks on international institutions[2] can be seen as part of a wider populist rejection of internationalism, resonating with the politics of Brexit in the United Kingdom (UK) and many other examples in Europe and other regions.[3] The recent decision by the United States (US) to leave the Human Rights Council is a landmark moment in this regard.[4] At the domestic level, we

---

1 Former United Nations High Commissioner for Human Rights, Zeid Ra'ad Al Hussein, 'Opening statement and global update of human rights concerns: 38th Session of the Human Rights Council' (*United Nations Human Rights Council,* 18 June 2018) <www.ohchr.org/EN/HRBodies/HRC/Pages/NewsDetail.aspx?NewsID=23206&LangID=E>.

2 *See generally* Ishaan Tharoor, 'Trump renews his battle with U.N.' *The Washington Post* (Washington, 24 September 2018).

3 *See generally* Matthew Googwon, 'Why a far-right party with white supremacist roots is on the rise in Sweden' *The Washington Post (Washington, 10 September 2018); Ishaan Tharoor,* 'Washington wakes up to "authoritarian" populism in the U.S. and Europe' *The Washington Post* (Washington, 10 May 2018); Joshua Kuralantzick, 'So you thought the global populist wave was ending? Think again' *The Washington Post* (Washington, 16 February 2018).

4 Julian Borger, 'US quits UN human rights council — 'a cesspool of political bias' *The Guardian* (London, 19 June 2018).

are also seeing widespread populist attacks on the institutions of democracy itself and on the rule of law, including open hostility in the populist media against the judiciary and against parliamentarians. It is notable that popular media attacks in Britain on the institutions of the European Union have followed the same pattern as earlier campaigns against the Council of Europe and the European Convention on Human Rights on issues such as prisoner voting.[5]

We are also witnessing a growing critique of human rights bodies and institutions from the political left.[6] The perceived alignment over recent decades of the human rights movement with centre-left governments, such as those led by Bill Clinton and Tony Blair, has shorn it of credibility with much of its natural support base and reduced its claim to impartiality. In the aftermath of the military disasters and the economic crisis of the early twenty-first century, the human rights movement is seen by many as being trapped in a failing and intellectually impoverished centrism. Worse still, the claim of international institutions as protectors of human rights has been undermined by regressive policies, particularly with regard to the EU and its role in advancing and imposing economic austerity and oppressive controls on migration.

Most significantly, traditional human rights actors face a challenge of relevance when confronted with the experienced human rights violations of inequality, racism, and nationalism. Scepticism of the left, which arises from the impotence of social democracy to develop effective responses to the War on Terror or the toxic debate on global migration, is reinforced by centre-left governments support for unilateral military interventions. At a time of deepening global crises, the irrelevance of human rights has been described by the Indian writer, Pankaj Mishra, as a 'seductive anti-politics'.[7] Older critiques of the human rights movement from a colonialist analysis have also prompted some larger International Non-Governmental Organisations (INGOs), such as OXFAM, to move their headquarters to the global South, but many face criticism of suppressing the voice and perspective of those most affected by current global rights' violations.

3. Leading the Resistance

Of course, this is not the full picture and there are defences to many of these criticisms. Throughout this period, there have been important voices and actors in the human rights movement which remained true to the mission of the UDHR. In South Africa and many parts of South America, activists have retained their

[5] *See generally* James Slack and Martin Robinson, '"This is for Britain to decide": Cameron pledges to fight diktat from unelected European judges who say prisoners MUST get the vote' *The Daily Mail* (London, 23 May 2012).

[6] Perhaps most prominent of which has been the work of Samuel Moyn. See generally Samuel Moyn, *The Last Utopia: Human Rights in History* (Belknap Press 2012); Samuel Moyn, *Not Enough: Human Rights in an Unequal World* (Belknap Press 2018).

[7] Pankaj Mishra, 'The People v Democracy: Why Our Freedom Is in Danger and How to Save It by Yascha Monuk' (2018) 40 (12) *London Review of Books* 9-13.

political potency from the fight against apartheid, through to reframing broader agencies for effective democracy, and economic equality. Civil liberties groups such as the American Civil Liberties Union and Liberty took important and principled stances in the face of the War on Terror.[8] The Council of Europe held military power to account on the issue of extraordinary rendition[9] and identified the human rights impact of European austerity policies.[10]

In many countries, including in eastern Europe, it is human rights organisations which are leading the resistance to autocratic governments, and which are being targeted for repressive measures as a result. The common thread in the repression which is now being witnessed in so many regions, is nationalism. This was, again, a theme in High Commissioner Zeid's outgoing address, where he stated:

> Is it not the case, for example, that historically, the most destructive force to imperil the world has been chauvinistic nationalism – when raised to feral extremes by self-serving, callous leaders, and amplified by mass ideologies which themselves repress freedom. The UN was conceived in order to prevent its rebirth. Chauvinistic nationalism is the polar opposite of the UN, its very antonym and enemy. So why are we so submissive to its return? Why are we in the UN so silent?
>
> The UN's *raison d'être* is the protection of peace, rights, justice and social progress. Its operating principle is therefore equally clear: only by pursuing the opposite to nationalism – only when States all work for each other, for everyone, for all people, for the human rights of all people – can peace be attainable.[11]

4. Shrinking Civic Space

This rise of aggressive nationalism is characterised by isolationism and hostility to the international system of human rights, but it is also expressed by restrictions on dissenting voices at home. This phenomenon has become known as 'Shrinking Civic Space', a term used to describe a range of policies used to restrict freedom of association, freedom of assembly, and freedom of

---

8 *See generally* Susan N. Herman, 'Taking Liberties: The ACLU and the War on Terror' (*The ACLU BLC*, 12 June 2011) <https://www.aclu.org/other/taking-liberties-aclu-and-war-terror>.

9 Committee on Legal Affairs and Human Rights, *Secret detentions and illegal transfers of detainees involving Council of Europe member states: Second Report* (Parliamentary Assembly of the Council of Europe June 2007).

10 Steering Committee for Human Rights, *The impact of the economic crisis and austerity measures on human rights in Europe* (Council of Europe 2016).

11 United Nations High Commissioner for Human Rights Zeid Ra'ad Al Hussein, 'Opening statement and global update of human rights concerns: 38th Session of the Human Rights Council' (*United Nations Human Rights Council,* 18 June 2018) <www.ohchr.org/EN/HRBodies/HRC/Pages/NewsDetail.aspx?NewsID=23206&LangID=E>.

expression; particularly when those rights are being exercised by civil society organisations.[12]

CIVICUS is the global alliance of civil society organisations and activists. Each year it publishes a 'State of the World' report which categorises countries in relation to their record of respect for these basic civil rights. Its most recent report found that 28% of the global population lived in States ranked in the worst category of 'closed',[13] with 17% of the global population living in the next worst category of 'repressed' States,[14] and a further 37% in States where civil rights were assessed as 'obstructed'.[15] Under CIVICUS's ranking, 14% of the population lived in States with the second best ranking of 'narrowed' civic space,[16] and only 4% in 'open' democracies.[17] Overall, CIVICUS describes a 'systematic and global crackdown on the conditions for civil society'.[18] The measurements used by CIVICUS in its reporting include issues relating to regulation of the media and interferences with a free press, the use of surveillance, the regulation of protests, and the regulation of elections and political activity.

These issues are also identified at the European level by the EU Fundamental Rights Agency in its report from January 2018, *Challenges facing civil society organisations working on human rights in the EU*.[19] The Agency identifies four different types of interference with civil society freedoms:

i. Violence and other attacks, including smearing of the reputation of civil society organisations and their personnel.
ii. Restrictions on participation in democratic process, such as excluding civil society from consultation on policy and access to government.
iii. Reduction in or obstacles to funding, including restrictions on foreign or international funding.
iv. Inappropriate or excessive regulation, including both direct and indirect restrictions on civil society activity.

---

12 In recent years the phrase 'shrinking civic space' has increasingly been used by international institutions such as the UN and the European Union to describe the phenomenon of a more difficult environment for civil society organisations to operate. The types of barriers to civil society activity which constitute this phenomenon are set out, for example, in the recent report of the European Union Fundamental Rights Agency, *Challenges facing civil society organisations working on human rights in the EU* (EUFRA January 2018).

13 CIVICUS, *State of Civil Society 2018: Year in Review: Top Ten Trends* (CIVICUS 2018) 4.

14 ibid.

15 ibid.

16 ibid.

17 ibid.

18 ibid.

19 European Union Fundamental Rights Agency, *Challenges facing civil society organisations working on human rights in the EU* (EUFRA January 2018).

5. Regulatory Interferences

The most significant type of restriction from an Irish perspective is that of regulatory interferences. Direct regulatory restriction refers to those laws that relate to NGOs and are aimed at restricting the activity of civil society. Examples include unnecessarily extensive procedures or laws regarding NGO certification. Indirect regulatory restriction differs as it refers to laws and rules, with a legitimate purpose, being applied in a way that restricts the activity of civil society. Examples of this indirect regulatory restriction include the use of counter-terrorism and money-laundering laws against civil society organisations and restrictions on funding for civil society or some categories of civil society activity.

Many States prohibit or restrict the ability of civil society organisations, or other categories of organisations from accessing funds from foreign or international sources. Such laws are often presented as being concerned with protecting political processes. From a human rights perspective, such laws can also constitute illegitimate interference with necessary civil society democratic participation. The UN has recently issued a set of general principles, entitled *Protecting Civic Space and the Right to Access Resources*, which unequivocally provides that, 'States must allow associations to seek, receive and use foreign funding as a part of their obligation under international human rights law to mobilize resources available within the society as a whole and from the international community'.[20] Nonetheless, 'foreign funding' laws retain strong political support in many countries, both where the object of these laws is to stifle civil society directly and where the application of political finance laws to civil society is indirect. Ireland is an example of the latter situation.

5.1 The Electoral Act

In 2001, the Electoral Act[21] extended the donation restrictions that previously applied only to election candidates and political parties to *all* contributions given 'for political purposes' to any 'third party'.[22] The Electoral Act prohibits 'third parties' from using any of the following sources of income for 'political purposes': (1) donations from foreign sources, (2) anonymous donations of more than €100, (3) cash donations of more than €200, and (4) donations of more than €2,500 from one source.[23] The donation restrictions include donations in kind, i.e. not just money but also the supply of voluntary services, any reduction in rates for the use of property or supply of services, and donations of property or goods.[24]

---

[20] Community of Democracies and UN Special Rapporteur on the Rights to Freedom of Peaceful Assembly and of Association, *Protecting Civic Space and the Right to Access Resources: General Principle 2* (Community of Democracies Project funded by Sweden).

[21] Electoral (Amendment) Act 2001.

[22] Electoral Act 1997, s 22.

[23] ibid.

[24] ibid.

Section 22 of the Electoral Act 1997 (as amended) defines 'political purposes' in a way that can potentially capture almost all advocacy work that civil society organisations in Ireland carry out. According to section 22(2)(a) (with our emphasis on provisions relevant to civil society organisations), 'political purposes' means:

i. to promote or oppose, directly or indirectly, the interests of a political party, a political group, a member of either House of the Oireachtas or a representative in the European Parliament, or;
ii. to present, directly or indirectly, the policies or a particular policy of a political party, a political group, a member of either House of the Oireachtas, a representative in the European Parliament or a third party, or;
iii. to present, directly or indirectly, the comments of a political party, a political group, a member of either House of the Oireachtas, a representative in the European Parliament or a third party with regard to the policy or policies of another political party, political group, a member of either House of the Oireachtas, representative in the European Parliament, third party or candidate at an election or referendum or otherwise, or;
iv. to promote or oppose, directly or indirectly, the interests of a third party in connection with the conduct or management of any campaign conducted with a view to promoting or procuring a particular outcome in relation to a policy or policies or functions of the Government or any public authority.

It is this fourth category that has proven problematic. This broad definition extends the rules on donations to potentially apply to a very broad range of advocacy activities. The problem would appear to arise from poor drafting, in that there is no indication that the Oireachtas intended such a broad application. In 2003, the Standards in Public Office Commission (SIPOC) itself sounded the alarm about the wide-ranging impact that s 22 could have on civil society freedom in Ireland. SIPOC stated in its 'Review of the Electoral Acts 1997 to 2002':

Because the definition of political purposes is so wide it may, unintentionally, cover, on an ongoing basis, any of the following:

1. local bodies such as Tidy Towns Committees, Residents / Tenants Associations, Community Organisations, etc.,
2. organisations such as Trocaire, Amnesty International, Threshold, the Society of St. Vincent de Paul, An Taisce, Credit Union Movement, Comhdháil Náisiúnta na Gaeilge, etc., representative associations such as ICTU, IBEC, ISME, IFA, USI, etc.,
3. other interest groups such as those representing vintners, lawyers, hoteliers, teachers, accountants, builders, doctors, nurses, etc.

The list is far from exhaustive. It is highly likely that, in conducting their day to day business, any of the above could be involved in activity which would fall within the definition of political purposes in that they would be attempting to promote or procure a particular outcome in relation to a policy or policies of the Government or any public authority, including a local authority.

5.2 Application and consequences of the Electoral Act

Despite this clear recognition by the regulator of the latent problems with the text of the Act, in recent years they have begun to apply the law broadly to civil society organisations engaged in general advocacy work. Among the examples that are known, in 2017 SIPOC ordered Education Equality, an all-volunteer organisation campaigning for equal treatment within the education system regardless of belief or religious affiliation, to return half of the €10,000 seed funding they had received from the Humanist Association for two years' expenses.[25] In a more high profile case, SIPOC also ordered Amnesty International to repay a large grant to the Open Society Foundation in December 2017.[26] Ultimately that case was resolved after Amnesty initiated judicial review proceedings against SIPOC.[27]

The consequences of the current regulatory framework for civil society organisations are very serious. According to the wording of the Electoral Act 1997,[28] civil society organisations that 'promote', 'oppose' or 'comment' on public policy risk criminal prosecution if they use donations above the threshold or any foreign donations to support their work, or if they fail to comply with the onerous procedural requirements attaching to small domestic donations. The possible *penalties* on 'third parties' for failing to comply with the Electoral Act 1997 include a maximum fine of a €25,394 and three years' imprisonment.[29] As well as those organisations that have faced orders to return funds, which SIPOC has deemed to be 'prohibited', and those organisations ordered to register as corporate donors for sub-granting, others have reported threats of prosecution and invasive and burdensome queries into their operations. Such queries, including SIPOC's direct correspondence with funders, have resulted in civil society organisations taking legal advice, often at considerable expense. The overall impact of such has been a serious 'chilling effect' on funders, and civil society more generally, when it comes to advocating on matters of public policy. The regulator has also indicated that it acts primarily in response to complaints from members of the public, which has encouraged campaigns aimed at smearing organisations through media and regulatory means.

---

25 *See generally* Jack Power, 'Humanist group reported to Sipo over €10,000 donation' *The Irish Times* (Dublin, 16 December 2017).

26 *See generally* Sarah Bardon, 'Amnesty International ordered to return donation from billionaire George Soros' *The Irish Times* (Dublin, 8 December 2017).

27 *See generally* Aodhan O'Faolain, 'Amnesty challenges Sipo order to return abortion campaign donation' *The Irish Times* (Dublin, 12 February 2018).

28 Electoral Act 1997.

29 Electoral Act 1997 , s 25(2)(b).

Ironically, while Irish civil society is experiencing these difficulties, Ireland is taking on a leadership role at the UN in defending civil society freedoms more generally. Ireland has also been one of the strongest supporters of the position of human rights defenders, through the leading role it played in the development of EU Guidelines on Human Rights Defenders, and through its support for Front Line Defenders, which has its headquarters in Dublin. Since 2013, Ireland has sponsored the Human Rights Council Resolution on Civil Society Space. In the context of widespread repression of civil society in many parts of the world, the leadership role played by Ireland is both welcome and significant.

6. Conclusion

If Ireland is to fulfil its necessary leadership role in defending democratic principles and European values, it is essential that we reflect our principles and values at national and international level. It is not tenable to sustain this principled international position without ensuring that Irish domestic law and policy meets the high standards that we call for from our international partners. We must ask ourselves whether Ireland has the political maturity to value dissent at home, as much as it advocates for strong civil society abroad? Certainly, there are examples of other EU States, such as the Netherlands, where governments fund initiatives to stimulate and sustain critical advocacy. Recently, the Irish Council for Civil Liberties (ICCL) undertook a joint report with CIVICUS, which examined and compared models of best practice in the regulation of political advocacy. This report highlighted the experience in other progressive EU States. The ICCL is now leading a coalition of civil society organisations working to reform the law in Ireland and to strengthen protection of civil society rights. Our aim is to maintain the protections that the Electoral Act 1997 provide for the integrity of the electoral process, while also ensuring that the regulations on funding are redrawn in such a manner as to avoid impacting on the general work of civil society outside of elections and referendums.

7. Bibliography

United Nations Human Rights Council (UNHRC). *Opening statement and global update of human rights concerns by UN High Commissioner for Human Rights Zeid Ra'ad Al Hussein, 38th Session of the Human Rights Council* (18 June 2018) www.ohchr.org/EN/HRBodies/HRC/Pages/NewsDetail.aspx?NewsID=23206&LangID=E

Al Hussein, R, *Opening statement and global update of human rights concerns by UN High Commissioner for Human Rights Zeid Ra'ad Al Hussein at 38th session of the Human Rights Council,* 18 June 2018

Bardon, S, *The Irish Times* 'Amnesty International ordered to return donation from billionaire George Soros' (Dublin, 8 December 2017)

Borger, J, *The Guardian* 'US quits UN human rights council–'a cesspool of political bias' (London, 19 June 2018)

CIVICUS, *State of Civil Society 2018: Year in Review: Top Ten Trends* (2018)

Googwon, M, *The Washington Post 'Why a far-right party with white supremacist roots is on the rise in Sweeden' (Washington, 10 September 2018); Ishaan Throor, The Washington Post* 'Washington wakes up to "authoritarian" populism in the U.S. and Europe (Washington, 10 May 2018)

Herman, SN, 'Taking Liberties: The ACLU and the War on Terror' (The ACLU, 12 June 2011)

Kuralantzick, J, *The Washington Post* 'So you thought the global populist wave was ending? Think again.' (Washington, 16 February 2018)

Moyn, S, *Not Enough: Human Rights in an Unequal World* (Belknap Press 2018)

Moyn, S, *The Last Utopia: Human Rights in History* (Belknap Press 2012)

Mishra, P, The People v Democracy: Why Our Freedom Is in Danger and How to Save It by Yascha Monuk (2018) 40 (12) *London Review of Books* Mishra, 9

O'Faolain, A, *The Irish Times* 'Amnesty challenges Sipo order to return abortion campaign donation' (Dublin, 12 February 2018)

Power, J, *The Irish Times* 'Humanist group reported to Sipo over €10,000 donation' (Dublin, 16 December 2017)

Slack, J and Robinson, M, *The Daily Mail*, '"This is for Britain to decide": Cameron pledges to fight diktat from unelected European judges who say prisoners MUST get the vote' (London, 23 May 2012)

'Secret detentions and illegal transfers of detainees involving Council of Europe member states: second report', Parliamentary Assembly of the Council of Europe, Committee on Legal Affairs and Human Rights, 7 June 2007

'The impact of the economic crisis and austerity measures on human rights in Europe', Council of Europe, Steering Committee for Human Rights (CDDH) (2016)

Thharoor, I, *The Washington Post* 'Trump renews his battle with U.N.' (Washington, 24 September 2018)

CHAPTER 11

THE 'CURIOUS GRAPEVINE': 70 YEARS OF NON-GOVERNMENTAL ORGANISATIONS IN THE UNITED NATIONS HUMAN RIGHTS SYSTEM

By Fiona McGaughey

1. INTRODUCTION

The United Nations (UN) human rights system has developed significantly in the last 70 years since the adoption of the Universal Declaration on Human Rights (UDHR).[1] One important aspect of these developments, is the critical role played by non-governmental organisations (NGOs) – a role often overlooked in traditional doctrinal scholarship. That it is overlooked by lawyers is perhaps not surprising as with the exception of the limited opportunities provided for 'consultation' with NGOs in Art 71 of the UN Charter,[2] there are almost no hard law provisions for the NGO role in subsequent treaties. NGOs began as almost extraneous to the international human rights system, but have carved out a role for themselves in the international human rights framework, which is welcomed by the UN,[3] but often resisted by States.[4] In the last 70 years, however, they have become increasingly important. In 1994, the UN Secretary General noted that 'NGO involvement has not only justified the inclusion of Article 71… but that it has far exceeded the original scope of these legal provisions'.[5] NGOs have been influential in drafting international legislation,[6] in bringing individual complaints to treaty bodies,[7] and in the

1 *Universal Declaration of Human Rights*, GA Res 217A (III), UN GAOR 3rd sess, 183rd, UN Doc A/810 (10 December 1948).
2 *Charter of the United Nations*, 4 October 1945, 1 UNTS XVI.
3 General Assembly 11 June 2004 *Fifty-eighth session Agenda item 59 Strengthening of the United Nations system*, UN Doc A/58/817, 3.
4 Eduard Jordaan, 'South Africa and the United Nations Human Rights Council' (2014) 36(1) *Human Rights Quarterly* 90.
5 United Nations Economic and Social Council, *General Review of Arrangements for Consultations with Non-Governmental Organisations: Report of the Secretary General* (UN Doc 70/1994/5) 26 May 1994.
6 Price Cohen, 'The Role of Non-Governmental Organizations in the Drafting of the Convention on the Rights of the Child' (1990) 12 *Human Rights Quarterly* 137; Zoe N Pearson, *Global Civil Society and International Law-Making: Mapping the Boundaries*, (PhD Thesis, Australian National University, 2002).
7 Hurst Hannum (ed), *Guide to International Human Rights Practice*, (University of

State reporting processes of the UN human rights treaty bodies and the Human Rights Council's Universal Periodic Review (UPR).[8]

This chapter will chart the growth of the NGO role in UN human rights bodies over the past 70 years. The history of the NGO role will be supplemented by some recent empirical research on the influence of NGO reports in the most well-established of the UN monitoring mechanisms, that of the human rights treaty bodies. The chapter draws on the author's semi-structured interviews with UN staff in the Office of the High Commissioner for Human Rights (OHCHR), treaty body members and NGOs. The empirical data indicates that NGOs play an important role in providing 'on-the-ground' expert information to treaty body independent experts, informing the questions they ask of States and the recommendations they make.

However, it is important to begin by noting that there is no universally accepted definition of 'NGO'.[9] However, the following definition suffices for our purposes: '…a non-profit, voluntary citizens' group which is organized on a local, national or international level…. Some are organized around specific issues, such as human rights, the environment or health'.[10] In this chapter, the organisations of interest are those who engage in advocacy work with UN human rights bodies.

2. NGOs and the UDHR Period

Seventy years ago, Eleanor Roosevelt who chaired the UDHR working group, predicted the importance of the NGO role. She famously stated that the rights in the UDHR would become known through a 'curious grapevine', namely NGOs.[11] This prediction is perhaps unsurprising, as although contemporary NGOs are prolific and play an extensive role in international law human rights law, they had established a relatively strong track record pre-1948. Then Secretary General Kofi Annan, at the 50th anniversary of the UDHR, stated:

> Before the founding of the United Nations, NGOs led the charge in

Philadelphia Press 1984); Loveday Hodson, *NGOs and the Struggle for Human Rights in Europe* (Hart Publishing 2011).

8 Fiona McGaughey, 'Advancing, retreating or stepping on each other's toes? The Role of Non-Governmental Organisations in United Nations Human Rights Treaty Body Reporting and the Universal Periodic Review' (2017) 35 *Australian Yearbook of International Law* 187; Fiona McGaughey, 'The Role and Influence of Non-governmental Organisations in the Universal Periodic Review – International Context and Australian Case Study' (2017) *Human Rights Law Review* 421.

9 For more analysis of the complexities of defining NGOS, see K Martens 'Mission Impossible? Defining Non-governmental Organizations' 13:3 *Voluntas: International Journal of Voluntary and Nonprofit Organizations* (2002) pp 271-285.

10 UN Department of Public Information, *What is an NGO* <https://outreach.un.org/ngorelations/content/about-us-0> accessed 16 April 2019.

11 William Korey, *NGOs and the Universal Declaration of Human Rights: A Curious Grapevine* (Palgrave 1998).

> the adoption of some of the Declaration's forerunners. The Geneva conventions of 1864; multilateral labour conventions adopted in 1906; and the International Slavery Convention of 1926; all stemmed from the world of NGOs who infused the international community with a spirit of reform.[12]

The existence of NGOs and their advocacy role with international organisations prior to the UN is also evident from the engagement of NGOs with the UN's predecessor, the League of Nations (the League). The Covenant establishing the League had limited provisions on NGOs, such as Article 25 on creating national Red Cross organisations.[13] Informally, NGOs were well recognised by the League, invited to sit on selected committees (although without voting rights), and to attend meetings.[14] There was a more strained relationship between the League and NGOs later in the League's existence – one possible explanation for the lack of initial NGO involvement in the creation of the UN. The Dumbarton Oaks draft of the UN Charter did not include provisions related to NGOs. This omission was addressed by NGOs at the San Francisco Conference in 1945, where there were an estimated 1,200 voluntary organisations in attendance.[15] These organisations, which we now refer to as NGOs, were active contributors to the drafting of the Charter,[16] including the drafting of Art 71, which provides that the Economic and Social Council (ECOSOC) may:

> ...[M]ake suitable arrangements for consultation with NGOs which are concerned with matters within its competence. Such arrangements may be made with international organizations and, where appropriate, with national organizations after consultation with the Member of the United Nations concerned.[17]

As stated above, in the intervening years, the role of NGOs has far exceeded the scope of Article 71 — and the predictions of Eleanor Roosevelt. Article 71 is sometimes heralded as revolutionary as a hard law provision for an NGO role. However, Otto argues that it simply formalised the extensive NGO consultative relationships which had existed in the League.[18] NGOs' other significant contributions to the drafting of the UN Charter include ensuring that human rights were included.[19] Had human rights been absent from the Charter,

---

12 Kofi Annan, 'Address to the 51st Annual DPI-NGO Conference', (United Nations, New York 1998).

13 League of Nations, Covenant of the League of Nations, 28 April 1919.

14 Steve Charnovitz, 'Two Centuries of Participation: NGOs and International Governance' (1997) 18(2) *Michigan Journal of International Law* 183, 221.

15 Chadwick Alger, 'The Emerging Roles of NGOs in the UN System: From Article 71 to a People's Millennium Assembly' (2002) 8 *Global Governance* 93, 93.

16 ibid.

17 *Charter of the United Nations*, 4 October 1945, 1 UNTS XVI, Art 71.

18 Dianne Otto, 'Nongovernmental Organizations in the United Nations System: The Emerging Role of International Civil Society' (1996) 18 *Human Rights Quarterly* 107, 109.

19 Alger (n 15) 93.

there would have been no formal, legal foundation for the development of the UDHR and subsequent human rights treaties and bodies.

NGOs, predominantly Western NGOs, including representatives of Jewish and Christian organisations, were also active in the drafting of the UDHR.[20] As Malik noted, these '…served as batteries of unofficial advisers to the various delegations, supplying them with streams of ideas and suggestions'.[21] For example, Art 16 of the UDHR on the Rights of the Family was influenced by Catholic groups and Art 18 on Freedom of Religion is often attributed to Dr Nolde, former Director of the Commission of the Churches on International Affairs of the World Council of Churches.[22]

3. NGOs Post-UDHR

Despite the provision for consultation with NGOs in Art 71 of the Charter, there were no subsequent hard law provisions for the NGO role, for example in UN treaties, until much later with Art 45(a) of the *Convention on the Rights of the Child.*[23] In fact, up until the 1980s, NGOs had a formal and limited role. In the 1990s, NGOs began to participate in world conferences and ECOSOC consultative status was widened to allow sub-regional, regional, and national NGOs to be accredited.[24] In 2000, the Millennium Declaration committed to '…give greater opportunities to the private sector, non-governmental organizations and civil society, in general, to contribute to the realization of the Organization's goals and programmes'.[25] In 2003, Kofi Annan established a panel of 'eminent persons to review the relationship between the United Nations and civil society'. The Chair was Fernando Henrique Cardoso, the former president of Brazil, and the subsequent report became known as the *Cardoso Report.*[26] The report acknowledged that governments do not always welcome the participation of NGOs but strongly supported 'civil society' participation.

20 Theo van Boven,'The Role of Non-Governmental Organizations in International Human Rights Standard Setting: A Prerequisite of Democracy (1990) 20 (2) *California Western International Law Journal* 207, 211.

21 Cited by van Boven, ibid.

22 ibid.

23 Contrary to what is often asserted, Art 45 a) does not provide for an NGO role *per se*, but rather that the Committee 'may invite… other competent bodies as it may consider appropriate to provide expert advice on the implementation of the Convention in areas falling within the scope of their respective mandates'. However, the Committee's rules 34, 70 and 74 of the Provisional Rules of Procedure, CRC/C/4 (14 November 1991) confirm that 'other competent bodies' includes NGOs.

24 Economic and Social Council, *Consultative relationship between the United Nations and non-governmental organizations,* ECOSOC Res. 1996/31, 49th plen mtg (25 July 1996).

25 General Assembly, 11 June 2004, *Fifty-eighth session Agenda item 59 Strengthening of the United Nations system*, UN Doc A/58/817.

26 *We the peoples: civil society, the United Nations and global governance: Report of the Panel of Eminent Persons on United Nations–Civil Society Relations*, UN GAOR, 58th session, Agenda Item 59, Strengthening of the United Nations System, UN Doc A/58/817 (11 June 2004).

It stated that constructively engaging with civil society is a *necessity* for the UN, not an option.[27]

3.1 The development of the NGO role in UN human rights treaty bodies

Meanwhile, since the 1970s, NGOs had begun carving out a role for themselves in contributing to the State reporting process of the new UN human rights treaty bodies. These treaties were introduced to give legal effect to the non-binding provisions of the UDHR and to introduce new rights and protect specific groups. There are currently nine core human rights treaties.[28] NGOs had begun to contribute information to the treaty bodies in order to inform their review of States' compliance with their treaty obligations. Each of the UN's nine core human rights treaties has its own Committee to monitor implementation of the treaty among States parties, primarily through considering periodic reports.[29] It is an often overlooked fact that the International Convention on the Elimination of Racial Discrimination (ICERD) is the longest standing of the UN human rights treaties, having been adopted before both the International Covenant on Civil and Political Rights and the International Covenant on Economic, Social and Cultural Rights. ICERD entered into force in 1969 and the CERD Committee began its work in 1970, leading the way for the drafting and operation of future human rights treaties. As discussed here, the CERD Committee was the testing ground for NGO involvement in State reporting.

In the early days, some CERD Committee members were resistant to NGO involvement — they were keen to preserve State sovereignty and not to interfere

---

27 ibid.

28 The nine core treaties are ordered by date of adoption by the General Assembly: *International Convention on the Elimination of All Forms of Racial Discrimination*, opened for signature 21 December 1965, 660 UNTS 195, (entered into force 4 January 1969) ('ICERD'); *International Covenant on Civil and Political Rights*, opened for signature 16 December 1966, 999 UNTS 171, (entered into force 23 March 1976) ('ICCPR'); *International Covenant on Economic, Social and Cultural Rights,* opened for signature16 December 1966, 993 UNTS 3, (entered into force 3 January 1976) ('ICESCR'); *Convention on the Elimination of All Forms of Discrimination against Women*, opened for signature 1 March 1980, 1249 UNTS 13, (entered into force 3 September 1981) ('CEDAW'); *International Convention against Torture and Other Cruel, Inhuman and Degrading Treatment or Punishment*, opened for signature 10 December 1984, 1465 UNTS 85, (entered into force 26 June 1987) ('CAT'); *Convention on the Rights of the Child,* opened for signature 20 November 1989, 1577 UNTS 3, (entered into force 2 September 1990) ('CRC); *International Convention on the Protection of the Rights of All Migrant Workers and Members of their Families,* opened for signature 18 December 1990, 2220 UNTS 3, (entered into force 1 July 2003); *International Convention for the Protection of All Persons from Enforced Disappearance*, opened for signature 20 December 2006, 2716 UNTS 3, (entered into force 23 December 2010); *Convention on the Rights of Persons with Disabilities*, opened for signature 13 Dec 2006, 2515 UNTS 3, (entered into force 3 May 2008).

29 The terms UN Committee and treaty body are both used in this chapter, with the same meaning.

in the internal affairs of the States parties.[30] To provide clarity, in 1972 the Chair of the Committee concluded '…it appears… that the Committee would continue the practice it had followed to date, allowing members to use any information they might have as experts'.[31] Therefore, use of unofficial information, such as NGO reports, was considered valid for those Committee members who wished to use it. The weakening of resistance to NGO involvement was bolstered in 1974. At the request of the CERD Committee, the UN Office of Legal Affairs advised that ICERD did not specify which sources the Committee would use, leaving it open for the Committee to use unofficial material from NGOs.[32] The use of NGO reports by the CERD Committee has been challenged by governments a number of times since, albeit unsuccessfully.[33] Most recently, UN proposals to align interaction of treaty bodies with governments, NGOs and National Human Rights Institutions as part of the treaty body strengthening process,[34] were vehemently rejected by some States who sought to use the opportunity to reduce the NGO role.[35]

In the 1990s, NGOs submitting reports and information to the CERD Committee became more common and the Secretariat began to provide support for this function.[36] The increased NGO participation was first noted in the Committee's annual report to the General Assembly in 1996, which acknowledged that NGO commentaries '…complemented the information available to members and helped improve the quality of the Committee's examination of those reports'.[37]

---

30 Felice D. Gaer, 'Implementing international human rights norms: UN human rights treaty bodies and NGOs' (2003) 2(3) *Journal of Human Rights* 339.

31 ibid, 343.

32 ibid, 342.

33 ibid, 342-343.

34 Office of the UN High Commissioner for Human Rights, *Non-exhaustive list of emerging proposals identified so far in the context of the treaty body strengthening informal consultations (including Dublin, Marrakesh, Poznan, Sion, Seoul, Pretoria, Bristol and Lucerne) and those of the Inter-Committee Meeting (ICM) and Meeting of Chairpersons (MC), as well as other proposals stemming from the process*, <http://www2.ohchr.org/english/bodies/HRTD/docs/ProposalsTBStrengtheningProcess.pdf> accessed 16 April 2019.

35 See, for example, submissions on the matter from China, Russia and Egypt: Government of China (2011), *Views of the Chinese Government regarding the human rights treaty body strengthening process*, (HRC/NONE/2011/184), para. 2.6; Government of the Russian Federation (2011) *Comments of the Russian Federation on the list of issues identified during the treaty body strengthening consultations, prepared by the Office of the United Nations High Commissioner for Human Rights,* (HRC/NONE/2012/1), para. 2; Government of Egypt, *The Future of the Treaty Body System: Egypt Position Paper* (undated) p 3.

36 Up until then, NGOs had to send the information to each Committee member individually, Lena J Kruckenberg, *The Unreal world of human rights: An ethnography of the UN Committee on the Elimination of Racial Discrimination* (Nomos Verlagsgesellschaft 2012).

37 United Nations Committee on the Elimination of Racial Discrimination, *Report of the Committee on the Elimination of Racial Discrimination General Assembly Official Records · Fifty-first Session Supplement No. 18* (1996) (A/51/18), p viii.

Therefore by 1996, NGOs had become important to the CERD Committee and the CERD Committee adopted general guidelines for interacting with NGOs.[38]

4. The Contemporary NGO Role

Scholars have placed NGOs in the UN human rights system on a spectrum ranging from important,[39] to essential,[40] or even elevated to a God-like status.[41] So how important are NGOs in State reporting to UN human rights treaty bodies? The author's previous work has established that there is evidence of NGO influence on treaty body concluding observations and on the recommendations of States in the Human Rights Council's UPR.[42] Given the significance of the CERD Committee in being the oldest treaty body and the testing ground for the NGO role, this section draws on data from semi-structured interviews with five CERD Committee members and 12 other international stakeholders including UN staff, government representatives and international NGOs. The interviews were recorded and transcribed, they were then coded and analysed using NVivo qualitative analysis software. The research was conducted in accordance with the University of Western Australia's ethics approval for the research, which required that interviewees be given the option of anonymity.

4.1 Treaty body State reporting and the NGO role

To explore the NGO role in treaty body State reporting, the CERD Committee will be examined for the reasons stated above. All Committees engage with NGOs in broadly similar ways — with some minor variations, such as the role for NGOs in Article 45 (a) of the *Convention on the Rights of the Child*, which provides that the Committee 'may invite... other competent bodies as it may consider appropriate to provide expert advice on the implementation of the Convention in areas falling within the scope of their respective mandates'.[43] The Chairs of the Committees co-operate with each other and the UN is working towards more simplified reporting with common working methods among the Committees.[44]

---

38 Kruckenberg (n 36) Ch. 5.2.

39 David P Forsythe, *Human Rights in International Relations* (2nd edn, CUP 2006) 203-204.

40 ibid, Michael Freeman, *Human Rights: an Interdisciplinary Approach* (Polity Press 2011); Laurie S Wiseberg, *The Role of Non-Governmental Organizations (NGOs) in the Protection and Enforcement of Human Rights* in J. Symonides (ed), *Human Rights: International Protection, Monitoring, Enforcement* (UNESCO Publishing 2003) 347-365.

41 Peter Willetts (ed), '*The Conscience of the World': The Influence of Non-Governmental Organisations in the UN System* (David Davies Memorial Institute of International Studies and the Brookings Institution 1996) 11.

42 McGaughey (n 8).

43 The Committee's rules 34, 70 and 74 of the Provisional Rules of Procedure, CRC/C/4 (14 November 1991) confirm that 'other competent bodies' includes NGOs.

44 Navi Pillay, *Strengthening the United Nations human rights treaty body system: A report by the United Nations High Commissioner for Human Rights* (United Nations 2012).

NGO reports may be submitted to the Committee by individual NGOs or by coalitions of NGOs.[45] NGOs may also contribute reports by developing the list-of-themes, which inform the treaty body's constructive dialogue and the follow-up procedure, whereby the Committee engages with the State on implementation of concluding observations.[46] The CERD Committee recommends concise reports and prefers coalition reports.[47] NGO reports are an informal part of the process and as such there are no formal restrictions on word limit; nor does the Secretariat translate NGO reports into the working languages of the Committee.[48] The lack of a word limit is problematic, as some Committee member interviewees expressed being inundated by NGO reports, some of which are 'very long'.[49]

Some CERD Committee members attend State-specific informal NGO lunchtime briefing sessions where NGOs present their concerns to the Committee members. This author's observation confirmed that lunchtime briefings were not always well attended by Committee members.[50] These short, one-hour meetings, held in a standard meeting room, without official interpreting, do not compare favourably with the formal, lengthy constructive dialogue held in conference rooms decked with interpreters behind glass partitions. It is clear that States parties are the primary actors and that NGOs remain soundly on a lesser and more informal footing. NGOs also meet informally with CERD Committee members on an *ad hoc* basis,[51] and it was this author's observation that the cafeteria at Palais Wilson[52] was a hive of NGO activity, where there were ongoing meetings between Committee members and NGO representatives.

Since 2012, all Committee members attend a weekly NGO briefing with NGOs from all States being reviewed in a given week.[53] Additional pressure to engage in a more structured way with NGOs came from the treaty body reform agenda,[54] and a meeting with NGO representatives at the Committee's 77th session, on 3 August 2010, where strengthening cooperation with NGOs

---

45 UN Committee on the Elimination of Racial Discrimination, *NGO Information Note* (84th session, 3 to 21 February 2014).

46 Daisuke Shirane, *ICERD and CERD: A Guide for Civil Society Actors* (The International Movement Against All Forms of Discrimination and Racism (IMADR), 2011) 25, 35.

47 ibid.

48 ibid.

49 CERD Committee Member Interviewee 5, interview conducted 30 April 2015, Geneva.

50 Author's observation of treaty body sessions, 2005, 2015, 2016.

51 Minority Rights Group (MRG) NGO interviewee 12, interview conducted 29 April 2015, Geneva; IMADR NGO interviewee 11, interview conducted 29 April 2015.

52 The UN building in Geneva where the majority of treaty body sessions are held.

53 United Nations General Assembly, *Report of the Committee on the Elimination of Racial Discrimination, Eightieth session* (13 February – 9 March 2012) General Assembly Official Records Sixty-seventh Session Supplement No 18 (A/67/18) para 65.

54 CERD Committee Member Interviewee 4, interview conducted 30 April 2015; CERD Committee Member Interviewee 5, (n 49).

was discussed.[55] As a result, weekly briefings were introduced, in which NGOs from all States under review can participate.

All NGO briefings are held outside of the formal review with governments. The meeting with the State under review, called the constructive dialogue, is held in public plenary sessions and generally spread across two half-day sessions lasting several hours in total. NGOs have no speaking rights at these sessions but can attend as observers.[56] In State reporting to UN Committees generally, the constructive dialogue has been described as 'the centrepiece of the exercise'.[57] It tends to take the form of diplomatic pleasantries on both sides, positive comments on progress and questions on areas of concern arising from the State's report from the Committee, and responses from the government. Despite the diplomacy, a government interviewee described treaty body constructive dialogues as 'like an inquisition'.[58] Constructive dialogues between the CERD Committee and the States parties can now be viewed online.[59] The questions asked of States parties may be informed by NGO reports,[60] or informal briefings.

The importance of the NGO role in treaty body monitoring is primarily the provision of critical, 'on the ground' information, offering a practical, cost-effective solution to fill a gap in the UN system. Leading human rights scholars have claimed that in their role of providing alternative information to UN Committees, NGOs play a significant role in State reporting.[61] The importance of information provided by NGOs has also been acknowledged by the UN Secretary General,[62] by Committee members in interviews for this study, and by Thornberry, an academic and former CERD Committee member.[63] Both Thornberry and Cushman argue that there is a lack of resources available to the OHCHR staff and Committee members to undertake fact-finding on the human rights situation in each State.[64] This was also a recurrent theme in interviews.[65] As one of the OHCHR staff members interviewed stated, 'People forget that the treaty body system does not have a fact finding tool of its own,

---

55 United Nations, *Report of the Committee on the Elimination of Racial Discrimination, Eightieth session* (13 February–9 March 2012) General Assembly Official Records Sixty-seventh Session Supplement No 18 (A/67/18), para 65.

56 For additional information on the constructive dialogue, see Michael O'Flaherty, *The UN and Human Rights, Practice Before the Treaty Bodies* (Martinus Nijhof 2002) Ch. 1.

57 Nigel S Rodley, 'UN treaty bodies and the Human Rights Council' in Helen Keller and Ger Ulfstein (eds), *UN Human Rights treaty Bodies: Law and Legitimacy* (CUP 2012) 336.

58 Australian Government Interviewee 13, interview conducted 29 April 2015, Geneva.

59 *Treaty Body Webcast*, <www.treatybodywebcast.org/category/webcast-archives/cerd/>, visited on 1 February 2016.

60 Forsythe, (n 39).

61 See for example, Wiseberg, (n 40) 350; Freeman, (n 40) 152.

62 See for example, United Nations Economic and Social Council (n 5).

63 Patrick Thornberry 'Confronting Racial Discrimination: A CERD Perspective' (2005) 5(2) *Human Rights Law Review* 239, 249.

64 ibid; Thomas Cushman, *Handbook of Human Rights* (Routledge 2012) 350.

65 OHCHR interviewee 6, interview conducted 28 April 2015, Geneva; MRG interviewee 12 (n 51); Human Rights Law Centre Domestic NGO interviewee 15, interview conducted

unlike Special Rapporteurs who move, who go and research and make reports but independent experts sit in Geneva'.[66] Furthermore, government reports are unlikely to highlight their own shortcomings, tending rather to be 'descriptive, formalistic, legalistic and self-congratulatory, rather than reflective and focused on substance and practical realities, and problems encountered'.[67] The gap for UN Committees includes this content on practical realities and problems; a gap filled by reports from civil society actors, predominantly NGOs, as borne out in the interview findings.

All OHCHR and CERD Committee member interviewees perceived NGOs to play an important role in State reporting. The words they used to describe NGOs ranged from 'important',[68] to 'very important',[69] and 'very useful'.[70] One used much more emphatic language such as 'critical',[71] and 'absolutely crucial'.[72] What was particularly valued by OHCHR staff and CERD Committee members was the provision of critical information. Most CERD and OHCHR interviewees perceived the NGO role as a balance in the State reporting system, resonating with a theme from the literature on NGOs in international law.[73] For example, as one OHCHR staff member stated in relation to NGOs, 'The treaty bodies get both sides of the story, they [the NGOs] are half of the story'.[74] This mirrors the views of a CERD Committee member who said: '…they're critical. At least from the perspective of the Committee in terms of their use and value to us, because without them we would only have one side of the story'.[75] The provision of 'on the ground'[76] or 'first hand'[77] information to complete the picture clearly emerged as interviewees' most valued role for NGOs.

Despite the overwhelmingly positive response to questions about the NGO role, most interviewees expressed some reservations about NGOs or about the reliability of NGO information. Scholarship on the NGO role in treaty body monitoring has not explored this reticence towards NGOs to the same degree as the positive commentary on the NGO role,[78] with the exception of some

23 September 2015, telephone interview; CERD Committee Member Interviewee 5 (n 49).

66 OHCHR interviewee 6, ibid.

67 Christof Heyns and Frans Viljoen, *The Impact of the United Nations Human Rights Treaties on the Domestic Level* (Kluwer Law International 2002) 25.

68 CERD Committee Member Interviewee 5 (n 49).

69 CERD Committee Member Interviewee 3, interview conducted 30 April 2015, Geneva; CERD Committee Member Interviewee 1, interview conducted 27 April 2015, Geneva.

70 CERD Committee Member Interviewee 1, ibid.

71 CERD Committee Member Interviewee 2, interview conducted 28 April 2015, Geneva.

72 ibid.

73 Laurie Wiseberg, 'Protecting Human Rights Activists and NGOs: What More Can Be Done?' (1991) 13(4) *Human Rights Quarterly* 525, 525; Steve Charnovitz, 'Nongovernmental Organizations and International Law' (2006) 100 *American Journal of International Law* 348, 348.

74 OHCHR interviewee 6 (n 65).

75 CERD Committee Member Interviewee 2 (n 71).

76 CERD Committee Member Interviewee 3 (n 69).

77 CERD Committee Member Interviewee 2 (n 71).

78 See for example, Wiseberg (n 73); Forsythe (n 39); Freeman (n 40).

general literature on NGO accountability,[79] and discussion of the complexities of the CERD Committee's engagement with NGOs.[80] In this regard, OHCHR staff and CERD Committee members ranged from those who were sympathetic to NGOs, open to NGO reports and quite trusting of their content,[81] to those who indicated quite high levels of scepticism of NGO information and motives. However, even the latter expressed support for NGO input once it could be verified. As one interviewer observed, 'Of course NGOs are important sources of information but sometimes, because they are partisans of ideas, sometimes they might be exaggerating…'[82]

Finally, within the context of a system beset by delays, backlogs, a lack of resources and questionable effectiveness,[83] OHCHR staff expressed frustration with the current system and a few of the CERD Committee member interviewees acknowledged that due to time pressures and the volume of information received, they cannot read all of the NGO reports.[84] One said: 'The problem for us, because we do have a problem, we have too much to read. At the last minute. They [NGOs] send it very late and we have more than the State party report. It's difficult for us'.[85]

4.2 NGO role in developing Concluding Observations

After the provision of information, OHCHR staff and CERD Committee member interviewees identified a second particularly useful aspect of the NGO role–suggesting recommendations for the Committee's Concluding Observations.[86] The unique understanding and expertise of NGOs, particularly domestic NGOs, was seen as invaluable by some interviewees. One Committee member gave the example of a submission from NGOs that had very focused recommendations about financing for housing to comply with Muslim law.[87] The interviewee felt that this particular recommendation would not have occurred to the Committee and suggested that proposing very precise, specific and 'implementable' recommendations is a useful role for NGOs.

---

79 Diana Hortsch, 'The Paradox of Partnership: Amnesty International, Responsible Advocacy and NGO Accountability' (2010) 42 *Columbian Human Rights Law Review* 119.

80 Thornberry (n 63).

81 For example, CERD Committee Member Interviewee 1 (n 69).

82 CERD Committee Member Interviewee 5 (n 49).

83 For more analysis of these issues, see the body of literature on treaty body reform / strengthening, including: United Nations General Assembly *Strengthening and enhancing the effective functioning of the human rights treaty body system* UNGA Res. A/RES/68/268, 68th session (9 April 2014); Michael O'Flaherty 'Reform of the UN Human Rights Treaty Body System: Locating the Dublin Statement', (2010) 10 (2) *Human Rights Law Review* 319.

84 CERD Committee Member Interviewee 4 (n 54); CERD Committee Member Interviewee 5 (n 49); CERD Committee Member Interviewee 1 (n 69).

85 CERD Committee Member Interviewee 5 (n 49).

86 CERD Committee Member Interviewee 2 (n 71); CERD Committee Member Interviewee 5 (n 49); OHCHR Interviewee 8, interview conducted 30 April 2015.

87 CERD Committee Member Interviewee 2 (n 71).

Interviewees were generally asked how the author's finding of strong correlation between concluding observations and NGO reports could be explained.[88] Interviewees' responses tended to link this strong reliance on NGO recommendations to a number of factors including the credibility or legitimacy of the NGO in question such as it being a 'specialised NGO',[89] or a key NGO within the country, or a coalition of NGOs.[90] Other interviewees focused more on the quality of the report itself. As one interviewee noted, '[i]t would relate to many things, it could relate to the quality. I cannot say it is a phenomenon but the most usable input has a higher chance of finding its way through'.[91] Some interviewees still maintained that 'there is not a direct link in the way you are suggesting',[92] and reiterated that NGO information is used during the constructive dialogue to pose questions to the State.[93] Geneva-based international non-governmental organisations interviewees noted that Committee members directly use NGO information in the constructive dialogue,[94] and in the concluding observations, particularly where an NGO has high credibility.[95]

Committee member and OHCHR reluctance to acknowledge the full extent of NGO influence is not surprising. Firstly, only the Committee has the authority to develop concluding observations.[96] Secondly, as noted above, there have been ongoing attempts by some governments to reduce or eliminate the NGO role in treaty body reporting, as one CERD Committee member noted, '[i]t is a delicate balancing act. There is no point in the outcome of a treaty body discussion being lauded by NGOs if it's ignored by the States parties. It's essential that that balance is found and that's challenging for both NGOs and States parties'.[97]

5. Conclusion

NGOs fought for inclusion in the drafting of the UN Charter, and as a result, consultation with NGOs is provided for in Art 71 of the Charter. They went on to contribute to the drafting of the UDHR and to human rights treaties. Seventy years after the adoption of the UDHR, we can reflect that the NGO role has exceeded what was anticipated in the early days of the UN. In particular, NGOs play an essential governance role in holding governments to account on their human rights treaty obligations by providing information and suggesting recommendations to UN treaty bodies. The information supplements reports

88 McGaughey (n 8).
89 CERD Committee Member Interviewee 3 (n 69).
90 CERD Committee Member Interviewee 2 (n 71).
91 OHCHR interviewee 6 (n 65).
92 CERD Committee Member Interviewee 1 (n 69).
93 ibid, CERD Committee Member Interviewee 3 (n 69); OHCHR interviewee 6 (n 65).
94 IMADR NGO interviewee 11, (n 51).
95 MRG NGO interviewee 12, (n 51).
96 Committee on the elimination of Racial Discrimination, 'Rules of Procedure', (UN Doc: CERD/C/35/Rev.3), Rule 67(3) in accordance with Art 9(2) *ICERD*.
97 CERD Committee Member Interviewee 1 (n 69).

provided by governments so that the Committee of independent experts can better assess the actual state of human rights on the ground. In this chapter, the importance of the NGO role was explored using semi-structured interviews and found that UN staff and treaty body members strongly value the NGO role and all saw it as ranging from 'important' to 'absolutely crucial'. This resonates with Wiseberg's assertion that the UN human rights machinery '...would grind to a halt were it not fed by the fact-finding of human rights NGOs'.[98]

6. Bibliography

Alger, C, 'The Emerging Roles of NGOs in the UN System: From Article 71 to a People's Millennium Assembly' (2002) 8 *Global Governance* 93

Annan, K, "Address to the 51st Annual DPI-NGO Conference," United Nations, New York, 1998

Charnovitz, S, 'Two Centuries of Participation: NGOs and International Governance' (1997) 18 (2) *Michigan Journal of International Law* 183

Steve Charnovitz, 'Nongovernmental Organizations and International Law' (2006) 100 *American Journal of International Law* 348

Cohen, P, 'The Role of Nongovernmental Organizations in the Drafting of the Convention on the Rights of the Child' (1990) 12 *Human Rights Quarterly* 137

Cushman, T, *Handbook of Human Rights* (Routledge 2012)

Forsythe, D, *Human Rights in International Relations* (2nd edn) (CUP 2006)

Freeman, M, *Human Rights: An Interdisciplinary Approach* (Polity Press 2011)

Gaer, FD, 'Implementing international human rights norms: UN human rights treaty bodies and NGOs' (2003) 2(3) *Journal of Human Rights* 339

Government of China, *Views of the Chinese Government regarding the human rights treaty body strengthening process* (HRC/NONE/2011/184) (2011)

Government of Egypt, *The Future of the Treaty Body System: Egypt Position Paper*, (undated)

Government of the Russian Federation, *Comments of the Russian Federation on the list of issues identified during the treaty body strengthening consultations, prepared by the Office of the United Nations High Commissioner for Human Rights,* (HRC/NONE/2012/1) (2011)

Hannum, H, (ed), *Guide to International Human Rights Practice*, (University of Philadelphia Press 1984)

Heyns, C and Viljoen, Frans, *The Impact of the United Nations Human Rights Treaties on the Domestic Level* (Kluwer Law International 2002)

Hodson, L, *NGOs and the Struggle for Human Rights in Europe* (Hart Publishing 2011)

Hortsch, D, 'The Paradox of Partnership: Amnesty International, Responsible Advocacy and NGO Accountability' (2010) 42 *Columbian Human Rights Law Review* 119

Jordaan, E, 'South Africa and the United Nations Human Rights Council' (2014) 36(1) *Human Rights Quarterly* 90

[98] Wiseberg (n 40) 354.

Korey, W, *NGOs and the Universal Declaration of Human Rights: A Curious Grapevine* (Palgrave 1998)

Kruckenberg, LJ, *The Unreal world of human rights: An ethnography of the UN Committee on the Elimination of Racial Discrimination* (Nomos Verlagsgesellschaft 2012)

Martens, K, 'Mission Impossible? Defining Non-governmental Organizations' (2002) 13:3 *Voluntas: International Journal of Voluntary and Nonprofit Organizations* 271

McGaughey, F, 'Advancing, retreating or stepping on each other's toes? The Role of Non-Governmental Organisations in United Nations Human Rights Treaty Body Reporting and the Universal Periodic Review' (2017) 35 *Australian Yearbook of International Law* 187

McGaughey F, 'The Role and Influence of Non-governmental Organisations in the Universal Periodic Review – International Context and Australian Case Study' (2017) *Human Rights Law Review* 421

O'Flaherty, M, 'Reform of the UN Human Rights Treaty Body System: Locating the Dublin Statement' (2010) 10 (2) *Human Rights Law Review* 319

O'Flaherty, M, *The UN and Human Rights, Practice Before the Treaty Bodies* (Martinus Nijhof 2002)

Otto, D, 'Nongovernmental Organizations in the United Nations System: The Emerging Role of International Civil Society' (1996) 18 *Human Rights Quarterly* 107

Pearson, ZN, *Global Civil Society and International Law-Making: Mapping the Boundaries*, (PhD Thesis, Australian National University 2002)

Pillay, N, *Strengthening the United Nations human rights treaty body system: A report by the United Nations High Commissioner for Human Rights* (United Nations 2012)

Rodley, NS, 'UN treaty bodies and the Human Rights Council' in Keller, Helen and Ulfstein, Ger (eds), *UN Human Rights treaty Bodies: Law and Legitimacy* (CUP 2012) 336

Shirane, D, *ICERD and CERD: A Guide for Civil Society Actors* (The International Movement Against All Forms of Discrimination and Racism 2011)

Thornberry, P, 'Confronting Racial Discrimination: A CERD Perspective' (2005) 5(2) *Human Rights Law Review* 239

Treaty Body Webcast, <www.treatybodywebcast.org/category/webcast-archives/cerd/ >

United Nations Committee on the Elimination of Racial Discrimination, 'Rules of Procedure', (UN Doc: CERD/C/35/Rev.3)

United Nations Committee on the Elimination of Racial Discrimination, *NGO Information Note* (84th session, 3 to 21 February 2014)

United Nations Committee on the Rights of the Child, *Provisional Rules of Procedure*, CRC/C/4 (14 November 1991)

United Nations General Assembly *Strengthening and enhancing the effective functioning of the human rights treaty body system* UNGA Res. A/RES/68/268, 68th session (9 April 2014)

United Nations General Assembly, *Report of the Committee on the Elimination of Racial Discrimination, Eightieth session* (13 February – 9 March 2012) General Assembly Official Records Sixty-seventh session Supplement No. 18 (A/67/18)

United Nations, *Report of the Committee on the Elimination of Racial Discrimination, Eightieth session* (13 February–9 March 2012) General Assembly Official Records Sixty-seventh session Supplement No. 18 (A/67/18)

United Nations General Assembly 11 June 2004 *Fifty-eighth session Agenda item 59 Strengthening of the United Nations system*, UN Doc A/58/817, 3

United Nations Economic and Social Council, *General Review of Arrangements for Consultations with Non-Governmental Organisations: Report of the Secretary General*, (UN Doc 70/1994/5), 26 May 1994

United Nations Committee on the Elimination of Racial Discrimination, *Report of the Committee on the Elimination of Racial Discrimination General Assembly Official Records · Fifty-first Session Supplement No. 18* (1996), (A/51/18)

United Nations Department of Public Information, *What is an NGO* https://outreach.un.org/ngorelations/content/about-us-0

United Nations Economic and Social Council, *Consultative relationship between the United Nations and non-governmental organizations,* ECOSOC Res. 1996/31, 49th plen mtg, (25 July 1996)

United Nations General Assembly 11 June 2004 *Fifty-eighth session Agenda item 59 Strengthening of the United Nations system*, UN Doc A/58/817

United Nations Office of the High Commissioner for Human Rights, *Non-exhaustive list of emerging proposals identified so far in the context of the treaty body strengthening informal consultations (including Dublin, Marrakesh, Poznan, Sion, Seoul, Pretoria, Bristol and Lucerne) and those of the Inter-Committee Meeting (ICM) and Meeting of Chairpersons (MC), as well as other proposals stemming from the process*, <http://www2.ohchr.org/english/bodies/HRTD/docs/ProposalsTBStrengtheningProcess.pdfhttp://www.treatybodywebcast.org/category/webcast-archives/cerd/>

van Boven, T, 'The Role of Non-Governmental Organizations in International Human Rights Standard Setting: A Prerequisite of Democracy (1990) 20 (2) *California Western International Law Journal* 207

We the peoples: civil society, the United Nations and global governance: Report of the Panel of Eminent Persons on United Nations–Civil Society Relations, UN GAOR, 58th session, Agenda Item 59, Strengthening of the United Nations System, UN Doc A/58/817 (11 June 2004)

Wiseberg, LS, *The Role of Non-Governmental Organizations (NGOs) in the Protection and Enforcement of Human Rights* in Symonides. J, (ed), *Human Rights: International Protection, Monitoring, Enforcement* (UNESCO Publishing 2003) 347-365

Wiseberg, L, 'Protecting Human Rights Activists and NGOs: What More Can Be Done?' (1991) 13(4) *Human Rights Quarterly* 525

Willetts, P, (ed), *'The Conscience of the World': The Influence of Non Governmental Organisations in the UN System* (David Davies Memorial Institute of International Studies and the Brookings Institution 1996)

INDEX